AF693657

DEFENDING YOURSELF AGAINST COPS

Dee Wampler

Foreword

We the People

"The Constitution is what the judges say it is."

Charles Evans Hughes

Every morning when we wake up we are protected by the Bill of Rights, yet some who advocate the Bill of Rights are perceived as "un-american". At no time in our history has it been more vital, stronger, or more meaningful.

The third century of the Bill of Rights begins at what history may record as the watershed moment when the nation reset its Constitutional compass and chartered as a fundamentally new course. The Constitutional momentum has shifted a significant distance the other way—towards more narrowed liberties.

Individual rights now flourish alongside the massive welfare state. Millions of Americans are receiving public assistance (welfare) in various forms. One in ten Americans are on food stamps. A succession of conservatives have recently been appointed to the Supreme Court, putting the nation on the threshold of a major turning point. To narrow the Fourth Amendment protection against unreasonable searches by permitting random stops of autos to search for drunk drivers, sweeps of busses to check for drugs, and government programs requiring mandatory drug tests.

It has cut back on the rights of criminal suspects and prisoners—upholding mandatory life sentences without parole for drug offenders—making it harder for prisoners to challenge their incarceration— permitting Prosecutors to tell the jurors about the impact of a crime on the victims.

Based on recent court decisions fundamental changes lie ahead in the 1990's.

The court is not the only force compressing American rights. Changes in society are pushing the nation towards more restrictions on our freedoms. Society has been willing to permit police to take shortcuts to conducting searches to unearth criminal evidence.

When our Constitution was adopted people agreed to support it only if basic rights were added *limiting the powers* of the government.

It is only the defense attorney, standing in the courtroom, who argues in defense of the Bill of Rights; constantly reminding the Judge and the jury to remember the protection of our fundamental guarantees.

Knowing what to expect can reduce your fears, make the process more knowledgeable, reduce surprise, and help you help your lawyer. Read on.

Chapter 1

What to Expect from My Lawyer

"The law and the stage—both are a form of exhibitionism."
Orson Welles

"The trouble with law and government is lawyers."
Clarence Darrow

"In all criminal prosecutions, the accused shall enjoy the right to a speedy and public trial, by an impartial jury...and to be informed of the nature and cause of the accusation; to be confronted with the witnesses against him; to have compulsory process for obtaining Witnesses in his favor, and to have the Assistance of Counsel for his defence."
Sixth Amendment
United States Constitution

Why Don't People Like Us?

"Hate evil, love good; maintain justice in the courts."
Amos 5:15

"The first thing we do, let's kill all the lawyers."
William Shakespeare, King Henry VI,
Part II, IV, ii.
(Anarchists plotting to kill the king)

There is a nastiness to lawyer jokes that reveals a real hostility. Anti-lawyer attitudes are not new to our culture, as cynical and unfavorable comments about lawyers can be found in the Greek culture of Plato, Renaissance Europe, and Cicero.

Given the quality of people that go into the law practice and the enormous achievements and high standards of integrity that most demonstrate such as Sir Thomas Moore, Abraham Lincoln, Louis Brandeis, Mahat Ma Gandi, and many others, makes the criticisms all the more disturbing.

Lawyers are aware of the endless slurs parading behind their backs. They work long hours to serve others, trying to maintain their integrity in a competitive setting when success is often measured in client satisfaction as opposed to "justice".

The vast majority of lawyers never see the inside of a courtroom serving instead as estate planners, opinion givers, deal makers, and negotiators.

Behind every dubious act of an attorney there is a client demanding even more aggressive action. Clients hire lawyers to find loopholes around regulations, avoid taxes, gain advantages over others, or simply get them out of trouble with little concern for the victim. Lawyers must learn to say "no" to clients and that there will be extreme pressure put to them when they do.

Litigants have "sour grapes" if they lose. The system is unfair and the other attorney took advantage. Most people trust their own lawyers but they hate the lawyer on the other side. Those who hate lawyers the most will be the first ones, in time of trouble to demand, "I want my Constitutional rights! Get me a lawyer!"

Over the centuries, lawyers have righted many wrongs and instituted social reforms accomplished by litigation.

Still...lawyer bashing continues. Critics claim lawyers have no regard for truth or fairness and will manipulate, distort, or conceal facts to gain an advantage. You really can't trust a lawyer since they are too clever. They say lawyers are condescending, use legal jargon to intimidate, confuse people about how the law works, are pompous, self-centered, abusive, are only interested in the dollar, and are not genuinely interested about their client or the legal system.

These descriptions apply to only a small percentage of the profession, and with slight modification apply equally to politicians, journalists, business executives, doctors, university professors, accountants, and preachers!

It is not up to an attorney to judge his client, but to the Judge and jury, and if a person is guilty, guilty of what?

Although hard to swallow, the question of guilt or innocence is irrelevant. What matters is what the D.A. can prove. "If they can't prove their case in court, they ain't got a case."

I didn't coin the phrase, "It is far worse to convict an innocent man than to let a guilty man go free," but I wish I did.

I do not minimize or excuse the terrible cost of crime, the agony and suffering of innocent victims of rape, child abuse, assault, murder, or theft. There is little excuse for most crimes. In our free society criminals are often free to prey on innocent victims.

This book is not about the victims. Many books and much publicity has been directed at the hapless victims of crime. This book is directed at innocent citizens who are charged as being criminals, their faces and names plastered across the news media for their neighbors to see—those who are jailed for months prior to trial who cannot afford bail or a good lawyer. This book is about *your Constitutional rights.*

Suppose you are arrested and charged with a crime. Your first step is to hire a lawyer.

Today's modern lawyer has received a great deal of legal education, but *advocacy and courtroom* education is still low. Many lawyers do not place faith in pretrial investigation of their cases or on legal argument in the courtroom. In law school, everything is unemotional.

Even the dullest case can be made emotional and exciting. You try to put the jury in the shoes of your client and sympathize with him no matter how bad he is. Lawyers should not be overly technical, relying on boring objections in front of the jury. It is time good lawyers realize that a bad man deserves a fair trial and the same legal rights as a good man. If you railroad a bad man and treat him unfairly in the criminal justice system, the next time they may railroad a good man and do the exact same thing to him.

The legal profession has its heroes and bums. There are too many lawsuits and too many lawyers.

The number of lawyers in the United States nearly doubled from 1975 to 1990, and could exceed 900,000 by the year 2000.

Does America need 70% of the world's lawyers? Is it healthy for our economy to have 18 million new lawsuits going through the system annually?

Incentives need to be provided for civil litigants to settle cases out-of-court, especially divorce and child custody disputes, and create uniform standards for punitive damage in tort cases. The need for reform is urgent.

Plea bargaining in criminal cases is not only entirely legal, but an important part of our system. If not for plea bargaining, our legal system would break down under the crush of sheer volume. Although plea bargaining is often informally spoken, it is seriously intended. Whether you approve or not, *listen understandingly to your lawyer* so you may understand the legal alternatives presented to you in your legal dilemma.

Every client charged with a crime has a *serious problem* that needs to be resolved. Does he need treatment for mental problems? Is he being influenced by the wrong kind of friends or co-workers? Did he act under extreme emotional disturbance? Was the act done in self-defense? There may be other "reasons" for the criminal act (involving family, environment, health, and social status).

Many contest the constitutionality of laws under which they are prosecuted, the rules of evidence, admission of physical evidence, and testimony the trial judge allowed. It is these cases, after all, that make new law and further extend and clarify the great constitutional questions that are being answered by judges on a daily basis as our society grows.

Though I personally challenge laws and rules of the court system, *I never dispute a jury verdict*. It is the nearest thing to *perfect justice* that man has devised. No one has ever claimed it is perfect. An accused is not entitled to a *perfect* trial, only a *fair* one. Jurors make small mistakes during trial but in the end, the nature and common sense of 12 people will decide your fate.

Behind every "crime", of which usually only the bare-bones facts are revealed in the media, there is at least one reason for the accused to justify the act committed. The jury is entitled to know this reason and judge the facts from both sides of the case before a final decision, not only as to guilt or innocence, but as to the amount of punishment.

RULE: IF YOU'RE GUILTY OR HAVE GUILTY KNOWLEDGE OF THE CRIME, YOU MAY WISH TO PROBE FOR WEAKNESSES IN THE PROSECUTION'S CASE, BUT EVENTUALLY PLEA BARGAIN, TAKING THE BEST OFFER YOUR LAWYER CAN NEGOTIATE. DISCRETION IS THE BETTER PART OF VALOR.

RULE: IF YOU ARE TRULY INNOCENT, DO NOT CONSIDER EVER PLEADING GUILTY! PLEAD NOT GUILTY, DEMAND YOUR RIGHT TO A TRIAL BY JURY (IF THE *FACTS* ARE IN DISPUTE) OR TO A TRIAL BY THE JUDGE WITHOUT A JURY (IF THE FACTS ARE NOT IN DISPUTE BUT *LEGAL* QUESTIONS ARE IN DISPUTE).

NOTWITHSTANDING, YOUR NATURAL RELUCTANCE AND FEAR, VALOR AND COURAGE ARE REQUIRED. BE STRONG IN YOUR RESOLVE.

Selecting Your Lawyer

> **"Lawyers are the only persons in the world for whom ignorance of the law is not punished."**
>
> Jeremy Bentham

You're in trouble and you need a lawyer:

1. On the telephone, he should seem ready, willing and able to help, friendly with immediate answers.
2. Make an office appointment. Nothing important was ever settled over the phone. If he is too busy to see you within 48-72 hours, select another attorney unless, he is sick, on vacation, or involved in a lengthy trial.
3. His office should be neat, staff attentive to business, and he should have a well-stocked library.
4. At your office conference he should not take telephone calls or interruptions. Your problem is the most important problem at hand.
5. Your attorney should be friendly and easy to get to know. If he doesn't know the law or can't answer your legal questions, *hire another attorney*.
6. Inquire if he has handled other cases similar to yours within the recent past. If not, *hire another attorney*.
7. Ask if he has tried recent jury cases. A knowledgeable trial attorney should try at least several jury trials annually. If it's been more than several years since he has been in the "arena", *hire another attorney*.
8. Discuss fee arrangements immediately. If he is unwilling to talk about the fee or is vague, hire another attorney. Inquire about extras, secretarial costs, photocopies, mileage, postage, or other expenses and have a definite understanding. Ask him

to confirm everything in writing with you. If he refuses, *hire another attorney*.

9. Before the office conference write out your questions and make sure you have his answers. Ask what actions or steps the attorney would take if you employed him. If he has no set course of action, is vague or indefinite, *hire another attorney*.
10. Demand a receipt for any fees paid.
11. Inquire of the attorney's *reputation* among your friends, neighbors, and relatives. Try to find a former client and talk to them. Go to the courthouse and find a policeman, clerk, secretary, or bailiff and ask the question:
    "If you were in trouble, who would you hire to be your lawyer?"
12. During your initial conference, if you don't feel comfortable with the attorney, *hire another attorney*. Wait. Get a second opinion.

Do not be swayed by television, radio, or yellow page ads. Some attorneys advertise because they have to—they don't have enough business by reputation.

Just because a lawyer is a law school graduate does not mean he specializes *in your problem*. Some lawyers are good, some aren't. Some are more knowledgeable than others.

If you have a close friend or relative that is an attorney, resist the temptation to hire him. It may ruin a good friendship. You'll do better and have more confidence in a lawyer that is yours, that you can discuss your personal faults, make confessions without embarrassment, in a strictly business relationship. Resist the temptation to employ an attorney because he is *cut-rate* or specializes in *bargain fees*. You will get exactly what you pay for.

Cooperating with Your Attorney

Once you hire an attorney, help him help you. You have placed your faith in him. Don't work against him. He has your best interests at heart.

1. Tell him the *truth*, even if it hurts. Don't lie or mislead him.
2. Keep all office appointments and appear promptly, and on time. Write out your questions in advance, and make sure you understand his answers.
3. Notify his secretary immediately if you change addresses or telephone numbers.
4. Feel free to *write out* any comments or suggestions on your case, so it becomes a part of his file.

5. If you agree to pay a fee, *pay it*. The less he worries about your fee, the more time he has to work on your case.
6. You may be emotionally upset and under stress. Don't take it out on your attorney or his secretary. He handles many other cases and can't handle your stress together with everyone else's. Treat his office in a businesslike manner.
7. Don't call his office unnecessarily. If you do call, leave a *definite message* with his secretary as to what you want.
8. In keeping a court date, appear early, dressed conservatively, and wait patiently for your attorney.
9. *Cooperate* and supply any evidence your lawyer requests. If he wants photographs, diagrams, good character letters, or wants you to attend AA, NA, ARTOP or other counseling, do it, and present written proof to him. If requested, supply him names, addresses and phone numbers of witnesses.

RULE: IF YOU ARE CHARGED WITH A CRIMINAL OFFENSE, WHETHER OR NOT YOU ARE GUILTY, IT MAY MEAN YOU NEED TO CHANGE YOUR LIFESTYLE BY CHANGING YOUR FRIENDS, ATTITUDE, OR YOUR DAILY ACTIVITIES. JUDGES AND JURIES ADMIRE PEOPLE THAT TRY TO HELP THEMSELVES. TRY TO ADJUST, MAKING THE NECESSARY CHANGES, TO ENSURE THAT YOU NEVER GET INTO TROUBLE AGAIN.

How To Be a Trial Lawyer

"A lawyer and an actor are akin. It is true I have no mask, I have no set lines, I have no black cloth, and I have no floodlights to help bring illusion, but out of the miseries and the joys of the strivings and experience of men, I must create an atmosphere of living reality so that it may be felt and understood by others, for that is advocacy."

Barrister Sir Edward Hall

Jurors want the truth. They want to know they haven't been fooled, and that they have been fair and render a good brand of justice as they can. Too often clever trial lawyers stand in the way of these goals.

The jury is the most intelligent, best informed and wisest collective mind in the courtroom. The average juror is about 40 years old. The 12 jurors will possess collectively among them 500 years of exquisitely varied life experiences. The worker who scrubs the latrines of the saloon for a living and goes home to a cold bowl of cereal and an empty bed knows more about the human condition than all of the Ph.D.'s I can haul into the courtroom.

The most successful trial lawyers are the ones who have the requisite technical skills, and also have mastered the highest art of all—the art of *truly being themselves* in the courtroom.

The successful trial lawyers in this country have one thing in common—they totally put themselves into their clients' cases, including a deep sense of caring.

Accident investigation must be thorough and complete, especially in serious matters, since civil suits often follow.

Dispatchers use the "ALERT" system which captures and indexes detailed information and automates deployment, call-taking, dispatching and record keeping.

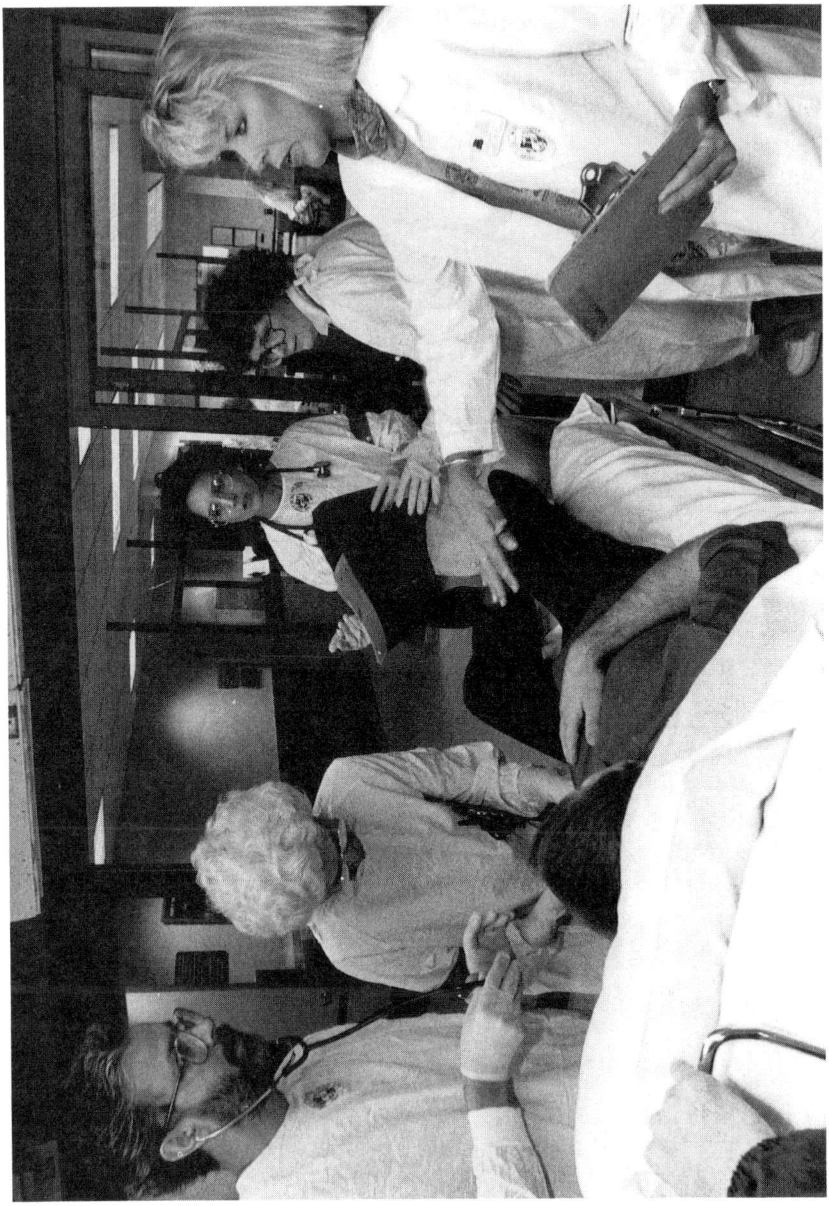

Code Blue Trauma team Dr. Beaton directs Joy Razbourn, RN, Arlene Wallace, RN, and Laurie Easter, RN. (Photo courtesy of John S. Stewart and Lester Cox Hospital, Springfield.)

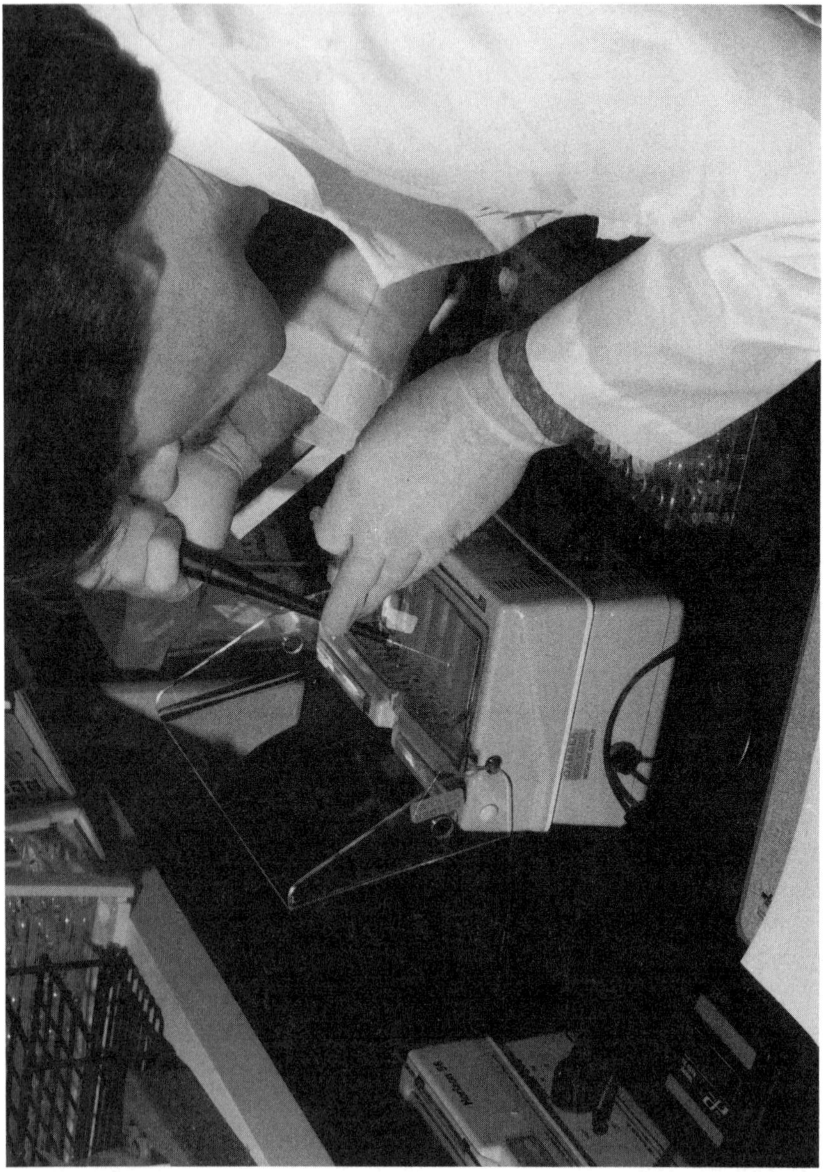

Forensic chemist Cary Maloney loading a test gel to determine the quality of DNA at the Missouri State Highway Patrol Crime Laboratory in Jefferson City.

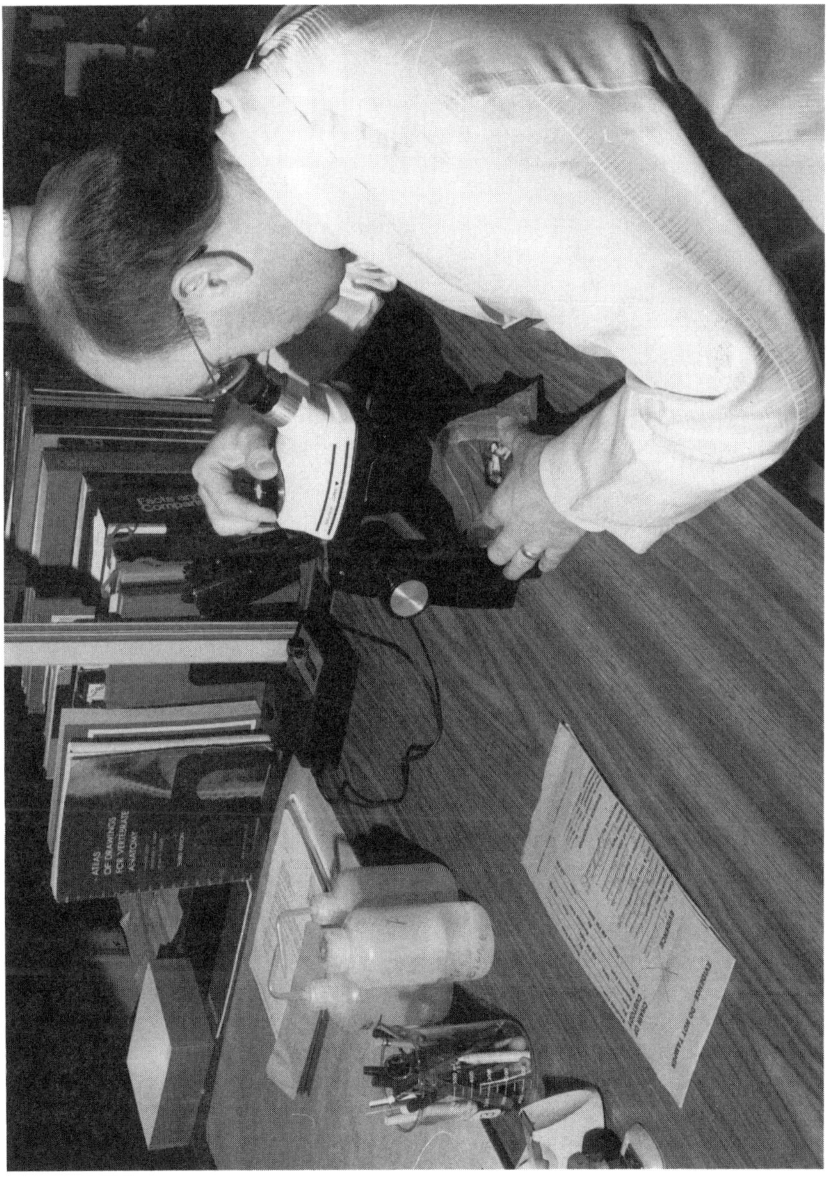

Senior Forensic Chemist Everett Markway performs a microscope examination of marijuana at the Missouri State Highway Patrol Crime Laboratory in Jefferson City.

HOLY
BIBLE
CONCORDANCE

Chapter 2

What to Expect at Trial

"Courage is being scared to death—and saddling up anyway."

John Wayne

"Innocent and guilty are harder to separate than Siamese twins."

Charlie Chan

"Justice, though due to the accused, is due to the accuser also. The concept of fairness must not be strained till it is narrowed to a filament. We are to keep the balance true."

Justice Benjamin N. Cardozo

Due Process of Law

"The right of an accused in a criminal trial to due process is, in essence, the right to a fair opportunity to defend against the state's accusations. The rights to confront and cross-examine witnesses and to call witnesses in one's own behalf have long been recognized as essential to due process."

Chambers vs. Mississippi,
U.S. Supreme Court, 1973

You should argue your right to *due process* and a large number of Constitutional rights: To present a defense, to present witnesses on your behalf, to know and understand the criminal charges against you and the state's case in advance of trial, and the right to fully cross-examine witnesses and present your *theory of the case.*

Few rights are more fundamental than your right to present witnesses in your behalf that put before the jury evidence that will influence the determination of guilt.

To preserve the public interest demands and a full and truthful disclosure of critical facts, all American citizens are guaranteed *due process of law.*

The Presumption of Innocence and Reasonable Doubt

A hallmark of the American criminal justice system is the *presumption of innocence* accorded every accused person, and the necessity that the state prove its case beyond a reasonable doubt.

These majestic phrases–presumption of innocence and reasonable doubt–serve the two highest values of the criminal justice system: fairness and certainty. *Fairness* requires no one be compelled to prove his innocence or even produce evidence in his defense; the entire burden is borne by the government. *Certainty requires no person be condemned by criminal conviction without the highest level of confidence that he is guilty.*

> **RULE: EVERYONE IS PRESUMED INNOCENT UNTIL PROVEN GUILTY. AN INDISPENSABLE PART OF THE RIGHT OF A SPEEDY AND PUBLIC TRIAL AND AN IMPARTIAL JURY IS NOT TO BE "DEPRIVED OF LIVE, LIBERTY, OR PROPERTY, WITHOUT DUE PROCESS OF LAW." AND PERSON EVER FACED WITH THE AWESOME POWER OF GOVERNMENT IS IN GREAT JEOPARDY.**

What is reasonable doubt? It is based on reason which arises from the lack of evidence. The purpose of a reasonable doubt standard is to communicate to the jury the *degree of confidence* that society expects of the decision maker in the most serious kind of lawsuit–the criminal trial.

What explains reasonable doubt? The witnesses testify. The Prosecutor rails. The Judge instructs. The jury listens. But there is only one person in the courtroom who brings reasonable doubt to life, who transforms it from the abstract to the palpable, from the evident to the irresistible. That person is the defense lawyer, in who the Constitution has entrusted care of the golden thread. Each time a jury utters the words, *not guilty*, that assignment is vindicated.

In our Constitutional scheme, the role of ultimate guardian of the liberties of the people is given to the U.S. Supreme Court. That court is obligated to honor the values implicitly and explicitly contained in the U.S. Constitution.

It is a sad fact that every day in some American courtroom a person who is not guilty under facts, or the law, or both, is unjustly convicted. The reasons vary: prejudice, ignorance, mistake, judicial indifference, police ineptitude, chicanery, prosecutorial over zealousness or defense counsel under zealousness. But in each case the presumption of innocence and the requirement of proof beyond a reasonable doubt are inadequate to prevent a miscarriage of justice.

How to Act in the Courtroom

You are on a stage. The jury watches you carefully for body language, inappropriate behavior, or mannerisms. Never laugh, smirk, or appear to be enjoying yourself. A trial is an unpleasant and serious matter. Everyone, including the jurors, would rather be somewhere else and not at the courthouse. From the time you park your car in the courthouse parking lot, you run the risk of seeing potential jurors. Dress conservative, act polite, and look pleasant.

If humorous things occur in the courtroom, do not laugh! Be serious. Write notes or whisper to your attorney when necessary.

In voir dire, make written notes of the jurors you *do not like* so that you can later make sure your attorney takes them off the jury panel.

During testimony, pay close attention and tell your attorney of any wrong answers or inconsistencies from the witnesses.

Keep a careful eye towards the jury. Establish eye contact and try to read what the jury is thinking. During the trial, make a list of errors. If the Judge overrules your lawyer and makes other rulings, make a *list of trial errors* so your attorney can put this in his *Motion for New Trial.* If you are convicted, you assist your lawyer in drafting motions for the new trial since he will have not have had an opportunity to read the transcript.

Always testify in your case if you can. It is your life on trial and you are entitled to have a part in the jury decision.

Sit erect and face the jury when answering.

Forget about the Judge and lawyers as they do not decide your fate. *Look at the jury.*

Answer the questions direct and simple. If you do not know the answer, say, "I don't know." If you make an error, correct it when you realize it.

It is better for a jury to see the attorney is honest and that the client not trying to hide anything, than the opposite. In the process, the criminal justice system is bettered since it is, after all, an earnest search for the truth. The rewards come in knowing that, as the client's representative, the lawyer had a direct part in helping another human being in a unique way.

Much of the success in winning a favorable verdict depends upon selecting a jury that will side with your client. Twelve of your peers will listen and weigh all of the evidence presented and reach a verdict of "guilty" or "not guilty".

Lawyers classify potential jurors into categories to create a favorable group dynamics for their cause. Major categories are: *leaders, followers, fillers, negotiators, and holdouts.* If the attorney is familiar with body language, he can better assess and select prospective jurors and detect subtle attitudinal differences among them...information which may be useful later when trying to convince them to side with his client.

Jurors and Jury Trials

> **"The power of the jury on occasion to deliver an accused person from both the police and the letter of the law is the sole reason for its existence as an institution."**
>
> George Barnard Shaw

Good trial attorneys are part actor. Their stage is the courtroom, their audience the Judge and the jury. From the moment lawyers enter the court, they start an unmatched, albeit subtle, command performance to convince the jury to side with their client. To accomplish this goal, the astute attorney must look, act, and think like an attorney every second he is on stage. He is a master story teller.

Prospective clients should be extremely careful in choosing a lawyer to represent them, for if he forgets his lines, the client could spend the rest of his life in jail. There is no room for mistakes or it may become a theater of the absurd.

Jurors are uncomfortable, nervous and confused in this strange new environment but all the time they ask questions like, "Do I like him?" "Can I trust him to tell me the truth?" "Is he an honest attorney?" "Is his client guilty?"

The purpose of *voir dire* is to find 12 jurors that are free of feelings, beliefs, and prejudices so they can deliberate without these beliefs "nagging" them, causing conflicts of interest. It is unfortunate when a juror, while deliberating in the jury room might say to his fellow jurors, "My sister was assaulted a few years ago; therefore, I'm going to automatically vote for guilty in this case." The client ends up the biggest loser as the result of such jurors' partialities.

Nonverbal behavior such as facial expression, body postures and gestures give clues as to real feelings for anything hidden we may be trying to conceal. We often "give ourselves away" as the way we cock our heads, avoid another's gaze, or orient our bodies. Correct interpretations of nonverbal cues enables you to conduct an ongoing analysis of what is really going on during a trial.

Near where the jury sits (the jury box) is an area that may feel *off limits* to attorneys. It is important for the attorney to *break into* this area by walking up to the box, standing as near as he can to the jury and speaking in a conventual manner. Once inside this invisible circle, the jury will better accept the lawyer. It is as if every person in the courtroom has an invisible hula-hoop around them and somehow one hoop is not supposed to intersect with another. Once the lawyer causes the hoops to intersect and *bump into* each other on a friendly basis, he is more acceptable within the jury's social circle.

Winning the Juror's Hearts and Minds

There is a mysticism about jury trials. Trial lawyers who lose cases often say, "I don't understand it. They liked me. They were eating out of my hand." But the lawyers have unwittingly fooled themselves.

As the lawyer and client discuss their case, it must be evaluated with the jury in mind. The jury is always in the picture. "How is my client going to play? Will the witnesses be believable?" "How am I going to present my case?" The defense lawyer is the script writer, producer, and director and style of presentation may ultimately influence whether the case is won or lost.

In *voir dire*, the lawyer selects the jury for a job, much like a job interview. The lawyer and client should carefully watch and listen to what people say and observe their appearance in answering questions. It is important that the lawyer establish a "commonality between the jurors and himself."

If a lawyer can sell himself and have credibility, the jury will follow his arguments in closing arguments. Trust must be established with the jury. You should reaffirm your persuasiveness and trustworthiness throughout the trial. If juries perceive you as genuine they will trust you. If they are not genuinely interested in you, your client is in trouble.

Lawyers use the acronym of "SOFTEN" to avoid the superficiality appearance syndrome:

S = Smile
O = Open Posture
F = Forward Lean
T = Touch
E = Eye Contact
N = Head Nod

Lawyers must overcome juror's common negative perception of attorneys as dishonest. A juror must be treated as you would wish to be treated. Don't believe for one minute that you can fool jurors, likewise you will not later be fooled by their verdict.

RULE: IN A JURY CASE, PAY CLOSE ATTENTION TO THE JURORS. MAKE CAREFUL WRITTEN NOTE OF THE JURORS YOU *DO NOT LIKE*, AND TELL YOUR ATTORNEY SO THEY CAN BE REMOVED.

RULE: IF THE JURY LIKES THE ACCUSED AND HAS A GOOD FEELING, *THEY WILL LOOK FOR AN EXCUSE TO ACQUIT*. IF THE JURY DISLIKES THE ACCUSED, THEY WILL SEIZE UPON ANY AVAILABLE REASON TO CONVICT.

Obtaining Information

Before going to court, you may need to obtain information of another person. Here are a variety of ways:

1. The county *Recorder of Deeds* maintains real estate deeds, loans, liens on personal property (UCC filings), marriage licenses, and other information.
2. The county *Assessor* has descriptions, measurements and value of land, houses and personal property.
3. The *Department of Revenue* has all traffic convictions (places and dates, detailed driver's license information, photographs, Social Security numbers), and car ownership details.
4. The county *Circuit Clerk* has all information on prior or pending civil cases, including depositions and interrogatory answers in (divorce and personal injury information) and criminal cases.

5. The County *Clerk* has voter information, which includes voter history, also all liquor licenses granted, and wage of county employees.
6. The city and county *health departments* and licensing offices can supply a variety of facts.
7. *Probate Court* has information concerning guardianship, incompetent persons, and detained descriptions and values in estates.
8. The Missouri *Secretary of State* has detailed information on corporations plus general literature.
9. The *Attorney General's office* has useful literature on many subjects.
10. *Credit agencies* have credit reports.
11. Ask polite questions of police, deputy sheriffs, elected officials, public employees, and county/city secretaries, and gain a wealth of *off the record* information and advice.
12. All city, county and state offices, for small fees, will supply certified copies of important documents, usually admissible in court.
13. Federal *Congressmen and Senators*, and State representatives and senators will be happy to obtain information for you, upon request, as a part of their constituent service. (Contact their staff employees who are always eager to please.)
14. Write *federal agencies* and get free information from the Department of State, Interior, Energy, Education, Labor, Defense, Commerce, Agriculture, Treasure, Securities, and Exchange commission, Transportation, General Services Administration, Environmental Protection Agency, Commission on Civil Rights, Veteran Administration, Postal Service, Small Business Administration, Occupational Safety and Health Review Commission, National Science Foundation, National Foundation for the Arts and Humanities, Interstate Commerce Commission, Federal Trade Commission, etc.
15. The *Government Printing Office*, Washington, D.C. 20401 has free or inexpensive booklets.
16. The *Fair Credit Reporting Act* gives you the right to know what information is distributed about *your credit* and to correct errors.
17. The *Freedom of Information Act* is an easy way to get information held by federal agencies. You must receive a response in 10 working days. (You cannot obtain classified and secret documents, personnel rules, confidential business information, investigatory files invading privacy or exposing confidential sources.)

18. Employ a *private detective* who has confidential sources.
19. The official *Manual of the State of Missouri* is 1500 page voluminous book listing or picturing every state employee with addresses, wages and job title. All personnel in the state in the Executive branch is listed, including photographs and personal history of judge.
20. High school, college and public *libraries* have voluminous information, including year book collections with photographs and information on students, Missouri statutes, and cases which are generally unavailable except at lawyers' offices.
21. *City directories* list neighbors, employment, and telephone numbers by neighborhood.
22. The State *Bureau of Vital Statistics* keeps death and birth certificates, divorce records and other facts on millions of persons.

Perjury of client

> **"The lawyer must always be ethical. He can be tough and dirty, but he must play within the rules. The defense lawyer must never lie, cheat, or steal."**

If you're thinking of falsely testifying at trial, think twice. You won't succeed in fooling the jury. Perjury in itself is a felony, although it is rarely filed. If a lawyer participates in the telling of a lie, it is subordination of perjury.

What will happen when you tell your lawyer you intend to lie at your trial:

1. Your lawyer will try to convince you otherwise.
2. If you insist, the lawyer is obligated to tell the Judge and Prosecutor (but not the jury).
3. You will be asked questions in the narrative when you tell your story from the witness stand.
4. Your lawyer should not argue or develop further your lies but should instead argue other defenses.

> **RULE: DON'T EVER LIE. DON'T EVER TELL YOUR LAWYER YOUR INTENT TO TESTIFY AT TRIAL AND LIE. YOU CAN'T FOOL THE JURY ANYWAY.**

You have selected your lawyer, your case is fully investigated and you're getting ready for trial. You'll need some knowledge of the law. Read on.

5
7
8
9
7 8 9 X 9 8 7
9
8
7

MINNESOTA
L'ETOILE DU NORD
WISCONSIN
STATE
MISSOURI STATE
HIGHWAY PATROL
SERVICE AND PROTECTION
IOWA
STATE
PATROL
POLICE
DEPT
POLICE

Chapter 3

Court Procedures

"America the beautiful—home of the brave and the land of the fee."

"In the Halls of Justice, the only justice is in the halls."

Lenny Bruce

"For justice, we must go to Don Carleone."

The Godfather

Tricks Prosecutors Play

"It isn't what people don't know that's important, it's what they know for sure but isn't true."

Will Rogers

The Prosecutor may prosecute with earnestness and vigor—indeed he should do so. But while he may strike hard blows, he is not at liberty to strike foul ones. It is as much as his duty to refrain from improper methods calculated to produce wrongful convictions as it is to use every legitimate means to bring about a just one.

Prosecutors wield great power and sometimes engage in misconduct. They are less subject to judicial or bar association oversight. Some types of prosecutorial misconduct have become almost normal.

Private attorneys and public defenders sometimes engage in similar misconduct, but there are important differences in their jobs. Undeterred prosecutorial discretion is terrifying:

1. Prosecutors are perceived by juries as prestigious and honorable.
2. They have powerful strategic and financial resources that give them distinct advantages.
3. They enjoy powerful decision making powers (charging crimes, plea bargaining, granting immunity, subpoenaing witnesses to Grand Juries and determining sentences).
4. The Prosecutor is elected to political office by the very persons on the jury.

Instead of clamping down on misconduct and imposing remedies of reversal of convictions or dismissal of charges, Appellate Courts use the *harmless error review* (although the Prosecutor erred it did not affect the jury verdict) overlooking misconduct, (claiming it was "invited" by the defense lawyer), ignoring misconduct where the defense lawyer failed to formally object, or indulging in the fiction of *curative instructions* (the Judge attempts to tell the jury to disregard and not consider what they have just heard.) (Similar to telling you you are forbidden to ever think about elephants.)

Other tricks that Prosecutors sometimes use are:

1. *Assassinating your character.* Attacking your character makes a conviction more likely, such as portraying you as dangerous or undesirable, or you associate with bad persons, inferring you have a criminal record and are more likely to have committed the crime;
2. *Introducing improper evidence.* Presenting false, misleading, or inadmissible evidence. It deceives the jury. Asking loaded questions with innuendos, referring to polygraph tests, withdrawn guilty pleas, guilty pleas of co-conspirators are all improper tactics;
3. *Inflaming juror prejudice.* Appealing to passions and prejudices by placing inadmissible evidence before juries, offering gruesome photographs or using inflammatory rhetoric, exhorting juries to "win the war on crime," inciting them to vengeance, or appealing to racial, ethnic, national, or religious prejudice, or appealing to wealth or class bias;
4. *Use of the media.* The Prosecutor and media often have a cozy relationship where the Prosecutor releases prejudicial information to them, and they print information from unnamed sources, and are able to slant stories trying the accused in a newspaper article instead of the courtroom. Quoting the results

of scientific tests and statements of witnesses helps form the public's decision about guilt even before any of the evidence is ever introduced into court, some of which may not be legally admissible;

5. Violating the privilege against self-incrimination. It is improper to infer because of your silence at trial, or failure to explain conduct to the police after arrest that you should be assumed guilty. Prosecutors come as close as they can stating their own case is uncontradicted, unrequited (an indirect reference to your failure to testify).
6. *Name calling* against your lawyer. Attacks on the defense lawyer are quite usual, belittling him, gaining an advantage before the jury by running him down claiming his objections were made in bad faith, or he always uses the same defense, does not care about the case, or has no confidence in his own client. In *sandbagging*, the Prosecutor makes new arguments and raises new theories for the first time during rebuttal summation so your lawyer has no chance to answer.
7. *Exploiting prosecutorial prestige* by stressing their own personal integrity and of their office by arguing they represent the government, and they are merely prosecuting a charge "brought by a Grand Jury". They insinuate their case is truthful and improperly vouch for their witnesses.
8. *Misrepresenting the record.* Prosecutors often refer to matters outside the record not entered into evidence, implying they are incriminating or insinuate issues of fact have already been decided. This lessens the jurors' sense of responsibility. They refer to the availability of pardon or executive clemency, the availability of appellate review, encourage the jury to go ahead and convict, and if there is any error a later Appellate Court can correct it.
9. *Hiding evidence.* Rules require all police reports to be turned over to defense counsel prior to trial, but often are hidden. The defense lawyer will learn of the information which might be helpful, but not until it is too late. On appeal the burden is on your lawyer to show the evidence would have likely made a difference and the jury verdict would have been different.
10. Once you win a case, the Prosecutor has unbridled discretion in *filing new charges* and can keep refiling almost without limits. He can plea bargain and make unbelievable sweetheart deals with

other criminals to force them to testify against you without restriction.

The Criminal Charge

You are entitled to know the nature, substance, and specific conduct of the criminal charges against you. A criminal charge must follow the statute, but must also *sufficiently inform* so you can *prepare your defense* and prevent a retrial on the same charges. Generic (general) charges are not allowed. A definite or precise date and hour is not required, but the mental state must be stated (willfully, knowingly, intentionally, negligently).

Amendments or changes in the criminal charge are allowed unless you are shown to be prejudiced.

You must file a *Motion for Bill of Particulars* which requests the state to make the charge more specific. In Associate Circuit Court the charge is a *complaint*. In Circuit Court, it is called an *information*. If a grand jury makes the charge, it is an indictment.

The Opening Statement

> **"Except ye utter by the tongue words easy to be understood, how shall it be known what is spoken? For ye shall speak into the air."**
>
> St. Paul

> **"Hollow words, I deem are the words of ills."**
>
> Aeschylus

The opening statement does not entitle lawyers to argue their case, but merely preview for the jury what the attorney believes the evidence will be. It helps make chronological order of the case easier for a jury to understand.

The Prosecutor *must* give an opening statement and outline his evidence. The defense attorney *need not* make an opening statement, but makes a serious mistake by not doing so. In the vast majority of the cases when an opening statement is not given by a defense attorney, the client ends up being convicted. Notwithstanding each juror's answer at voir dire surveys by trial attorneys constantly show that jurors *do* hold it against the accused if he does not testify or present evidence to explain his side of the case.

The opening is an outline of the expected evidence, and attorney comments are not evidence in and of themselves.

Talking to the jury in the opening statement is an opportunity by expression, gesture and mannerism to try the case, make points and advance arguments to the jury perhaps by a mere inflection of the voice.

The prosecution will make reference to the *victim* in an attempt to get sympathy and prejudice. The defense counsel will use his client's first name and tell the jury good things about his case, and touch his client's shoulder to *humanize him*.

RULE: JURORS TEND TO FORM MIXED OPINIONS ABOUT THE CASE EARLY IN THE OPENING STATEMENTS, THE VAST MAJORITY, MORE THAN 75% OF THOSE OPINIONS ARE NEVER CHANGED DURING A TRIAL.

By the end of the opening statements most of the jury panel have made a tentative decision as to how they are leaning without hearing one drop of evidence. The defense attorney should get his theory in early so the jury can be pondering his case.

The Closing Argument

"It's never over till it's over."

Yogi Berra,
New York Yankees (1946)

"Good idea not to accept gold metal until race is won."

Charlie Chan

Closing arguments is the time for the trial attorney to show his colors. Nothing could be more boring than an attorney who reads his closing statement from typewritten pages or who merely reviews the testimony of the witnesses. The lawyer should *argue* the facts.

Most attorneys would be astounded to proceed to the lectern and argue without any prepared notes. Juries are impressed by the attorney who speaks from the heart, who knows enough about his case that he can call the witnesses' names and argue their testimony *without the use of notes*.

It is simple enough for the attorney to outline the argument on paper and memorize the outline with several broad themes of the case. Once this is accomplished, rehearsal once or twice in front of a mirror the night before together with the trial attorney's innate ability to convince and persuade should be sufficient for the attorney to spend 20-30 minutes in front of the jury without the benefit of notes.

Even the most complicated case should be reduced down to attacks on the credibility of key witnesses, false reliance by the state on the evidence, or proof by defendant's witnesses which cause a reasonable doubt.

Sex in the Courtroom

A woman has a much better chance than a man of acquittal on a murder charge. Of course, if she happens to be a blond, her chances rise about 45 percent.

There have been few studies done on the significance of sex in the courtroom but, as in real life, it is an important and moving force.

The quality of participants in the trial between the prosecutor and defense attorney is important. Whether a particular attorney is handsome, homely, honest, timid, soft-spoken, arrogant, or a shyster depends upon the juror's perception.

Attorneys should let the jury see their good side, especially to break the solemnity and seriousness of the occasion.

It is important to physically lay hands on your client, put your arm around his shoulders and talk to him, mention his wife, family, military and work record, to let the jury know he is a *human being* and *living person*, and not just a "defendant".

When representing a young male, you want other young males and females on the jury who will relate to the same lifestyle. When representing an older client, you want older jurors who will be more understanding. If representing a white collar defendant, you want older, more conservative, white collar jurors. When representing a blue collar defendant, you want younger, factory, blue collar type jurors.

Older women can relate to younger male defendants as their sons and grandsons. It is important if your client is a good looking male or female to get members of the *opposite sex* on the jury who might have a natural physical attraction. If you represent an attractive female, avoid female jurors whenever possible.

The Prosecutor wants a jury that vote together (like sheep) as a group to convict the defendant. The defendant will seek a jury of independent-thinking people (woman wearing hats, men wearing white socks) who will not be stampeded by appeals for law and order to make an example out of your client.

RULE: MAKE SURE THE JURORS SELECTED AGREE:

1. THAT THEY PRESUME YOUR CLIENT NOT GUILTY TO START WITH.
2. THAT THE PROSECUTOR HAS THE TOTAL BURDEN OF PROOF.
3. THAT THEY AGREE WITH BEYOND A REASONABLE DOUBT AS THE STANDARD OF PROOF.
4. THAT YOUR CLIENT DOES NOT HAVE TO TESTIFY OR PROVE HIS INNOCENCE.
5. THAT THE JUROR HAS NO AX TO GRIND OR SCORE TO SETTLE BY MAKING YOUR CLIENT AN EXAMPLE.
6. THAT THE JUROR HAS NEVER BEEN A VICTIM OF A SIMILAR CRIME.
7. THAT THEY AGREE TO BE TOTALLY IMPARTIAL.
8. THAT THEY WOULD BE SATISFIED WITH A PERSON LIKE THEMSELVES ON THE JURY IF THEY WERE THE ACCUSED.
9. THAT THEY HAVE NO REASON TO HOLD ANYTHING AGAINST YOUR CLIENT.
10. THEY HAVE NO RELATIVE IN LAW ENFORCEMENT.
11. THAT THE JURY VOTE MUST BE UNANIMOUS AND THEIR VOTE IS JUST AS IMPORTANT AS ANYONE ELSE'S, AND NOT TO SURRENDER THEIR VOTE IF THEY ARE IN THE MINORITY.

Televised Trials

Television is here to stay in our nation's courtrooms. Most states now permit some TV coverage, and Federal Courts are experimenting.

The intolerable circus in *Texas vs. Billie Sol Estes,* (U.S. Supreme Court, 1962), had cables and wires across the courtroom floors. Microphones and cameras were prominently displayed and beamed at the jury and witnesses. Proceedings were disrupted by TV crews.

The Court ruled the *judicial serenity and calm* is a Constitutional right to which every accused is entitled. To hold otherwise is a *desecration of the courtroom.*

Television has now progressed where a camera can unobtrusively be located in a tiny hole in the rear of the courtroom. The idea that the *majesty of the law* or that *courtrooms belong to Judges only* is wrong.

Cable viewers have many opportunities to view real trials which are far different from make-believe television dramas.

Missouri trials will soon be on television and citizens will benefit by seeing justice well served.

Suppression Hearings (the Exclusionary Rule)

> **"I ask you, Ladies and Gentlemen, would a police officer jeopardize his career by lying under oath?"**

All illegally seized evidence is excluded from court. If *evidence* is found or *confession* obtained after an illegal search or eyewitness identification is obtained after an illegal lineup, *none of the evidence may be used.* This is known as the *Fruit of the Poisonous Tree Doctrine.*

There is a growing reluctance to apply the *Exclusionary Rule*, and some believe the rule may soon be abandoned.

You have a *reasonable expectation or privacy* that your property will be free from intrusion, and that expectation must be a reasonable one which society is prepared to recognize.

Rules for pretrial suppression hearings are:

1. *Motions to Suppress* raise a collateral issue, independent of your guilt or innocence, and normal rules of evidence may not apply. The trial judge hears the evidence without a jury.
2. Motions must be filed in writing and in advance of trial. You must prove the illegality of arrest or search. The state has the automatic burden of proof.
3. The evidence must be sought to be used by the state at trial, must be relevant, and must have been seized by police and not a private citizen.
4. If no Motion to Suppress is filed prior to trial, the Judge assumes you have no objection.
5. You must have a possessory interest or reasonable expectation of privacy (*standing to complain*).
6. If you testify, your testimony cannot be used against you at trial unless you testify differently at trial.
7. Hearsay testimony is admissible to explain the basis for police action.

When a confession is obtained, your lawyer will file a *motion to suppress* that the statement was coerced, that you were not properly advised of Miranda rights, or you did not make an intelligent waiver of your rights. Physical evidence should be suppressed if there was an illegal arrest or the search.

You will invariably learn information at your hearing that will aid you at trial.

Associate Circuit Courts

Most prosecutions begin in the Associate Circuit Court of the county that has venue (where the crime occurred). They have jurisdiction to try misdemeanors and to hold felony preliminary hearings.

The Court has jurisdiction to accept misdemeanor pleas of guilty or to try the case. Trials are normally before the Judge, but can also be before a jury.

If a jury has been requested, or once requested and waived, the trial is *on the record*, tape recorded and the appeal goes directly to the Court of Appeals instead of Circuit Court.

Preliminary Hearings

The preliminary hearing is held in Associate Circuit Court and a *critical stage* of a criminal proceeding. The purpose is to test the existence of *probable cause* for filing of felony criminal charges in Circuit Court. You can see the evidence against you and cross-examine the witnesses for later use at trial.

You have a meaningful opportunity to defend.

A smart move is to tape record the preliminary hearing:

> the tape can be used to impeach a witness later at trial, and
> the tape cannot be used by the Prosecutor if his witness later becomes unavailable.

If probable cause is found to exist, you are *bound over* to Circuit Court to stand trial at a later date. If you are not bound over, you are discharged by the Judge, but the charge may later be refiled by the Prosecuting Attorney, if he so desires, for a new preliminary hearing.

Pretrial Discovery (State Court)

The exchange information, reports, physical evidence, and witnesses' statements after the preliminary hearing or grand jury indictment.

The Prosecutor must disclose any information which might reduce the crime, lessen the punishment, or tend to show your innocence. If he fails to disclose something that might make the trial fundamentally unfair (might have created a reasonable doubt) and was not disclosed, an appellate court will reverse the conviction and order a new trial (the *Brady* Rule). A criminal trial is a *search for the truth* and not a mere poker game to be won by the most skilled lawyer. The purpose of pretrial discovery is to minimize surprise.

You have the right to the following:

1. Names and addresses of the state's witnesses
2. Written statements of witnesses
3. Grand jury transcripts
4. Reports of scientific tests by experts
5. Papers, and objects the state intends to use at trial.
6. Prior criminal convictions of state's witnesses
7. Electronic surveillance tapes
8. The rap sheet of the accused (the Hoover sheet)
9. Psychiatric reports
10. The right to scientifically test evidence
11. The identity of eye-witness informants

If the Prosecutor produces his existing file, it is substantial compliance with the discovery rules.

The State has the right to know the following:

1. Reports or statements of your experts
2. Names and addresses of defense witnesses
3. Papers, and objects you may use at trial.
4. Whether you intend to rely on insanity
5. If you intend to rely on an alibi, the names of witnesses and information as to the place that you claim to have been at the time of the offense.
6. Names of all good character witnesses

Either attorney may interview the other parties' witnesses without the consent of the other attorney. A witness has the right not to talk with either attorney, but you refusal to be interviewed can be mentioned at trial.

Pretrial Discovery (Federal Court)

Discovery in federal varies from state to state, but are under the same general rules interpreted by different U.S. Attorneys throughout the nation.

Federal Rule 16 provides for discovery and inspection by both the government and the defendant of each other's files.

The *Jencks Act* limits obtaining copies of reports or statements made by a witness until the witness has *actually testified* on direct examination in the trial of the case.

This is a bad law. The government may have voluminous pages of testimony and statements and if your attorney is not given an advance look, before trial, to meaningfully prepare cross-examination questions, handling him a bundle of reports after the witness testifies, while the jury is seated in the jury box, is of no value.

The U.S. Supreme Court in *Brady vs. Maryland* reminds us:

> "...the essential task of a criminal trial is to search for the truth...this search is not furthered by rules which turn the trial into a mere poker game to be won by the most skilled tactician."

These cases require disclosure of evidence that is favorable to the accused and important to guilt or punishment. Such evidence is called *impeaching* or *exculpatory* if it would be helpful to the accused.

Mercifully, some U.S. Attorneys adopt an *open file policy* broader than what the law allows, which gives you a semblance of a fair trial.

Media Publicity

> **"Now where do I go to get my good reputation back?"**
>
> Ray Donovan, Former Secretary of Labor,
> leaving the courtroom after being acquitted of bribery

Prosecutors and police can demoralize an accused by talking about him in the press. It makes life hell, embarrasses his family, and ostracizes him from the community. The Prosecutor speaks through press releases, speaking indictments and criminal charges (long rambling criminal charges), speaking motions (getting facts into the media in legal motions which they know are not otherwise admissible), and bail and pretrial detention hearings.

> **RULE: IT IS DIFFICULT TO REPRESENT A DEMORALIZED PERSON. GOVERNMENT PROSECUTORS WANT YOUR CLIENT TO SURRENDER, QUICKLY PLEAD GUILTY, AND ROLL OVER ON THEIR FRIENDS.**

It is important the new media have access to non-prejudicial information about a crime. The press needs police cooperation to accurately and fairly report the concurrence of a crime. The following suggestions are reasonable guidelines that protect the interest of the state and accused while also giving facts to the public:

1. Information necessary to aid in the suspect's apprehension.
2. A warning to the public of any dangers that an at-large suspect might present.
3. Name, age, residence, occupation, and family status of those arrested.

Lawyers are careful about what they say outside the courtroom prior to trial. Ethical rules prohibit attorneys from making statements to the press intended to influence the public.

Few Prosecutors understand they are to release no prejudicial information about the accused, without also adding that *the accused is presumed innocent.*

Conduct of Trial

> **"Three things belong to Judge: to hear courteously, to answer wisely and to decide impartially."**
>
> Socrates

It is duty of the trial Judge to maintain dignity, order and decorum in the courtroom.

Although the Judge normally leaves questioning to the attorneys, he has the power to call and question a witness. The Judge exercises judicial self-restraint. He may not indicate his belief of guilt or innocence, nor commit on the evidence.

The court, in its discretion, may exclude trial witnesses from the courtroom. (The *Rule as to Witnesses.*) This insures their testimony will not be influenced by what they have heard in the courtroom.

The accused should not appear in jail clothes, but can be shackled or handcuffed if he demonstrates hostility.

> **RULE: THE JUDGE IS ALWAYS TO APPEAR NEUTRAL AND SHOW NO FAVORITISM TOWARD EITHER SIDE. THE BEST JUDGE IS ONE WHO LISTENS TO BOTH ARGUMENTS AND DECIDES THE CASE STRICTLY ACCORDING TO LAW.**

Witnesses

Once a witness testifies, he is subject to full rights of cross-examination by the opposing lawyer. Attorneys have the right of cross-examination of witnesses within proper bounds. The scope of cross-examination is *limited* to matters brought out in the direct examination and only in rare cases may new evidence be introduced.

An attack on the believability of a witness is called *impeachment*. Discrediting a witness may be accomplished as follows:

1. Showing bias or prejudice
2. Showing incapacity as witness
3. Showing bad reputation for honesty
4. Showing the witness has been convicted of a crime
5. Proof of prior inconsistent statements
6. Showing facts inconsistent with his testimony
7. Showing he has been promised money, leniency or favors

Impeachment by Prior Convictions and Bad Conduct

A witness may be cross-examined and *impeached* by a prior misdemeanor or felony conviction.

There is an absolute right to ask such questions, no matter how old or remote the crime except in federal court which limits prior convictions only to felonies within the preceding ten years and which involved fraud.

Evidence may be shown that on a prior occasion the accused committed acts which constitute a crime (even though he may not have been actually convicted.) Admittedly, this may be prejudicial and inflame the passions of a jury; however, evidence of *prior bad acts* helps to establish motive, intent, absence of accident or mistake, and are admissible.

The Prosecutor cannot call a witness to testify who is expected to take the Fifth Amendment, but the defendant may. If a deposition or prior sworn testimony is available, and if the witness is otherwise *unavailable* to attend trial, his prior testimony may be read to the jury.

Once asked about prior inconsistent statements, a witness' credibility can then be *bolstered* by asking about *prior consistent statements.* Any evidence to bolster a witness is admissible if offered in rebuttal.

If a witness is asked whether the accused has ever been in *trouble* or *arrested*, the *door is "opened"* and the witness can then be asked questions and specifics about prior arrests, and confrontations with police, regardless of whether a conviction followed.

Witnesses may be cross-examined as to any matters referred to in direct examination or within *fair preview* of direct examination, and otherwise inadmissible evidence may be received into evidence by way of cross-examination where the witness *opens the door.* Great latitude is given to show bias, motive, ill feeling, prejudice, or interest on the part of any witness.

RULE: IF YOU TAKE THE WITNESS STAND, BE PREPARED TO BE ASKED EMBARRASSING QUESTIONS.

Good Character Witnesses

The law presumes a person of good character would have been less likely to have committed the crime than one of bad character. Therefore, evidence of the good character of defendant by witnesses who are familiar with his reputation in the community for truthfulness, honesty, good moral character, and being a law abiding citizen, is admissible. It is not what the witness personally knows, but what he has heard others say.

A witness may be shown to be a good friend of the accused or asked about other aspects of the accused such as prior arrests that did not result in convictions. Accordingly, a good character witness can hurt a defendant. Most witnesses do not understand their testimony is based on their knowledge of the reputation (which is what others say) (gossip) and not on what the witness personally knows about the accused.

RULE: IF YOU ARE ON TRIAL THINK TWICE BEFORE PRESENTING GOOD CHARACTER WITNESSES. YOU OPEN THE DOOR TO POSSIBLE EMBARRASSING EVIDENCE, PRIOR ARRESTS OR BAD ACTS. PRESENT GOOD CHARACTER EVIDENCE ONLY IF YOU ARE SQUEAKY CLEAN.

Eyewitness Identification

One of the best types of proof is eyewitness identification. Factors considered by the court in determining the reliability of the identification include:

1. the opportunity to view the criminal at the time of the crime
2. the witness' degree of attention
3. the accuracy of the prior description of the criminal
4. the level of certainty demonstrated by the witness at the confrontation
5. length of time between the crime and confrontation

Privileges:

"Many links frequently compose the chain of testimony which is necessary to convict an individual of a crime...that no witness be compelled to furnish any one of them against himself..."

Chief Justice Marshall, U.S. Supreme Court, 1807

The law has, for many years, recognized certain conversations to be private and secret. Proof of what was said at these conversations cannot ever be admitted into evidence. Once it is shown a witness is getting ready to answer a question using privileged information, an appropriate objection is made and the Judge will forbid an answer.

1. Attorney-Client Privilege

Any conversation between an attorney and a client is privileged. The client asserts the privilege and can prohibit his lawyer from ever testifying against him or in any court where the testimony might come into evidence. Any time a lawyer is asked questions about what a client has said to him, the lawyer will refuse to answer. Once it is shown the communication was made confidentially to the attorney to obtain legal advice, then it is forever secret.

If the third persons are present and are closely identified with the client, the conversations, remain privileged, but if third persons were present and there is proof the conversation was not intended to be private, the privilege is deemed waived.

The only exception is the *fraud exception* where the attorney is actually becoming involved in a crime with a client, or the *tax* reporting exception where information you give to your lawyer in preparing a tax return is not privileged.

2. Husband-Wife Privilege

Neither spouse may testify against the other as long as they are legally married. It may be invoked only by the witness spouse.

The confidential conversation survives death or divorce if the communication was intended to be confidential. The purpose is to preserve family by preventing spouses from becoming adversaries in criminal proceedings against one another. Exceptions are:

1. Where spouses are joint participants in a crime;
2. Where the crime occurred *before* the marriage;
3. Where spouses are involved in divorce case;

4. Where the crime was child molestation or wife beating.

3. Doctor-Patient Privilege

Conversations occurring between you and your doctor are privileged. The purpose is to protect you so you may admit to illnesses to receive medical treatment and for the doctor to inquire about your medical background to properly treat you.

4. Clergyman-Penitent Privilege

The privilege of making a *confession* to your priest or minister is protected by state and federal law that anything said is private and confidential.

5. Informant-Identity Privilege

This privilege is not absolute and may be granted or denied at the discretion of the Judge. The name of an information might be disclosed if relevant and helpful to the accused, although there is no absolute right to disclosure.

The government will claim privilege because it values confidential information given it. Heavy burden rests of the accused to show the identity of the informant is necessary to his defense.

6. Journalist Privilege

A journalist does not have an absolute privilege under the First Amendment to refuse to testify before a grand jury to answer questions relevant to an investigation into the commission of a crime, but does not have a privilege to refuse to divulge his sources.

The burden is on the moving party to prove:

1. That an effort has been made to obtain the information from other sources
2. The only access available to the information is through the journalist
3. The information is critical to the case

Most states have a *shield law* which protects against compelled disclosure of sources and information in which news announcers and reports refuse to testify or answer questions as to the source of their information.

7. Grand Jury Secrecy

The privileged nature of state and federal grand jury matters prevents grand jurors and lawyers from telling things that occurred before a Grand Jury.

8. Accountant-Client Privilege

There is no accountant-client privilege unless the accountant was employed by your attorney and is working under the attorney.

9. Fifth Amendment Privilege

A citizen has the unqualified right to take the *Fifth Amendment* and refuse to answer questions or give some information which might *form a link in a chain* which will *tend to incriminate* you. This includes authenticating records and files in which there is not a Fifth Amendment privilege if, by identifying or authenticating the records, you tend to incriminate yourself.

There is no Fifth Amendment privilege on behalf of a *corporation,* especially as to records that are *required to be kept by law.*

10. Hotline Privilege

Evidence of hotline calls are privileged communications when a person calls the Division of Family Services to report child abuse or neglect.

Right to Counsel

Everyone has *the right to consult with a lawyer* at any time and *no one* can interfere with that right. When police first knock on your door, or while being questioned at a crime scene, or while standing by your car on the highway, police can never interfere with your right to refuse to talk unless an attorney is present. You have the absolute right to *say nothing,* and have an attorney present if and when you do talk.

Even under arrest for DWI you have the right to *talk to an attorney* by telephone before you take the breathalyzer test.

> **RULE: SINCE YOU ARE INVOLVED IN A LEGAL MATTER, IT IS A GOOD IDEA TO CONSULT A PERSON SKILLED IN LEGAL MATTERS. WAIT BEFORE YOU TALK. SOLEMN REFLECTION AND SOUND LEGAL ADVICE NEVER HURT ANYONE.**

Failure to Talk

> **"The genius of the Constitution is that it sides with the citizen against the government."**

If you take the Fifth Amendment as soon as you are arrested, it cannot be commented on at trial. If you testify at trial, you cannot be cross-examined as to your failure to come forward sooner.

You *always have the right to remain silent*, and no adverse comment can be made at any time about your decision to claim your Constitutional right.

> **RULE: WHEN IN DOUBT, TAKE THE FIFTH AMENDMENT. YOUR FAILURE TO TALK CANNOT BE USED AGAINST YOU.**

Bail should be sufficiently high to give a *reasonable assurance* that you will appear, but should not be used as an instrument of oppression.

Should you fail to appear, the Court declares the bond in default, issues a *capias warrant* for your arrest, and the Prosecutor will certify the forfeiture to Circuit Court for final judgment and execution on the sureties. If the bondsman can later show good reason to have the forfeiture set aside, when you appear, he may get his money returned.

The Judge can release you on your own recognizance (known as "ROR") or allow you to sign an unsecured bond.

Conditions can be placed on you such as:

1. ordering supervision
2. placing restrictions on travel, association or residence
3. requiring reports to bailiff at regular intervals
4. requiring a 10% cash bond
5. forbidding contact with the victim or witnesses
6. any other reasonable conditions

When released on bond, your custody is transferred to the bondsman. If you willfully fail to reappear, you are guilty of a separate crime.

> **RULE: AT BAIL HEARING, DO NOT CONCENTRATE ON GUILT OR INNOCENCE. DISCUSS YOU PREVIOUS GOOD RECORD, EMPLOYMENT, SCHOOLING, FAMILY, AND STRONG TIES TO THE COMMUNITY AND**

THAT YOU WILL RESPONSIBLY RETURN TO COURT WHENEVER ORDERED.

Citizen Opinions

Citizen (non-expert) witnesses can testify to their opinions to prove:

1. Identity of a person
2. Speed of an automobile
3. Temper of animals
4. Recollection of the weather
5. Color, weight, light or darkness
6. State of feeling between persons, whether friendly or hostile
7. Appearance of a person, whether healthy or sick
8. Race to which a person belongs
9. Reputation
10. That a sound was one of "distress"
11. Sanity or insanity
12. Intoxication
13. The value of property

Interpretation of Criminal Laws

Criminal laws are to receive a sensible, reasonable, and logical result, and should not receive meaningless, and absurd constructions. Words should not be taken out of context but used in their plain and ordinary meaning.

All criminal laws are *strictly construed* against the state and in favor of the accused and are interpreted *liberally in favor* of the accused. If there is any doubt that the offense charged is covered by the law, you must be acquitted.

Bail Bonds

> **"Excessive bail shall not be required, nor excessive fines imposed, nor cruel and unusual punishments inflicted."**
>
> Eighth Amendment, U.S. Constitution

You have the right to a reasonable amount of bail set by the Court, unless the charge is murder. After conviction, bail is often increased, since it may be more probable you would fail to appear.

The bondsman is the one person you like to see after being arrested. He is a licensed businessman who pledges his financial assets to the court to ensure that you do not have to remain unjustly imprisoned after arrest and before trial. Courts recognize his importance and dependability by relinquishing you to the bondsman who guarantees your later appearances in court.

The bondsman benefits several people. His client is allowed to return to the job, of critical importance when he is the family breadwinner. The family stays together, ensuring the shared support so vital at that time.

For a small percentage of the bail amount, the bondsman keeps the accused and his family from having to pay the full amount of bail and further sacrifices while the wheels of justice sometimes grind slowly.

The bondsman helps the Sheriff since it reduces the jail population and saves taxpayer costs.

There are five *ways to make bail*:

1. Pay the full amount of the bail to the court (which is money later returned).
2. Post a property bond, which normally includes the following:
   a. the property must be within the county or state.
   b. an attorney must often be hired immediately.
   c. property abstract, title insurance, and current tax statement must be gathered together.
   d. the value of the property must sometimes be 200 percent of the bond amount.
   e. letters of appraisal are required from appraisers and real estate experts.
   f. you must wait in jail for these things to happen.
3. Post 10% cash bond (if the judge consents).
4. Hire a bail bondsman (which costs you 10% of the total bond).
5. Obtain a ROR (Release on own recognizance).

RULE: IF THE BOND IS SMALL, CALL A BONDSMAN. IT'S CHEAP AND QUICK. IF THE BOND IS LARGE AND YOU ARE SHORT OF MONEY, WAIT UNTIL YOUR FORMAL ARRAIGNMENT IN COURT. YOUR LAWYER MAY GET THE BOND LOWERED AND MAY GET THE JUDGE TO APPROVE A PROPERTY BOND (WHICH DOES NOT COST) OR A ROR.

Surrendering on a Warrant

RULE: NEVER SURRENDER YOURSELF ON YOUR OWN. IF YOU LEARN THAT YOU ARE WANTED, CONTACT AN ATTORNEY IMMEDIATELY FOR ADVICE.

Your lawyer will arrange for you to turn yourself into court when it is in open session at the earliest opportunity.

If you turn yourself in to the FBI, DEA, Highway Patrol or city detectives, you will be questioned, thrown in jail, and a high bond recommended. There will be *no opportunity* to make a property bond (placing your real estate for bond rather than paying a bond fee to a professional bondsman), or an ROR (release on own recognizance), or have your bond amount lowered. By the time you are taken to court in a jail uniform, you're upset and fearful.

If you surrender to a Judge in the presence of your lawyer, your bond might be lowered or more favorable arrangements made or a combination of conditions which will reasonably insure your appearance in court. It will save you money and be more dignified. You can then be routinely booked at a later time, asked routine booking questions, and released.

Grand Jury

Grand Juries are impaneled in both state and federal court for two purposes:

1. To investigate the conduct of public affairs and officials and
2. To decide whether evidence is persuasive enough to justify bringing to trial someone accused of committing a crime.

A Grand Jury returns a *Presentment* or *True Bill* which becomes a basis for the subsequent court criminal charge. The federal juries consist of no less than 16, nor more than 23; the state juries have 12.

The jury can issue subpoenas, take hearsay testimony in secret and makes its decision in secret. The Prosecutor dominates the proceedings. If evidence of guilt is unimpressive a *No Bill* is recorded, which seldom occurs.

This does not prevent the Prosecutor from trying again before another Grand Jury or investigating new and different charges.

Indictments are sometimes sealed (secret) until the accused is taken into custody.

> **RULE: THE GRAND JURY IS A TOOL OF THE PROSECUTOR AND CONTROLLED BY HIM. THE PROCEEDINGS ARE SECRET. YOU MAY NOT KNOW THE PROSECUTOR IS INVESTIGATING YOU UNTIL IT IS TOO LATE. MUCH OF HIS EVIDENCE IS HEARSAY. HE NEED NOT PRESENT FAVORABLE EVIDENCE ABOUT**

YOU. THE PUBLIC TENDS TO LEND GREATER IMPORTANCE TO GRAND JURY INDICTMENTS, BUT IT IS NOT JUSTIFIED.

Federal Pretrial Detention

Some Federal Prosecutors will ask for *pretrial detention* if you are:

1. A risk to flee
2. A danger to the community
3. Likely to be convicted.

It is often used to harass or punish you by keeping you in jail for a few days before a formal bond hearing. Perhaps you'll panic and confess. You'll have trouble getting your lawyer's fees together. You'll have no chance to meaningfully interview and hire an attorney.

At the hearing, stay clear of the facts of the case. A jury will listen to the facts later and decide guilt. Simply present facts of your personal life, employment, marriage, children, and ties to the community to convince a Judge that you will later appear for court.

How to Handle a Grand Jury Subpoena

RULE: IF SERVED WITH A GRAND JURY SUBPOENA, DO NOT PANIC!

Being served with a grand jury subpoena should not ruin your day. Read the subpoena carefully to determine whether they only want documentary evidence or whether they want you to testify. You may ask questions of the person serving you, but he will tell you to call the prosecutor's office. You may call the U.S. Attorney's Office, but you will be encouraged to make an appointment to come in and "discuss" your information with one of their investigators so as to "avoid having to appear before the Grand Jury." This is attractive enough that many people will, without seeking advice of a lawyer, make incriminating statements. Resist this temptation!

If you are 1000% innocent and have no guilty knowledge, or are a mere records' custodian of documents being sought, go to the prosecutor's office and discuss the matter. Arrangements can be made for you to produce the materials to federal agents so that a grand jury appearance is not necessary.

If, however, you have some guilty knowledge of the crime, make an appointment with an attorney who is knowledgeable of federal grand jury matters. Seek his advice which will probably include the alternative of *taking the Fifth.*

You lose nothing by taking the Fifth. If you do refuse to answer, it cannot be mentioned or used against you. Once the prosecutor learns you are going to take the Fifth, they may not call you before the jury.

The Grand Jury sits in a private room with the Prosecutor and an official court reporter who transcribes the proceedings. Do not be nervous. If you have a question, you can step outside and consult with your lawyer who is not permitted inside the Grand Jury room.

If you have been subpoenaed, it may mean you are *not a target* since often, targets are not subpoenaed but are investigated by calling other witnesses.

You do not have a Fifth Amendment right to refuse to produce *business records*. You can gather these together at your convenience, deliver them to your attorney's office, and let him deliver them to the Prosecutor.

RULE: THE LESS YOU HAVE TO SAY TO A PROSECUTOR, OR THEIR INVESTIGATORS–THE BETTER YOU ARE.

Juveniles

Special courts have exclusive jurisdiction of all crimes where a juvenile (under 17) is involved. In minor violations, the child is released to the parents. In more important crimes the child is ordered to a juvenile detention home.

The court holds a hearing within 4 days. The child may not be held more than 7 days unless a formal Petition is filed.

Proceedings prior to the juvenile petition are *detention hearings*. The court receives testimony relevant to the necessity for detention and may review written reports, social reports, and appoint a *guardian ad litem*.

RULE: THE JUVENILE OFFICER MAY MAKE *INFORMAL ADJUSTMENTS* BY GIVING ADVICE TO THE JUVENILE, REFERRING HIM TO APPROPRIATE PUBLIC OR PRIVATE AGENCIES THAT PROVIDE COUNSELLING.

If a formal Petition is filed, the juvenile is entitled to be represented by an attorney. A juvenile hearing is not open to the public and persons are present only if they have a direct interest in the case. The evidence is decided by the Judge. The case must be proved beyond a reasonable doubt. The juvenile is afforded rights during the trial and, if convicted, has the right of appeal similar to regular criminal trials.

Strict adherence to Constitutional safeguards, such as Miranda warnings, is not required because of the informal nature of juvenile procedures.

In *In Re: Gault* (1967), the U.S. Supreme Court ruled a juvenile has the right to remain silent and consult an attorney.

When police determine an arrested person is a juvenile, he is taken immediately to a juvenile officer and is not rereleased to police until a juvenile Judge has so ordered.

Juvenile files are secret and can never be opened.

Extradition

If you are wanted for a felony in another state, you can be arrested and held 20 hours until an arrest warrant is filed alleging you are a *fugitive form justice.* The governor's office will not issue warrants until they are sure a felony warrant has been issued by the demanding state, and the warrant is based upon probable cause.

You may waive the right to contest the extradition and the demanding state is notified to transport you to their state.

If you refuse to waive extradition, the demanding state will contact its Governor's office which will forward its warrant required for extradition to the governor of Missouri. The Governor may then issue a *Governor's Warrant* directing the Sheriff to deliver you to the demanding state.

The same procedure is allowed if you flee from Missouri to another state. You are not entitled to be released on bail.

The Governor may call upon the Attorney General or county Prosecutor *to investigate the demand for your extradition* and decide whether *you ought to be surrendered.*

Guilt or innocence is not inquired into by the governor except to properly identify you as the person charged with the crime. If you decide to test the legality of the arrest, you are given a reasonable time to apply for Writ of Habeas Corpus.

The *Uniform Mandatory Disposition of Detainer Law* gives you the right to demand a speedy trial within 180 days. If the trial is not held within such time or additional reasonable time as the court may allow, the court dismisses the charge.

You must do more than merely write letters expressing a vague desire for disposition of charges; you must comply with strict requirements of the law.

RULE: IF YOU ARE ARRESTED ON A FUGITIVE WARRANT FROM ANOTHER STATE, *DO NOT* WAIVE EXTRADITION. MAKE BOND, EMPLOY A LAWYER, AND STALL AND NEGOTIATE YOUR CASE. MAYBE THE DEMANDING STATE WON'T EXTRADITE YOU. IF THEY DO, AND A GOVERNOR'S WARRANT IS RECEIVED BY YOUR SHERIFF, GO AHEAD AND TRAVEL TO THE DEMANDING STATE ON YOUR OWN, REPORT TO THE COURT, AND TURN YOURSELF IN ACCOMPANIED BY YOUR LAWYER AND BONDSMAN.

Courtroom Demeanor

> **"When I use a word it means just what I choose it to mean—neither more nor less."**
>
> Humpty Dumpty

A criminal trial is a serious event.

Our system strives to guarantee a fair trial by impartial Judge and jury, and represents the entire history of democratic process and its achievements of individual freedoms. Demeanor in the court must not only reflect a serious attitude, but an appreciation of the proceedings, and it demands respect in every word and deed.

Your performance in court will be seriously judged by the jury:

Appearance. Be clean, well groomed, shaved, and conservatively dressed.

Demeanor. A sincere businesslike attitude should always be displayed, demonstrating a positive, decisive, and knowledgeable attitude. Proper manners are essential.

Language. Slang, profanity, or coarse language should never be used.

The Prosecutor will first ask questions on direct examination, to relate facts to the court and jury as firsthand knowledge.

After the direct, the defense will cross-examine. The functions are:

To bring out the whole truth and not just facts favorable to the Prosecution

To uncover omissions in testimony that have the effect of leaving unfair or misinterpreted conceptions

To bring out bias

To demonstrate uncertainty
To show unfamiliarity with facts
To show prejudice

If you are telling the truth, you will be successful under the most rigorous cross-examination. You should not only be sure as to the truth but also as to the limits of your own knowledge.

Always be alert for leading questions in the answer is suggested by the questions.

Observe the following rules:

1. Stand upright when taking the oath. Say, "I do," in a clear voice.
2. Sit erect in the chair. Do not make movements that might catch the eye of the jurors and distract them.
3. Be polite and courteous, especially toward the opposite attorney. Do not regard either attorney as an enemy.
4. Listen carefully to every question; think before answering. If the question is not understood, ask the attorney to repeat it. Speak clearly and distinctly. Never cover the mouth or chew anything.
5. Answer only the questions asked; do not volunteer any information. Do not try to outwit or mislead either attorney.
6. Look at the jury when answering a question. Don't look at an attorney for help. Try not to be overly partisan.
7. If memory is not clear on a point, say so. If a mistake is made, correct it.
8. Do not laugh or smile when a question is asked and do not attempt to be humorous or clever in answering.
9. Temper should always be kept under control. Do not show anger.
10. Use a "yes" or "no" response if possible, however, answers that need explanation may be given.
11. If an attorney mistakes testimony or facts, promptly and courteously correct him.

Trail Objections

During the jury trial both lawyers will voice various objections.

If an objection is "sustained," then the question is to be disregarded and the answer shall not be considered in evidence. If the objection is overruled, the Judge does not find merit in the objection and the answer is for the jury to consider. Some common objections are:

Argumentative. When an attorney argues with the witness.

Asked and Answered. A later repetition of the same question calling for the same answer.

Assuming Facts Not in Evidence. The framing of a question in a manner that certain facts not in evidence must be assumed as true by the witness before answering.

Bolstering. A question that attempts to bolster testimony before the testimony is attacked, such as, "You are telling the truth, aren't you?"

Best Evidence Rule. The best documentary evidence available and procurable, as opposed to secondary documentary evidence, must be admitted. For example, an original document is the best evidence, as compared to a photocopy.

Beyond the Scope. Testimony outside the scope of inquiry. Often the objection is raised on cross-examination and pertains to facts not brought out on direct examination.

Calling for Conclusion. Questioning where a conclusion must be drawn from the question before it can be answered. "Isn't it a fact," or "as a matter of fact," and similar questions call for a conclusion.

Compound Question. A question requiring a number of answers.

Cumulative. Seeking repetitious evidence that is unneeded.

Hearsay. Testimony that rests on the *truthfulness* of someone not on the witness stand or of the second source, rather than firsthand evidence. Hearsay is secondary indirect evidence and is based on what a third party has told the witness.

For example, Witness A testifies to the truth of Fact X because B told A it was true. This testimony is inadmissible because: B is not available to testify and be cross-examined, observed or judged by the court and not under oath.

Hearsay excludes out-of-court statements offered to prove the *truth* of what was said.

Exceptions to the Hearsay Rule. There are many exceptions to the Hearsay Rule, which may allow the evidence under some other theory. The rationale underlying exceptions embraces (1) the necessity for the exception to serve the ends of justice, (2) the guarantee of trustworthiness of evidence.

Out-of-court statements made by persons who were not involved in a trial may not be admitted into evidence "for the truth" of what was said. Such information may come into evidence for the purpose of *explaining conduct* and other exceptions. But any oral or written statement or non-verbal conduct of a person intended to be an assertion as to the truthfulness of a fact is not admissible.

Exceptions to the hearsay rule are so great that the rule should be that hearsay is admissible in the following instances:

Hearsay exceptions include:

1. Present sense impression
2. Excited utterance
3. Then existing feelings
4. For diagnosis or treatment
5. Recorded recollections
6. Regular records
7. Absence of expected regular record entry
8. Public records
9. Vital statistics
10. Absence of a public record
11. Church records
12. Marriage, birth and death certificates

13. Family records
14. Property records
15. Ancient documents
16. Market publications
17. Learned treatises
18. Pedigree reputation
19. History and boundary reputation
20. Character reputation
21. Conviction of a crime
22. Judgment
23. Dying declarations
24. Statement against interest
25. Numerous other exceptions

Immaterial. Facts which are not essential or necessary.

Irrelevant. Evidence which does not relate to the matters at trial which neither prove or disprove the issues at trial.

Leading and Suggestive. A question that suggests the answer for the witness:

Example: "You arrived at the accident and saw the defendant's vehicle cross the double yellow line, isn't that true?"

1. When a witness is hostile or adverse,
2. When the witness is a child
3. If the witness' memory needs to be refreshed.

Improper Foundation. A proper foundation must be laid before facts may be admitted into evidence. In the instance of photographs, the laying of proper foundation includes the date and time photographs were taken, and whether the picture accurately represents the scene as it was when the picture was taken.

Improper Impeachment of Own Witness. You cannot argue with your own witness, unless he gives surprise or hostile testimony.

No Corpus Delicti. Offering facts into evidence before proof that a crime has been committed.

Prejudicial. Evidence that unnecessarily inflames the passions of the jury, such as bloody photographs or evidence of another unrelated crime.

Self-Serving. Evidence may not be offered that only furthers the witness' own cause.

Strike. Delete and remove from the official court record.

RULE: I'VE RARELY FOUND IT BENEFICIAL TO REPEATEDLY JUMP UP AND DOWN LIKE A JACK IN THE BOX AND MAKE TECHNICAL OBJECTIONS IN FRONT OF A JURY. JURIES GROW WEARY OF LAWYERS CONSTANTLY INTERRUPTING WITNESSES, TRIALS BEING DELAYED AD INFINITUM. JURORS ARE GIVING THEIR PRECIOUS TIME AS A PART OF THEIR DUTY AND WISH TO SIMPLY HEAR THE EVIDENCE AND MAKE AN INFORMED DECISION. HEARING LAWYERS' WRANGLE OVER FINE POINTS OF LAW IS A TRAVESTY ON THE SYSTEM OF JUSTICE. LITTLE IS GAINED BY A CONSTANT BARRAGE OF OBJECTIONS. OCCASIONALLY, AN OBJECTION WILL TEND TO SHOW THAT THE JUDGE IS ON MY SIDE (IF I WIN MY OBJECTION), TO DISRUPT OPPOSING COUNSEL'S TRAIN OF THOUGHT AND RATTLE HIM IN FRONT OF THE JURY, OR SHOW OPPOSING COUNSEL IS NOT WELL PRESENTED.
THE LESS OBJECTIONS THE BETTER.

The Ten Commandments of Cross-Examination

There are important rules lawyers use in cross-examination.

1. Be brief.
2. Ask short questions using plain words.
3. Ask only leading questions.
4. Don't ask a question if you don't know the answer.
5. Listen to the answer.
6. Don't quarrel with the witness.
7. Don't permit the witness to explain.
8. Don't allow the witness to repeat direct testimony.
9. Avoid asking the "one question too many."
10. Save the explanation for summation.

A lawyer should not be afraid to cross-exam, to fail, or to be embarrassed. It will happen no matter how experienced an attorney is.

You never know what is going to happen when a witness takes the stand, and it's an extremely rare fight when both sides don't land at least a few punches.

A lawyer will try to control the witness by controlling the questions. You can control the subject matter and must control yourself. If you succeed then you can control the outcome of the case.

Stare Decisis

> **"It is revolting to have no better reason than a rule of law than that so it was laid down in the time of Henry IV."**
>
> Former U.S. Justice
> Oliver Wendell Homes (1887)

The cornerstone of our legal system is that prior judgments and court opinions, sound in principle and workable in practice, are *heavily relied upon* in the law and are cited by lawyers and Judges as legal authority.

In deciding legal questions, courts look for prior case decisions to see if a nearly identical case has been decided answering the same legal question.

This does not mean courts refrain from reconsideration of prior decisions. Legal research by lawyers and Judges can take many hours or days, to determine minute points of law, checking prior court decisions in other states, and all federal courts throughout the United States.

Lawyers look for cases to prove prior *precedent* and if they can find an identical case have a much better chance of persuading the Judge. A *white horse cased* is one that is identical, or a *case on all fours* is exactly opposite. *Supporting* or *distinguishing* authority is cited in legal *briefs* and supplied to the opposing lawyer.

Accomplice Testimony

Accomplices may testify against each other as long as they are not co-defendants in the same criminal case.

Where an accomplice has given a confession and testifies, the confession is admissible against him. But when the accomplice testifies, that portion of his confession implicating another accused must be cut out or erased from the confession under the *Bruton Rule*.

RULE: YOU CAN BE CONVICTED OF YOUR OWN CONFESSION, BUT NOT BY THE CONFESSION OF ANOTHER PERSON ON TRIAL WITH YOU.

The Sunshine Law

"I think heroic deeds were all conceived in the open air..."

Walt Whitman
Leaves of Grass

"It is the public policy of this state that meetings, records, votes, actions, and deliberations of public governmental bodies be open to the public unless otherwise provided by law...which shall be liberally construed and their exceptions strictly construed to promote this public policy."

Missouri Law

The law sets out specific instances when a meeting, record, or vote may be closed. Public meetings are to be held at reasonably convenient times and in places accessible to the public.

At least 24 hours prior to a meeting, a notice must be prominently posted in the office of the body holding the meeting. The notice must include the time, place and agenda of the meeting.

Public records are to be kept open and available to the public for copying. The custodian for the records, must act on each request for access to a public records be acted on no later than the end of the third business day following the date of the request. If access to the record is not granted, the custodian must provide a written statement explaining why access is not granted.

A governmental body is permitted to close its meetings, records, and votes relating to the following:

1. Litigation
2. Leasing, purchase, or sale of real estate where public knowledge might adversely affect the transaction
3. Hiring, firing, disciplining or promoting an employee
4. Welfare cases of identifiable individuals
5. Software codes for electronic data processing
6. Individual identifiable personnel records
7. Records which are protected from disclosure by other law

If a court finds a governmental agency has violated the Sunshine Law, it may declare void any action taken in violation of the law, and fine a person up to $300 and order payment of costs and attorney fees to the party successfully establishing a violation.

Allocution

You have the right to personally speak to the Judge prior to being sentenced. This right, before sentencing is *ancient in the law*, usually depicted in westerns as asking the cattle rustler if he has anything to say before he is strung-up and hung.

Years ago it was thought sometimes the executioner might spare the condemned man.

In current day courtrooms, it is appropriate for you to speak a few words before sentence is pronounced as long as the words are *humble, conciliatory, apologetic,* and *not threatening* or challenging. You can make a Judge mad and increase your sentence by saying the wrong thing. Sometimes the wisest use of the tongue is to keep it in your mouth.

Dismissal of Charges

If you are charged but the case later dismissed (*nolle proseque*), found not guilty, or imposition of sentence suspended, all court *records are closed.*

You cannot thereafter be guilty of perjury for giving a false statement by reason of failure to recite the arrest or trial in response to any inquiry made for any purpose (employment applications).

Privacy of Arrest Records

Arrest records are considered private if you are not charged within a few days after arrest.

Absent giving consent for someone to look at your records, the arrest records are closed, but not *expunged.*

Police always have access to the records. It is possible to ask the court to expunge the arrest records, as courts have considerable equitable powers, but unless good reasons exist, courts are reluctant to erase them.

They remain law enforcement records forever.

RULE: FORGET ABOUT HAVING YOUR ARREST RECORDS DESTROYED AT THE POLICE STATION. IT ISN'T GOING TO HAPPEN.

Crimestoppers

Fighting crime isn't just a job for the police. Everyone can join the battle through Crimestoppers. This citizen supported program allows people to anonymously tell about criminal activity without getting involved.

You can call Crimestoppers and tip off police without giving your name. Cash rewards of up to $1000 are paid. Calls have led to the arrest of suspects in all types of crimes.

When you call the police, no one will ask your name, but you will be assigned a code number. You will be asked to call back after police have had time to investigate your tip and determine if information led to arrest. You always identify yourself by your code number. Unlike many reward programs, Crimestoppers pays on arrest and not for conviction.

The board of directors is made up of community citizens, and police are not generally involved. Rewards are paid by board members at an undisclosed location, at a time and day agreed upon with the coordinator and the informant. No signatures are required.

Free Speech

> **"Free speech would not protect a man in falsely swearing "fire" in a theater, and causing panic."**
>
> Justice Oliver Wendell Holmes, Jr. 1919

> **"Free speech means the right to yell "theater" in a crowded fire."**
>
> Abbie Hoffman

You can't yell "fire" when nothing is burning, but does the First Amendment give citizens a blank check? There are certain exceptions to free speech:

1. Libel and Slander

You may be sued for damages by spreading a *defamatory falsehood* in print (libel) or with spoken words and gestures (slander).

The burden of proof varies depending upon whether the person suing is a private citizen or a *public figure*, (a government official, celebrity, community leader). Public figures must prove the defamation was not only false but was made with *actual malice* or *reckless disregard* for the truth. Statements of opinion are usually deemed *fair comment* as the Supreme Court held there is no such thing as false idea.

2. False Advertising

Federal law prohibits making false claims about a product if those claims are a *material factor* in a consumer's decision to buy it.

It in famous 1961 Rapid Shave case they advertised their shaving cream could be used to shave sandpaper. The sandpaper shown in the TV ad was a "mock-up" and was, therefore, ruled improper.

3. Obscenity

For decades, courts have wrestled with laws defining *obscenity* and *pornography*, attempting to draw the fine line to protect constitutionally protected First Amendment rights, but to isolate hardcore pornography.

The Amendment guarantees the right of free speech, which, through the Fourteenth Amendment, protects citizens of each state.

A special problem are search warrants authorizing mass seizures of books and magazines, so as not to operate as a prior restraint on protected reading materials. A *prior adversary hearing* prior to the seizure, or a prompt post-delivery hearing is required.

What is obscene depends upon each case:

1. Whether the average person applying contemporary community standards finds the work taken as a whole appeals to prurient interests?
2. Whether it describes in a patently offensive way sexual conduct specifically defined by state law?
3. Whether it lacks serious library, artistic, political, or scientific value?

The jury is entitled to rely on its knowledge of what is contemporary community standards.

RULE: NUDITY, ITSELF, THE NAKED MALE OR FEMALE BODY, IS NOT OBSCENE.

Notary Public

The Missouri Secretary of State regulates and licenses state notary publics. A notary is authorized to swear to and verify signatures, to take acknowledgements, administer oaths, and to certify documents.

A notary must be licensed by the state, insured and bonded, and keep strict records in a permanently bound journal every time a notary seal is placed on a document.

In criminal trials, *notarized papers are not admissible* contrary to popular belief. Just because a document is sworn to, does not make it admissible in court since it is hearsay (an out of court document being admitted for the truth of its contents).

It is a criminal offense for a notary to knowingly or recklessly commit misconduct in notarizing signatures. Careful attention must be made to properly identify the person whose signature you are notarizing.

A notary public has no legal training. It is a crime for a notary to render legal advice or engage in the unauthorized practice of law.

> **RULE: PEOPLE THINK NOTARIZED STATEMENTS CAN BE USED AT TRIAL. THEY CAN'T. SUCH STATEMENTS ARE HEARSAY AND HAVE NO LEGAL VALUE.**

Child Review Death Team

When a child under 15 years of age dies, the coroner or medical examiner shall determine the necessity for a *child death review* and notify the child death team. The team includes public officials and representatives of public health care service providers. Missouri law provides for the enactment of rules and regulations to aid in the identification of suspicious deaths of children as to whether there should be an autopsy. They have access to juvenile and DFS records and are immune from civil lawsuit.

Wiretaps and Bugs

State and federal law enforcement agencies electronically monitor millions of telephone conversations yearly, with nearly 1,000 bugs and telephone taps. The number of taps in Missouri is increasing drastically as the sophistication of law enforcement officers and knowledge of Missouri's wire tap law increases.

The controversial *roving wiretaps* allow police to monitor targets wherever they go, providing secret operations in which undercover agents plant miniature transmitters everywhere from a boat hull, barn, or at a highway intersection.

Federal authorities notify you that you have been secretly recorded, but they don't disclose where you were recorded, why, or what you said.

Electronic surveillance is an important investigative tool helpful in penetrating secrecy surrounding organized crime and narcotics rings.

An average court-ordered wiretap would be as follows:

> After a long investigation into a narcotics or illegal gambling organization, police secretly tap a conventional home telephone, remaining in place for one month, picking up 35 calls a day, of which most are considered innocent. The remaining incriminating conversations overheard each day, however, lead to your arrest.

The cost of a month long wiretap is about $53,000, or in federal court about $81,000, most of the money paying salaries of police and federal agents who monitor the bugs continuously, tuning in on tape machines only during incriminating conversations. Federal law forbids taping telephone calls that do not concern criminal activity.

> **RULE: ACTUAL WIRETAPPING IS RARE AND DIFFICULT TO DO. YOU RUN A MUCH GREATER RISK OF HAVING YOUR CONVERSATIONS SIMPLY VOLUNTARILY RECORDED BY THE OTHER PERSON ON THE LINE.**

Talking on the Telephone

The telephone is a wondrous invention and used properly can save you dollars and hours of time in conducting normal business affairs. Placing business orders, answering customers' questions, and keeping in touch with long distance family members, the telephone has revolutionized the nation. Hand-held mobile phones and car telephones are now a necessity.

In criminal prosecutions, the telephone can be a dangerous instrument which police and Prosecutors regularly use to ensnare participants in crimes:

1. Police commonly use informants who pretend to be good friends of yours. They are paid money, promised plea bargains, dismissal of current cases, or made other promises to enlist his help in telephoning you to record the conversation. Simple recording devices available at stores in all cities can be used to tape record all calls you make or receive. These portable recording devices can be carried and telephone calls recorded at other phones, including pay telephones. The informant will regularly engage you in incriminating conversation, enticing you to admit to past, present, or future criminal activity. Many criminals attempt to talk in "code" by using other names for drugs or stolen property, but these incriminating conversations, when taken together with the attendant criminal conduct, will demonstrate a pattern to the jury that your conversation was directly intended to carry out a crime.
2. The *controlled delivery* drug cases, the drug transporter is arrested and drugs seized. It is common for police to have the informant telephone the intended designation of the drugs, making 2-3 phone calls explaining the reason for the delay in delivery.

3. The caller will regularly include conversation which directly relate to the day, date, hour, and nature of contraband being discussed so the tape is "self contained" or "consistent" and will make sense when played later to the jury.
4. Once the tape is recorded, it is preserved and marked, for the chain of custody. A typist transcribes the conversation. At trial, the transcript is not admissible into evidence, but is passed to the jury for their aid in listening to the conversation. The tape is played by use of a loud speaker system, simple jam box, or an elaborate tape recording where each juror is given a separate pair of headphones.

Anyone involved in criminal activity should be extremely careful in telephone conversations especially when dealing with someone you do not trust or suspect may be an informant. Any tape recording, made with the permission of *one willing participant* to the conversation, is legal. State and federal wire-tap laws prohibit a stranger to the conversation to intercept and divulge your phone call. It is even illegal for you to wire your own business or personal phone and record your spouse, employees, or others who may be using your own telephone.

> **RULE: IF YOU ARE INVOLVED IN ANY CRIMINAL ACTIVITY, IT IS A BAD IDEA TO DISCUSS IT OVER THE TELEPHONE. YOU RUN THE RISK OF MISPLACED TRUST AND FAITH THAT HE WILL TAPE RECORD THE CONVERSATION. AFTER YOU LEARN THIS LESSON, YOU WILL HAVE MANY YEARS IN THE PENITENTIARY TO CONSIDER YOUR MISTAKE.**

Scientific Reliability of Machines

In any type of testimony concerning the operation of a machine such as a breathalyzer or radar gun, there must be proof that the machine was in *proper working order* and had been previously tested for accuracy (the *laying of the necessary foundation*).

> **RULE: AN EASY WAY TO WIN A SPEEDING TICKET IS TO CHALLENGE THE PROPER WORKING ORDER OF THE RADAR GUN.**

Ballistics

Evidence of shot patterns made by guns and striations or markings on bullets positively identify the particular gun as a murder weapon.

The barrel of a gun has tiny marks or scans that make ridges and scratches on a bullet. A bullet is fired into cotton, preserved and examined under a microscope and then compared with a bullet found in a deceased person.

RULE: BULLETS ARE LIKE FINGERPRINTS, POSITIVELY INDENTIFIABLE, AS COMING FROM THE SAME GUN.

CRIME VICTIM'S COMPENSATION

To determine if you are eligible for the *Missouri Crime Victim's Compensation Fund*, the eligibility requirements are:

1. The incident occurred in Missouri or you are a Missouri resident injured in a state with no compensation program.
2. The incident was reported to police within 48 hours of its occurrence, or is a child sexual assault or abuse case and was reported within 48 hours of discovery.
3. Your claim is filed within one year.
4. You must be a victim, guardian of a minor victim, or family member of a deceased victim.
5. You suffered physical death as a result of a crime.
6. You cooperated with law enforcement officials during their investigation and prosecution.
7. The claim is not for property loss.
8. Economic loss (medical expenses, wage loss) totals $50 or more and has not, or will not be paid in full by other sources.
9. You were not an accomplice or did not commit a crime in connection with the incident.
10. The claim is not for pain and suffering.
11. If the incident involved a car, the person who committed the act must have intended to hit you or was driving while intoxicated.

Missouri: A Modified No-fault Divorce State

"If befriend a donkey, expect to be kicked."

Charlie Chan

"There is no winning in a divorce case; only degrees of losing. A 'civilized divorce' is a contradiction in terms."

Danny DeVito in
War of the Roses

If the court rules that there is *no reasonable likelihood that a marriage can be preserved* and is *irretrievably broken,* it can order a decree of divorce or legal separation.

Once suit is filed and personally served, the children immediately come under the jurisdiction of the court and may not be removed from the county or from the parent who has possession of them at the time the case is filed.

If either party believes the other is destroying or concealing property, or disturbing the peace or causing mental or physical harm, a *temporary restraining order* may be obtained.

All matters involved in the divorce, including child custody, visitation, and division of property are decided by the Judge.

Years later, there is a *substantial change of circumstances,* the same court can change the divorce decree.

The guiding principle is the best interest and welfare of any minor children and all orders have their well being in mind, including completely denying visitation if it would endanger or impair a child in any way.

Divorce matters are civil and police rarely become involved except to keep the peace. If police are convinced a restraining order is being violated, a full report should be made, and the parties advised to contact their attorneys.

Police may provide *standby assistance* while one spouse separates from another.

> **RULE: IN A DIVORCE CASE NO ONE WINS. EVEN TEMPORARY VICTORIES MAY MEAN NOTHING. THE SOONER YOU SETTLE THE DISPUTES WITH THE ONE PERSON IN THE WORLD YOU CHOSE TO MARRY, THE BETTER YOU ARE. GET A LAWYER, TELL HIM THE TRUTH—THEN TAKE HIS ADVICE.**

Grandparents are not given specific rights to ask for visitation and may employ an attorney and *intervene* in the litigation.

Adult Abuse Law

Police are required to enforce adult abuse laws to stop domestic violence. They must immediately respond to calls, and no longer have an option as to what to do. He must let her know her rights, resources, and inform her how to get an order of protection. The officer must arrange for transportation from the scene or to a hospital or shelter.

If police have probable cause to believe abuse is going on, he must arrest the abuser, whether or not the woman signs a complaint. If the officer decides not to arrest, he must provide a written report stating why.

If both parties claim to have been assaulted, the officer must attempt to identify and arrest the person believed to be the primary physical aggressor.

It a second call is made within 12 hours at the same address, an arrest must occur. The law includes family and household members, former spouses, and any persons related by blood or marriage.

Ex parte orders of protection can be served which provide temporary court protection before a divorce can be obtained.

Police, arresting in good faith, are granted immunity from civil lawsuit alleging false arrest, false imprisonment, or malicious prosecution.

Police may arrest a person who refuses to surrender custody of children when ordered to do so by an order of protection, and requires immediate delivery of the children.

There are loopholes in these laws. There are no rights under the law for gay relationships, for dating relationships, or for couples who have never lived together.

Child Abuse Hotlines and Investigations

The DFS has a Central Registry Unit that receives confidential reports of suspected incidents of child abuse. A central file is maintained of all reports for cross-checking. The toll-free hotline is open 7 days a week, 24 hours a day (800-392-3738).

Certain occupational groups (teachers and doctors) are required by law to make hotline reports.

Once a report is made, it is referred to a DFS county office and an investigation commences within 24 hours to detect potential abuse and to help the child. If the child is reported to be *in immediate danger* the social worker must personally observe the child and a preliminary finding is made to see abuse is substantiated.

RULE: NATIONAL STATISTICS SHOW A HIGH PERCENTAGE OF ALL HOTLINE CALLS ARE UNSUBSTANTIATED. NONETHELESS, A TREMENDOUS AMOUNT OF GOOD HAS BEEN DONE FOR THE SAFETY OF SOME CHILDREN WITH THE USE OF THE HOTLINE,

UNLESS IT IS USED BY *ANGRY RELATIVES* OR FIGHTING SPOUSES TO GAIN A TRIAL ADVANTAGE IN A DIVORCE CASE.

Business burglary showing damaged cash register provides an interesting trial exhibit for the prosecution. (Photo courtesy Jefferson City Police Department.)

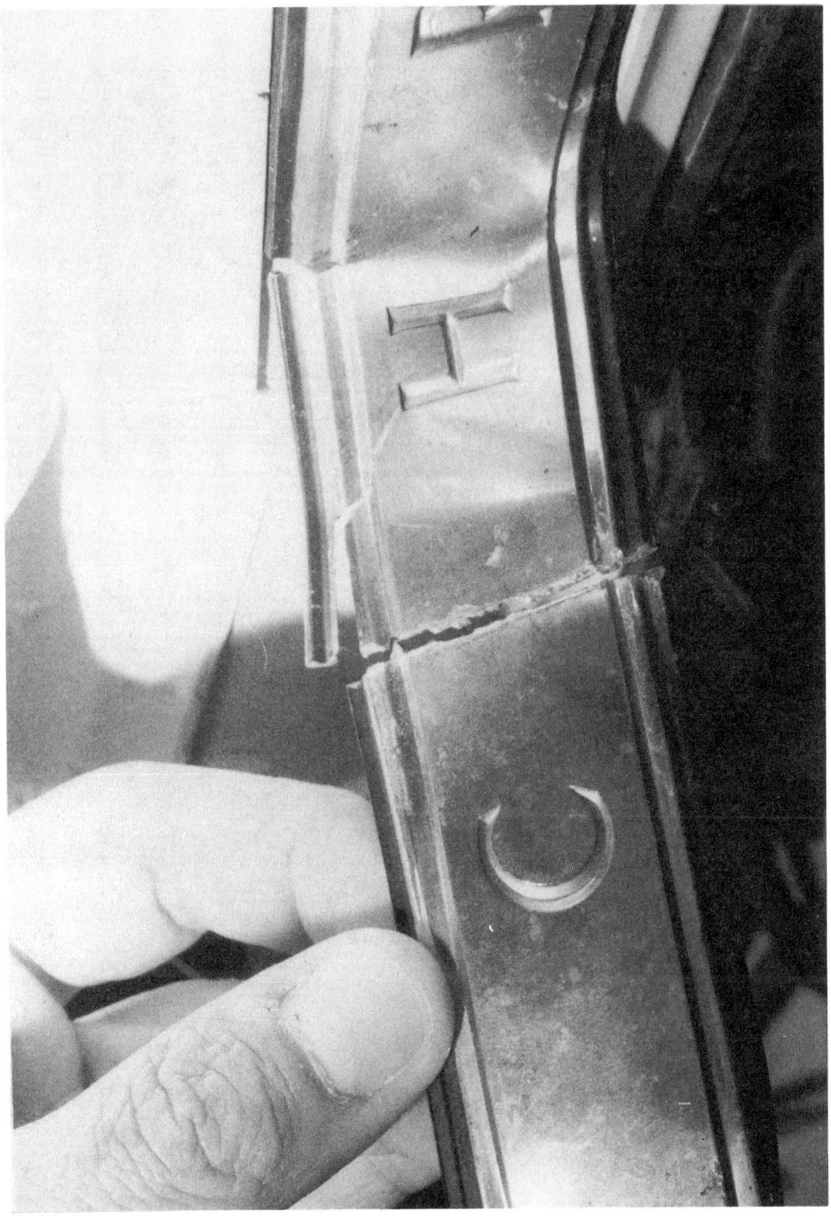

Leaving scene accident-close up photo of recovered evidence to suspect vehicle (Carthage P.D.).

Tire Track Evidence at a high school burglary resulted in a solved case (Marshall Chief of Police James B. Simmerman).

Leaving the scene accident - Det. Guy Blankenship shown matching evidence recovered to suspect vehicle (Carthage P.D.).

Bob Lawrence searching recovered stolen vehicle for hidden VIN number (Jasper County Sheriff's Office).

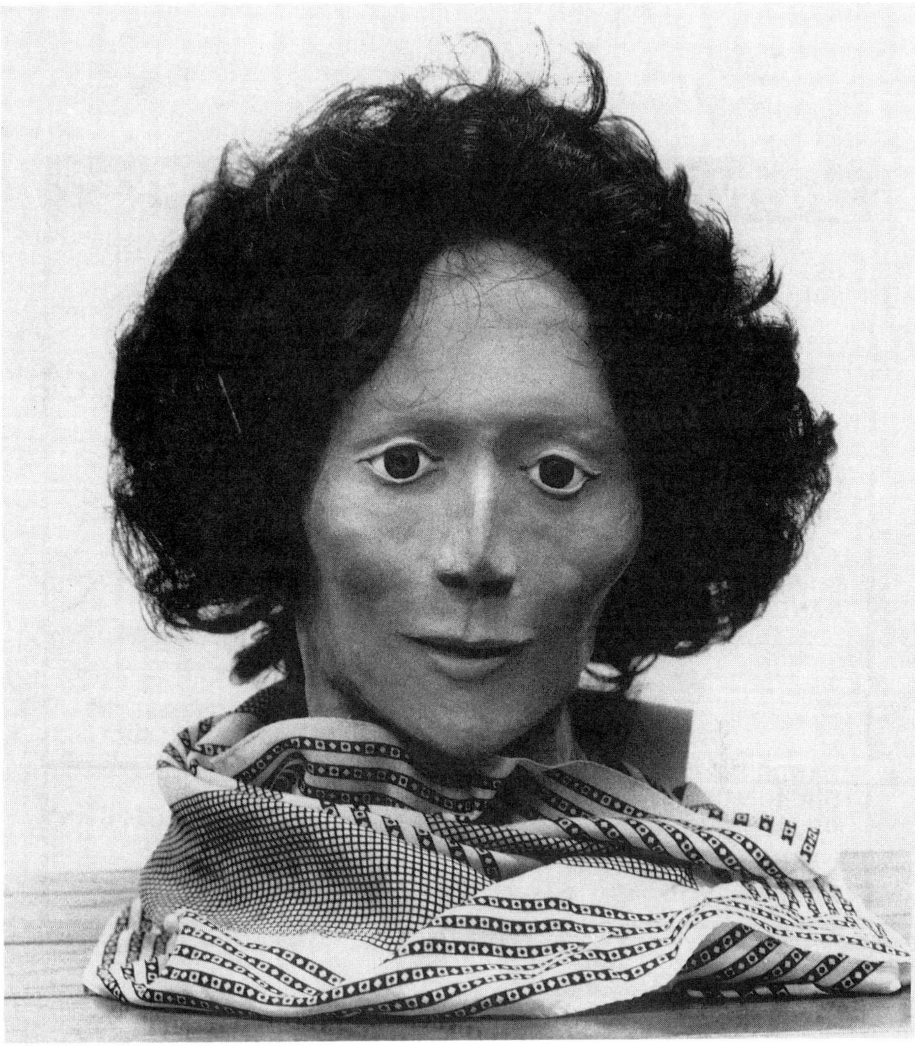

Greene County Sheriff John Pierpont and Dr. Erwin Busiek, Medical Examiner, used a mock up of skeletal remains to attempt to identify a skull found near a highway.

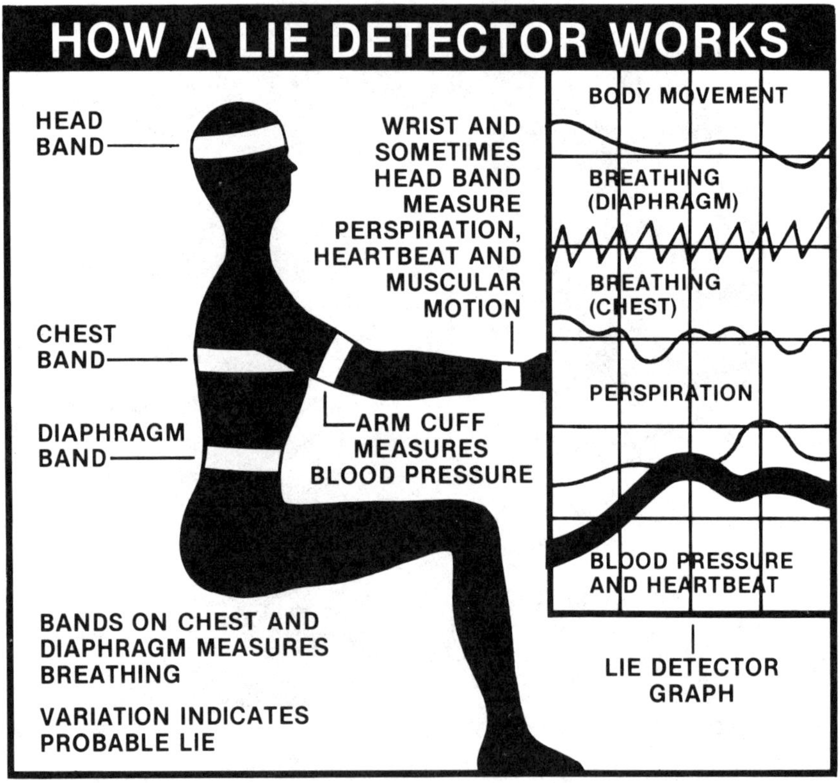
HOW A LIE DETECTOR WORKS
HEAD BAND
WRIST AND SOMETIMES HEAD BAND MEASURE PERSPIRATION, HEARTBEAT AND MUSCULAR MOTION
BODY MOVEMENT
BREATHING (DIAPHRAGM)
BREATHING (CHEST)
PERSPIRATION
BLOOD PRESSURE AND HEARTBEAT
CHEST BAND
ARM CUFF MEASURES BLOOD PRESSURE
DIAPHRAGM BAND
BANDS ON CHEST AND DIAPHRAGM MEASURES BREATHING
VARIATION INDICATES PROBABLE LIE
LIE DETECTOR GRAPH

BRING ME MEN TO MATCH MY MOUNTAINS

EQUAL JUSTICE UNDER LAW

IN GOD WE TRUST

Chapter 4

Defense!

"Why did I stab him 25 times? Because I couldn't turn off the electric carving knife, that's why."

"None of us were driving, Officer, we were all in the back seat."

There are a large number of defenses available in a criminal trial. Your defense depends upon the facts in your case and the truth of what happened. Some commonly used defenses include the following:

Self-Defense

When considering *self-defense* there is a major distinction between deadly and non-deadly force. The reasonable belief of the defender, under the circumstances *as they appear at the moment,* is required for self-defense, acting as a *reasonable man* given his particular belief at the time.

If non-deadly force is being used against you, you are not permitted to use deadly force. It is the use of deadly force that causes most of the difficulties in self-defense cases.

Since Henry VIII (1532), governments have attempted to define self-defense, in which the familiar phrase *retreat to the wall* was first used, which implies a person must retreat as much as possible before using deadly force in self-defense.

RULE: YOU MAY STAND YOUR GROUND AND USE DEADLY FORCE IF IT REASONABLY SEEMS NECESSARY TO PROTECT YOURSELF OR OTHERS.

Liberty itself is threatened if a law abiding citizen can be forced from a place where he has a right to be seems to be that a person should retreat as far as he can and then kill the other only as the only possible means of saving his own life. Some states have adopted the *no retreat rule*, others the *retreat rule*, where a person must elect to take an obviously safe retreat, if available, unless he is in fear of his life at the time.

RULE: TO CLAIM SELF-DEFENSE YOU MUST PROVE YOU OR YOUR FAMILY WERE REASONABLY PLACED IN FEAR OF YOUR LIVES.

General Denial

"Selling drugs? I didn't say I was 'selling drugs.' I said I was selling 'rugs'."

You have no duty to testify, present evidence, or to give an opening or closing argument. You have the complete right to sit silently in the courtroom during the entire case.

There are cases where the defense lawyer will use this strategy of merely cross-examining the state's witnesses, testing their credibility and memory. At the end of the case your lawyer argues the Prosecution *failed to prove the charges beyond a reasonable doubt.* If all 12 jurors unanimously agree with each other, you are free. The Prosecutor has a high burden of proof.

The reasonable doubt sufficient to acquit is doubt which would cause a reasonable man to hesitate to act in the more important affairs of his own life. Beyond a reasonable doubt does not mean beyond any shadow of a doubt.

The jury may suspicion or surmise that you are guilty. You may be the most likely suspect, may have been caught with stolen property nearby, and are in a compromising position. You may have made admissions or confessions that indicate you have guilty knowledge of the crime. Notwithstanding, the jury still must be firmly convinced of your guilt. The government must prove *each element* of the crime offense beyond a reasonable doubt.

Alibi

Even if the offense was committed as charged, if you were at another place you could not have been the person who committed the crime.

The burden of proof is on the Prosecutor to prove your *presence at the scene* of the crime. You have the burden of proof to come forward to prove that you were somewhere else. If you can satisfy the jury of a *reasonable doubt* of your presence at the crime scene, you are entitled to an acquittal.

The Prosecutor can present rebuttal witnesses, attacking the credibility or your alibi witnesses. You must reveal the names of your witnesses to the Prosecutor in advance of trial.

He will investigate and check out their stories, as to how they happened to remember where they (and *you*) were at another place months earlier.

Circumstantial Evidence

Circumstantial evidence means that *direct eyewitness* identification or testimony *may not be required* to convict you.

Circumstantial evidence may completely prove the case as long as every circumstance is *consistent with* the hypothesis of *guilt* and *inconsistent with innocence*, and must exclude every reasonable hypothesis that would establish you to be innocent.

RULE: SOMETIMES IN THE APPELLATE COURT, CASES CAN BE DISMISSED WHEN THAT COURT SIMPLY DOES NOT FIND THE PROSECUTOR'S EVIDENCE TO BE SUFFICIENT ENOUGH FOR THE JURY TO HAVE VOTED FOR GUILTY.

RULE: CIRCUMSTANTIAL EVIDENCE CASES ARE LEGAL IF ALL OF THE FACTS ARE CONSISTENT WITH GUILT. IF A VICTIM SWEARS IN COURT THE CRIME WAS COMMITTED AND POINTS YOU OUT AS THE PERPETRATOR, A SUBMISSIBLE CASE IS MADE AGAINST YOU. THEN IT IS UP TO THE JURY.

Motive

You may defend on the grounds you had no reason to do the crime. The existence of criminal intent (known as scienter) is essential. It is presumed you intended the natural and probable consequences of your act. The element of knowledge is rarely capable of direct proof and the jury must view *all the facts* to determine whether there is criminal intent or guilty knowledge. It may be proved by indirect evience and inferences reasonably drawn from circumstances surrounding the incident. Wide latitude is given the Prosecutor to prove motive.

RULE: STRANGELY THE PROSECUTOR IS NOT REQUIRED TO PROVE MOTIVE BUT MAY LET THE JURY

SPECULATE. IT THEN FALLS UPON YOU TO KNOW LACK OF ANY MOTIVE OR REASON TO HAVE COMMITTED THE CRIME. THIS MAY BE YOUR BEST DEFENSE.

Speedy Trial

Once criminal charges are filed you have the right to have your case quickly resolved. To demand your 6th Amendment right to a speedy trial, you must make known your wish by filing a *Demand for Speedy Trial.*

The U.S. Supreme Court in *Barker vs. Wingo* (1972) provided a 4 factor balancing test. The conduct of the prosecution is weighed to determine whether you are denied your constitutional rights:

1. the length of the delay
2. the reason for the delay
3. your assertion of your right for a speedy trial
4. prejudice to your case from the delay

Federal courts attempt to try your case within two months. State courts are required to try your case in 6 months from the date your case if filed in Circuit Court but are many exceptions which stop (toll) the speedy trial from ticking, which makes the law meaningless. If you claim police delayed their investigation *before* charges were filed, you ask for dismissal because of *pre-indictment delay.*

RULE: MANY CASES ARE DELAYED FOR YEARS AT A TIME, BUT PRECIOUS FEW ARE EVER THROWN OUT BY THE JUDGE FOR FAILURE TO RECEIVE A SPEEDY TRIAL. FIRST, FEW DEFENDANTS EVER REALLY WANT A SPEEDY TRIAL. DELAYS ALWAYS WORK TO THE ADVANTAGE OF THE DEFENDANT. SECOND, THE MOST DIFFICULT OF THE FOUR PART BALANCING TEST IS SHOWING HOW *YOUR CASE WAS PREJUDICED*, I.E., THAT EYEWITNESSES TO THE CRIME, WHO WOULD HAVE SUPPORTED YOUR TESTIMONY AND TESTIFIED TO YOUR INNOCENCE HAVE SINCE DIED OR CANNOT NOW BE LOCATED.

Intoxication

If you make the decision to drink alcohol, consume drugs, and become intoxicated, it is not a defense to a crime. Only if it was involuntarily induced (someone threatened or tricked you) is it a defense. Only if your intoxication is a disease sufficient to amount to a *psychosis*, is it a legal defense.

The jury is allowed to consider your degree of intoxication as a factor in *affecting your mental state* at the time of the crime and thus may *diminish your capacity* necessary to entertain one of the mental states required to commit the crime.

Ignorance of the Law

You cannot claim *ignorantia legis non exusat* (ignorance of the law), although a jury may consider it in determining your motive or in assessing punishment.

Entrapment

The Prosecution must prove your *predisposition and willingness* to commit a crime if the opportunity is presented to you to break the law. Entrapment defense exists to protect innocent citizens from *being drawn into criminal acts* by government agents.

To use this defense you must admit that you did in fact commit the crime.

The mere fact that undercover informants, police or others helped to provide a favorable opportunity to commit the crime is not entrapment. The jury will decide whether you were *predisposed* to commit the crime.

Sorrells vs. United States (U.S. Supreme Court, 1932), considered the *subjective view* which focused on your *state of mind* and whether you were predisposed to commit the crime. This subjective view is the current law, an *affirmative defense*, which must be raised and proved by the accused.

A minority of states use the *objective view* which concentrates exclusively on the conduct of the police. In this view your predisposition to commit the crime is irrelevant.

The government may not overstep the line between setting a trap for the *unwary innocent* and the *unwary criminal*. They must establish you were predisposed to commit the crime for which you were arrested prior to first being approached by government agents.

The state may use undercover agents to enforce the law, but may not originate a criminal design or plant in you a predisposition to commit the crime.

The government's quest for convictions should not cause the arrest of innocent law-abiding citizens.

Defending on the Facts Verses the Law

One of the first decisions in defending yourself is to decide whether to defend on the *facts* or the *law*:

1. *Facts.* If there is a factual dispute, as to whether you were present or have an alibi, whether the contraband was in fact stolen or did amount to more than $150, or whether the eyewitness is correct in their identification or could be mistaken, then such a case needs to be tried before a jury. The jury is the great *fact finder* who will determine beyond a reasonable doubt whether the Prosecution witnesses should be believed. Cases involving factual disputes are best resolved by a jury!
2. *Law.* If you defend on legal grounds, you should go to trial before the Judge sitting alone without a jury. If you have filed a Motion to Suppress the warrantless search of your home, or to contest the validity of a Search Warrant, or to contest whether the Miranda warnings were legally given, a Judge can best determine these legal questions since he has to apply case decisions handed down over previous years and interpret statutes.

Even if you lose you still have the right of appeal to the Court of Appeals where a panel of Judges will again decide whether the Judge was correct in his rulings.

Pleading Guilty with the Right of Appeal. Your particular court may allow you to plead guilty, but preserve your right of appeal, giving you a *contingent* right of appealing legal questions to an Appellate Court. Other courts prefer that you enter *no contest* or *nolo contendra* pleas or, plead not guilty and ask for a *trial on the record* (TOR). A TOR occurs in just a few minutes' time where you plead not guilty but indicate to the Judge you are willing to let the police reports be read into evidence. The Judge then *finds you guilty* and pronounces sentence.

Battered Women

RULE: BATTERED WOMEN ARE CAUGHT IN A CYCLE OF VIOLENCE. TOO OFTEN, IT ACCELERATES UNTIL THE ULTIMATE VIOLENCE.

A third of all women's injuries coming into emergency rooms are no accident. Most are the result of deliberate, pre-meditated acts of violence. Frequently they occur over and over until the woman is killed.

Although family violence is one of America's most critical health issues, society repeatedly sweeps it under the rug. It is not just a "personal problem" to be settled among the family. Tragically, the victim returns home to be beaten again.

The existence of battered women has come to the limelight in the past few years, its progression towards public awareness paralleling the growth of the women's movement. There has been little public outcry against this brutality, jokes about wife beating no longer seem funny; some experts estimate that as many as 50% of all woman will be battered victims at some point in their lives. Most women do not leave the relationship, preferring to ignore their condition, because of complex reasons.

In the *Battered Wife Syndrome* a woman is repeatedly subjected to forceful physical or psychological behavior to coerce her to do something he wants her to do, without any concern for her rights. The couple normally goes through a *battering cycle* at least twice. (Any woman may find herself in an abusive relationship with a man once).

The cause of the problem is a general breakdown of the family unit and the moral fiber of the nation. It is possible to love your family and not hurt them either physically or mentally. Families must learn to accentuate the positive and ignore the negative behavior in each other without resorting to violence.

Recognizing yourself as a potential batterer includes some of the following characteristics:

1. Were you physically abused as a child?
2. Was your mother battered by your father?
3. Do you display violence against other people?
4. Do you play with guns or use them to protect yourself against other people?
5. Do you lose your temper frequently?
6. Do you commit acts of violence against objects?
7. Do you drink alcohol excessively?
8. Are you unusually jealous?
9. Do you become enraged when people do not listen to your advise?
10. Is there a sense of overkill in your cruelty or kindness?
11. Do you feel that you are being battered or are battering someone? If so, you should seek help immediately.

Are You Abused?

A woman who answers "yes" to any of these questions may be in serious trouble.

Does your partner:

1. Constantly criticize you and your abilities?
2. Become overprotective or extremely jealous?
3. Threaten to hurt you, children, pets, family or friends?
4. Prevent you from seeing family or friends?
5. Have sudden bursts of anger?
6. Deny you access to family assets or control all finances and force you to account for what you spend?
7. Use intimidation or manipulation to control you or your children?
8. Hit, punch, slap, kick, or shove you?
9. Prevent you from going where your want when you want?
10. Force you to have sex when you don't want to?
11. Humiliate or embarrass you in front of others?

We live in a violent world in a society riddled with violent images, and through television and the news media, we have become perpetual observers of violence. We grow more in accepting brutality and perceive it as normal. Once this happens, an emotional numbness sets in. Thus, people raised in this atmosphere of terror often fail to recognize the consequences of their own violent actions.

The tacit acceptance of pornography, the promotion of machoism and the breakdown of the family unit all create a climate for violence in the home between man and woman, turning love into terror.

Insanity

In 1843 England Daniel M'Naghten was a Scottish woodcutter suffering from the delusion that he was persecuted by the Pope and Prime Minister Robert Peal (who founded the London police force known as "Bobbies"). He set out to shoot Sir Robert but by mistake shot Peal's secretary Edward Drummond. Although there was public outrage, M'Naghten was found not guilty by reason of insanity.

What became known as the *M'Naghten Rule*, held a man is not responsible for his criminal acts if because of a disease of the mind does not know the *nature and quality of his acts* or does not know that they are *wrong*.

Missouri has a modified rule. If a suspect is *suffering from a mental disease or defect excluding responsibility* he is entitled to have a mental examination prior to trial. If all agree with the mental examination test results, the suspect is committed to the Division of mental diseases and is "acquitted" of the criminal charges. If the attorneys and Judge cannot agree on this procedure then it becomes a jury question. The *diminished responsibility* rule allows that a suspect may not be entirely crazy but only particularly crazy, enough that might lower his degree of mental capability. He may be guilty of a lesser crime which carries a lesser punishment due to a form of temporary insanity in which he may have been temporarily blinded at the moment of the crime.

A suspect must also be sane *at the time he stands trial.* If he is unable to cooperate with and assist his lawyer in his own defense, he is found to be insane and sent to a mental institution *until such time as he can later proceed to trial.* Thus, there are two stages in which a suspect must be found sane: (1) at the time of trial, in order to aid in his own defense; and (2) to be found guilty he must be found sane at the time of the crime.

When a heinous crime is committed, the smart police officer will begin a daily log on the suspect from the time he is taken into custody. This concerns his choice of food while in jail, whether the suspect used salt and pepper, and properly uses eating utensils. Does his zip his pants, does he properly use toilet paper (or does he scoop up the feces and smear it on the wall?). Does he tie his shoestrings, dress himself properly? What are his reading and writing materials while in custody? Is he interested in the scores of sports events, current events, stock market reports?

What are his relationships with other prisoners? Are his statements, conduct and comments to jailers and other prisoners appropriate under the circumstances? Daily logs should be made of the conduct of such prisoners during the first several weeks of their imprisonment after the commission of a criminal offense in order to sell to a jury at a later time the fact that this prisoner is just as sane as anyone else and "should fry in the electric chair" for his crime.

The war of the psychiatrists occurs in trials where both prosecution and defense produce expert witnesses. The psychologist does the testing–psychiatrists do the treating.

Juries weigh heavily expert evidence unless there is conflicting expert evidence, and in such an instance, where there is equally conflicting or impressive testimony on both sides of juries tend to totally disregard the conflicting testimony and decide the case as if there were no psychiatric evidence at all.

All persons are presumed sane. The suspect has the burden of proving that he is insane.

Once examined by a doctor, the Judge must decide whether the suspect "did know or appreciate the nature, quality, or wrongfulness for his conduct, or was incapable of conforming his conduct to the requirements of law." The defendant must enter a special plea setting up this defense within ten days of his Circuit Court arraignment.

Most crimes require some "state of mind" (*mens rea*) an element of the offense which must be proved, beyond a reasonable doubt. The issue of mental disease is important to determine whether the defendant did or did not have such a state of mind.

Four *mental states* required in Missouri are: (1) purposely, (2) knowingly, (3) recklessly, and (4) criminally negligent. If he is provoked, intoxicated, or acts in self-defense, he may not have the required mental state. It takes more than just suspicion and a mere emotional disturbance, alcoholism, or drug dependence. Amnesia is not a defense.

If the suspect has the *present sufficient ability* to consult with his attorney and a factual understanding of the proceedings against him, the trial proceeds just like any other trial for the jury to determine the issues.

> **RULE: IF YOU INTEND TO CLAIM INSANITY, YOU NEED TO BE IMMEDIATELY EXAMINED BY A PSYCHOLOGIST OR PSYCHIATRIST IMMEDIATELY AFTER YOUR ARREST. ALL NEIGHBORS AND WITNESSES SHOULD BE INTERVIEWED AND ALL EVIDENCE GATHERED. YOU WILL HAVE THE BURDEN TO CONVINCE THE JURY OF YOUR INSANITY.**

Commitment of the Mentally Ill

Laws provide for commitment of the mentally ill. If police arrest a suspect they believe is mentally ill and is likely to injure himself or others if allowed to remain free, the officer may petition the Court, even without medical certification, to have the person temporarily committed.

A person may also be involuntarily committed by a friend, relative, spouse, or guardian with the certification of two doctors. The person is then entitled to a hearing within five days to determine if he is mentally ill (likely to injure himself and others), or if he is otherwise in need of treatment and care because *he cannot make responsible decisions with regards to his own hospitalization.*

The Diagnostic Statistical Manual (DSM) is the bible for doctors to determine what *is* or *is not* a mental disease. The human brain is one of the most complicated bodily organs of which we know so little.

In the aftermath of the Vietnam War, for instance, *Delayed Stress Syndrome* has been discovered. In this syndrome, where a suspect has continued delusions from a period of time when he suffered a trauma or shock due to the death of others, or the loneliness and despair of his life due to the fact he survived and his friends didn't, a suspect may commit crimes to draw attention to himself, or to punish himself for being a survivor.

When defendants are acquitted by a jury on the grounds of insanity, it is mandatory they be confined to the Fulton State Hospital. There, a person remains confined forever unless and until such time as the Director certifies that he can *conform his conduct to the requirements of the law.* Every six months the patient can petition for a hearing on whether he has been cured to the extent allowed by law.

Thus, on some relatively minor, insignificant crime, it is possible a person be confined for life whereas on extremely serious felonies, it is possible a person could be confined for only a few months.

There have long been many arguments as to the quality of care given such individuals when they are confined at a mental institution. Then again, with many of the mentally sick individuals confined in mental institutions, there is little that can be done. Absent, prolonged and permanent administration of drugs, and the willingness of the person to voluntarily take drugs and submit himself to regular therapy when freed, there is often little else that can be done.

When a suspect faces a long prison sentence, it is wiser to go the insanity route particularly when there is sound medical testimony supporting it. If given a viable choice, juries would much prefer the lesser route, that is, to send him to a *hospital* rather than label him a criminal and send him to *prison*.

Ex Post Facto

For criminal law to be ex post facto, it must be retrospective, applying to events occurring *before* its enactment and must *disadvantage* the accused.

The Constitution seeks to give fair warning to citizens advance notice as to whether their conduct is against the law.

It is ex post facto if it:

1. Punishes as a crime an act previously committed which was innocent when done
2. Makes more burdensome the punishment for a crime after its commission
3. Deprives one charged with a crime with any defense available according to the law at the time when the act was committed.

Thus, you may not suffer any disadvantages from a new law that enacted since the commission of the original crime. If it is *substantially disadvantages* you by removing some existing statutory or legal right, it is forbidden.

The Good Faith Defense

The defense is largely used in regulatory and administrative law crimes where you rely on expert advice or make a mistake of law or fact and believed in good faith, you had a consent to act. The argument may be advanced in criminal trials and have some jury appeal.

You may also argue to the Judge or jury *collateral estoppel,* the matter of *issue preclusion* based on some final judgment between the parties where the same issues and facts were previously decided. *Equitable estoppel* does not require a prior adjudication or judgment by a court, but *collateral estoppel* means in a prior *civil* case a judicial or administrative determination was made adverse to the Prosecution. It is not *res judicata,* since this refers to a prior *criminal* case. You must claim, on some narrow ground, the Prosecution is now being permitted to reprosecute and litigate some fact or theory previously failed in a prior civil case. Collateral estoppel does not operate so much as an acquittal but to resolve a *particular issue* in which the Prosecution seeks to prove.

Double Jeopardy

Res Judicata or double jeopardy protect you from:

1. A second prosecution for the same offense after acquittal on the first
2. A second prosecution after conviction on the first
3. Multiple punishments for the same offense
4. Multiple prosecutions for the same offense (splitting or carving out different small crimes)
5. Prosecutions from multiple jurisdictions (municipal court, state court, federal court), (Waller vs. Florida, U.S. Supreme Court, 1970).

Duress

If coercion was present, imminent and impending, of such an extent as to induce a well grounded apprehension of death or serious bodily injury you may claim your act was a product of duress.

Statute of Limitations

The law requires that criminal conduct be prosecuted within a specified period of time. If you can prove that your criminal conduct, including the last of the overt acts occurred three to five years earlier, then the statute of limitations would have expired and the criminal prosecution is forbidden.

Extreme Emotional Disturbance

If a reasonable person of ordinary intelligence in your situation would have reacted with extreme emotional disturbance, and there is psychiatric evidence to prove this, it is a partial defense.

This defense is available to the ordinary person caught in events out of his control as long as there is a reasonable justification for his actions. You cannot hide behind the actions that you yourself have set in motion.

Unconstitutionality of Law

If you are being prosecuted under a law that is vague, indefinite, difficult to understand, it must be brought to the judge's attention immediately. If the judge agrees the law should be declared unconstitutional, the charges are dismissed.

Selective Prosecution

If you can prove that police, in the conscious exercise of selectivity of enforcement deliberately discriminated against you on the grounds of race, religion or some other arbitrary classification then your "equal protection rights" have been violated.

> You must show by a heavy burden (1) that others similarly situated have not been prosecuted but that you were signaled out and (2) that the police discriminatory selection of you was in bad faith to prevent the exercise of your constitutional rights.

Necessity

If you committed an act to prevent some significant imminent harm and there was no other adequate alternative, such as protesters charged with criminal protest at an abortion center, you can claim your act was done out of necessity. You must show that you were faced with two evils and chose the lesser one, that you acted to avoid imminent harm and reasonably believed your conduct would abate the greater harm, and that there were no legal alternatives available. More than mere civil disobedience is required.

Some incurably ill persons claim defense of medical necessity for growing and using marijuana.

Travelers' Exemption

Persons traveling on highways in a peaceable journey through the state can carry a weapon concealed, or an otherwise illegal weapon is legal, as long as you're on a *continuous lawful journey through the state.* If you had turned aside from the lawful journey to otherwise engage in some unlawful activity, you forfeit the benefit of this exemption.

Withdrawing the Guilty Plea

Tendering a plea of guilty to the court is a solemn act and is not to be lightly disregarded. There is no absolute right to withdraw a guilty plea either prior to or after sentencing, but if you believe an error was made and you have been wronged, the burden is on you to establish grounds which would justify allowing the withdrawal of the plea. The court will look at how much time has elapsed, the prejudice of the Prosecutor, and whether your initial plea of guilty was truly understanding and voluntary.

Police Misconduct

> **"Save for torture, it would be hard to find a more effective tool of tyranny than the power of unlimited and unchecked ex parte examination."**
>
> Judge Learned Hand

> **"Major Strasser's been shot...Round up the usual suspects."**
>
> Claude Raines, *Casablanca* 1942

"Decency, security, and liberty alike demand that government officials shall be subjected to the same rules of conduct that are commands to the citizen. In a government of laws, existence of the government will be imperiled if it fails to observe the law scrupulously. Our government is the potent, the omnipresent teacher. For good or for ill, it teaches the whole people by its example. Crime is contagious. If the government becomes a law breaker, it breeds contempt for law; it invites every man to become a law unto himself; it invites anarchy. To declare that in the administration of the criminal law the end justifies the means—to declare that the government may commit crimes in order to secure the conviction of a private criminal; would bring terrible retribution. Against that pernicious doctrine this court should resolutely set its face."

Olmstead vs. U.S.
(1928)
Justice Brandeis

The Judge may dismiss charges if the conduct of police is so outrageous that due process principles should absolutely bar a conviction.

The difference between passive tolerance of misconduct versus conscious direction by police is sometimes a fine one.

Violations and improper conduct by police that might form the basis of motions to suppress evidence include:

1. The continued questioning of a suspect after he insists on his right to a lawyer.
2. The planting of cellmate informants.
3. The conducting of secret interrogations with defendants without their attorney.
4. The use of psychological coercion to secure confessions.
5. The denial of means to contact a lawyer.
6. The making of promises regarding the outcome of the case.
7. Falsely advising a defendant that a co-defendant has confessed.
8. Failure to consider the physical condition of suspect including the probability of his being on drugs, alcohol, or suffering from a mental disability.
9. Conducting lineups without giving the defendant's lawyer an opportunity to be present.
10. Conducting physical examinations or special tests without knowledge of the lawyer.

11. Threatening you with placing your children in a foster home unless you confess.

Police Officer's Liability

Like an ordinary citizen, the police officer may be sued for civil damages. Civil liability of a police officer will take two separate aspects:

1. Liability for unintentional acts (negligence)
2. Liability for intentional acts (punitive).

In *unintentional* acts, a police officer is held to be the standard of care of the *ordinary and prudent man* in the similar circumstances. In determining whether a police officer's conduct meets the standard of care required of him, he is given the benefit of particular knowledge he has as a police officer, which caused him to act in the manner he did.

Many incidents of potential civil liability for negligence arise out of the officer's operation of motor vehicles. Traffic laws of the state exist for the protection of all its citizens. Ordinarily, one who violates a traffic law, which violation results in injury to an innocent person, may be held liable for his negligence. Police are given special authority to violate the state traffic statues. The driver of an emergency vehicle may:

1. Park improperly,
2. Run a stop light or sign, but only after slowing down as may be necessary for safe operation,
3. Exceed the speed limit so long as life and property are not in danger, and
4. Disregard regulations regarding direction of movement or turning in specified directions.

In order to qualify as an emergency vehicle, the siren or light must be "on" and the officer must be on a true emergency mission. Police do not have unlimited authority to violate traffic control devices. In chasing a fleeing suspect, the officer must weigh the possible advantages to be gained by apprehension of the suspect against the danger created to innocent citizens.

There are several *intentional* acts which may result in lawsuits. A common one is a *false arrest.* This may occur anytime a police officer makes an arrest for a felony where he lacks probable cause.

A police officer sued for *malicious prosecution.* This involves bringing a charge where probable cause is lacking and is brought with malice.

It is common for police to communicate among themselves and use terminology in referring to suspects which would, under other circumstances, be *slanderous* (spoken) and *libelous* (written). Usually (on grounds of public policy) these communications are privileged and not within the rules imposing liability for slander or libel.

Police may be sued by the victim of an alleged assault when the victim contends that the officer, without justification, used *unnecessary force and violence*. An integral part of a police officer's duty is the making of arrests. Those who are arrested do not always give the arresting officer their utmost cooperation. Courts permit the officer to use whatever force is reasonably necessary to effect an arrest.

> **RULE: EVERYONE WANTS TO SUE THE POLICE OFFICER, ESPECIALLY AFTER BEING CLEARED OF CHARGES. YOUR ODDS OF WINNING ARE SMALL, ARE GENERALLY A WASTE OF TIME AND MONEY. COORDINATE YOUR CASE WITH YOUR CRIMINAL LAWYER AND A NEW CIVIL LAWYER WHO BRINGS FRESH REASON. THERE IS NOWHERE FOR YOU TO GO TO GET YOUR GOOD NAME AND REPUTATION RETURNED.**

Civil Rights Lawsuits

Police may be sued in state or federal court, the most common being a federal lawsuit for willful deprivation of federally secured rights or the infliction of unnecessary punishments.

Officers, *acting under color of law*, are liable. Reasonable force may be used to arrest, secure, and detain an offender, but such acts are measured against how an ordinary, prudent, and intelligent person would have acted under the same circumstances.

You have the federally guaranteed right to be arrested, charged, tried by a court, and punished only if he is found guilty. Police do not have the right to punish on the spot, and to do so would deprive the person of the Constitutional right and to due process of law.

Police may not deprive you of any federally guaranteed rights, ("any rights, privileges, or immunities secured or protected by the Constitution or laws of the United States...") and this includes a review of all federal laws and Supreme Court decisions that have created federal rights.

The Protection of Federal Witnesses

The Federal Witness Security Program has protected 6,000 witness and 7,000 of their family members since the program started 20 years ago.

Since Joseph Valachi's appearance before the U.S. Senate in 1962, a Mafia member who gave public testimony about the interworking of the criminal organization, the government has come to realize the value of witnesses who provide inside information about criminal groups. Criminal organizations thrive on the cloak of privacy that masks membership and activities and the testimony of confidants within the groups can be devastating.

Entering the program from the time of their first appearance before a grand jury, they receive protection from the U.S. Marshal Service through the culmination of the trial. It includes around the clock protection whenever they return to an area where they're in greatest danger to give testimony or to attend to other business.

Relocation away from the threat area and the creation of new identities is another form of protection. This means a legal name change, new documentation, Social Security cards and driver's licenses. Arrangements for housing, medical care, job training and employment are included. Subsistence funding lasts about 18 months.

To date no protected witness has ever been killed.

Protected witnesses are not above the law themselves and must obey the law whenever they relocate and meet all their legal obligations. There is not exemption or immunity from prosecution for criminal offenses they might commit.

How to Talk to a Detective or a Federal Agent

"I'm from the government and I'm here to help you."

"The check is in the mail."

"Of course, I'll respect you tomorrow."

World's Biggest Lies

Great care should be taken if you are approached by a police detective or a federal agent such as F.B.I., D.E.A., U.S. Postal Service, U.S. Customs, U.S. Department of Agriculture, U.S. Fish and Wildlife.

How do you talk to a fed? Very carefully. If you are 1000% innocent, with no guilt knowledge of the crime–talk. If you are in anyway knowledgeable about the crime, say nothing. Demand your right to an attorney before you make any comments.

1. They Will Surprise You.

They will never call for an appointment. Surprise is an advantage to them, catching you off guard and unaware. Your mind is on other things. Suddenly, two friendly men politely request a few minutes of your time showing you an important looking badge.

You are embarrassed, frightened, and yet honored that someone so important would want a few minutes of your time and that you are important enough to have information that others want.

Demand to see their identification and that they give you a personal business card.

2. They Will Be Polite, Low Key, and Businesslike.

Detectives are not mean or antagonistic. They will be conservatively well dressed, will identify themselves and get to the point. They seldom smile or chat. They will request a private room where they can talk to you. You are hoping they will go away if given the "right answers". They will take brief notes but not tape record you. (Since this would have to be given to your lawyer.) Later, when they testify against you at trial, they can misquote you and it is *their word against yours* as to what was said. You will be the loser.

3. They Will Convince You It's in Your Best Interests to Talk.

They begin low key and work their way up. They only want a "few minutes" and only a few answers.

Once "the cat is out of the bag", that you have established a friendly attitude and begin to answer their questions, you're hooked! They'll take longer than a few minutes, ask pointed, planned questions, and watch your mannerisms and body language. They'll sense if you are lying or uncomfortable and as you talk, you will become increasingly uncomfortable. Once you start talking, it is hard to stop and request a lawyer. You'll feel guilty or unfriendly if you demand you Constitutional rights. They may or may not advise you of your Miranda warning rights (they're not required to since you are not "in custody").

If you think that they are not going to search your property or they do not have a grand jury subpoena in their pocket, simply demand, pointedly: "Do you have a grand jury subpoena in your pocket?" Place the burden on them.

Detectives are information gathering experts. They listen to your answers and gather information. *They do not give out information.* The surest way to counter a detective is to ask them questions:

1. "What is your purpose in being here?"
2. "Am I under a grand jury investigation?"

3. "Am I under investigation from your agency?"
4. "Who sent you here?"
5. "Why didn't you call me for an appointment?"
6. "What specific crimes do you believe that I have committed?"
7. "Who told you that?"

Quickly, you will learn they will "beat around the bush" without giving you a direct answer, and you'll know little more than vague generalities.

4. They Will Take No Written or Tape Recorded Statement From You.

At trial, they will establish a two-agent-one ratio with you, they will not permit anyone else to be present in the room who might act as your witness. If you do decide to talk to them, demand your right to have a friend or relative present.

When dealing with a dective turn on a tape recorder and record the entire conversation. *Ask them questions* and soon they will leave.

Rules when agents approach you:

1. Don't move. If they were rude enough to come unannounced to your home or business, make them talk to you in front of others. The will be uncomfortable.
2. Don't make an appointment or agree to see them later. You are not required to do this and are only inviting trouble.
3. Don't give them any documentary evidence or sign any statements. If so, demand that you be given a photocopy of the evidence or an immediate carbon copy. They won't like this and will refuse to comply.
4. Demand their personal business card. Since you are nervous, you will want their full names to give to your attorney.
5. When asked to talk, tell them you'll be glad to talk in the presence of your attorney. Answer nothing further. They have no right to ask the name of your attorney or to question your further. The law prohibits them from badgering you.
6. Be firm. If they pester, beg, badger, or intimidate, get mean! If they refuse to leave, threaten to call the police and prosecute them for trespass. Don't worry about making them mad. They already believe you are guilty.
7. After you talk with your attorney, reflect on your predicament, *then and only then,* if you want to talk, you

may do so. Your previous refusal to talk cannot ever be used against you or mentioned in court.

Criminal investigative agents go to work each day for one purpose: To detect, investigate, arrest, and convict "the guilty". At the time they're talking to you, "This means you!" They're satisfied when people are convicted and go to prison. This is their job. If you believe you can give them "snow job" and they'll go away, you are extremely naive. You'll pay for it later.

Just how far can they go? What are your legal rights? When can police enter upon your property, arrest, and question you? You need to know these answers because your arrest is frightening and will occur fast and unexpected.

Cpl. David Zulke, Patrolman Tom Dempsey, Cpl. David A. Henson, Sgt. Matt Brown and Cpl. Jack McMullin (left to Right) take "suspects" into custody (Springfield Municipal Airport).

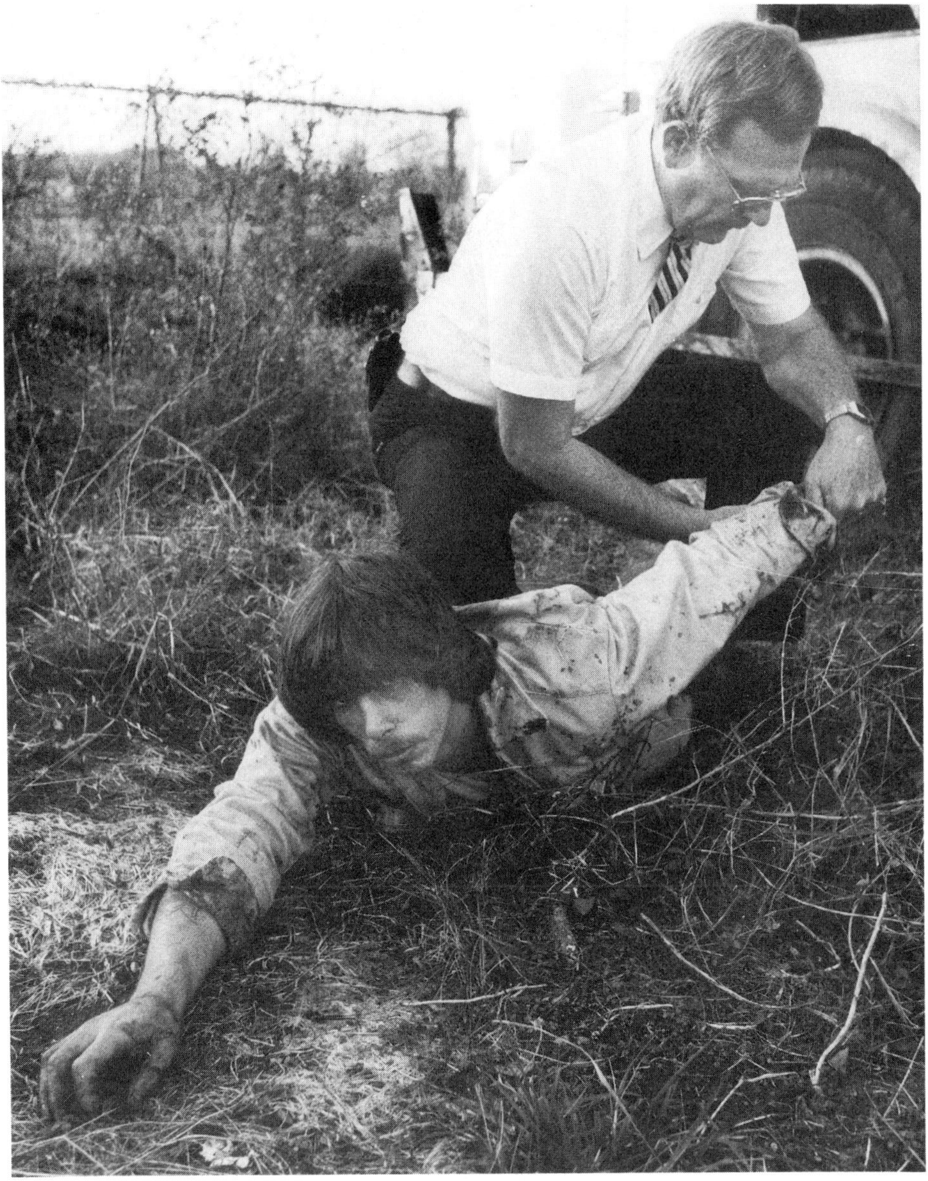

Greene County Sheriff John T. Pierpont captures a jail escapee Robert T. Bentley.

Detention officer Ernie Wells and Springfield Police Officer Jerry Plott conduct a thorough stop, frisk and patdown on an arrested subject.

Jackson County Sheriffs' Department arrested 3 suspects in a marijuana field, evidence difficult to deny when arresting officers carry a camera.

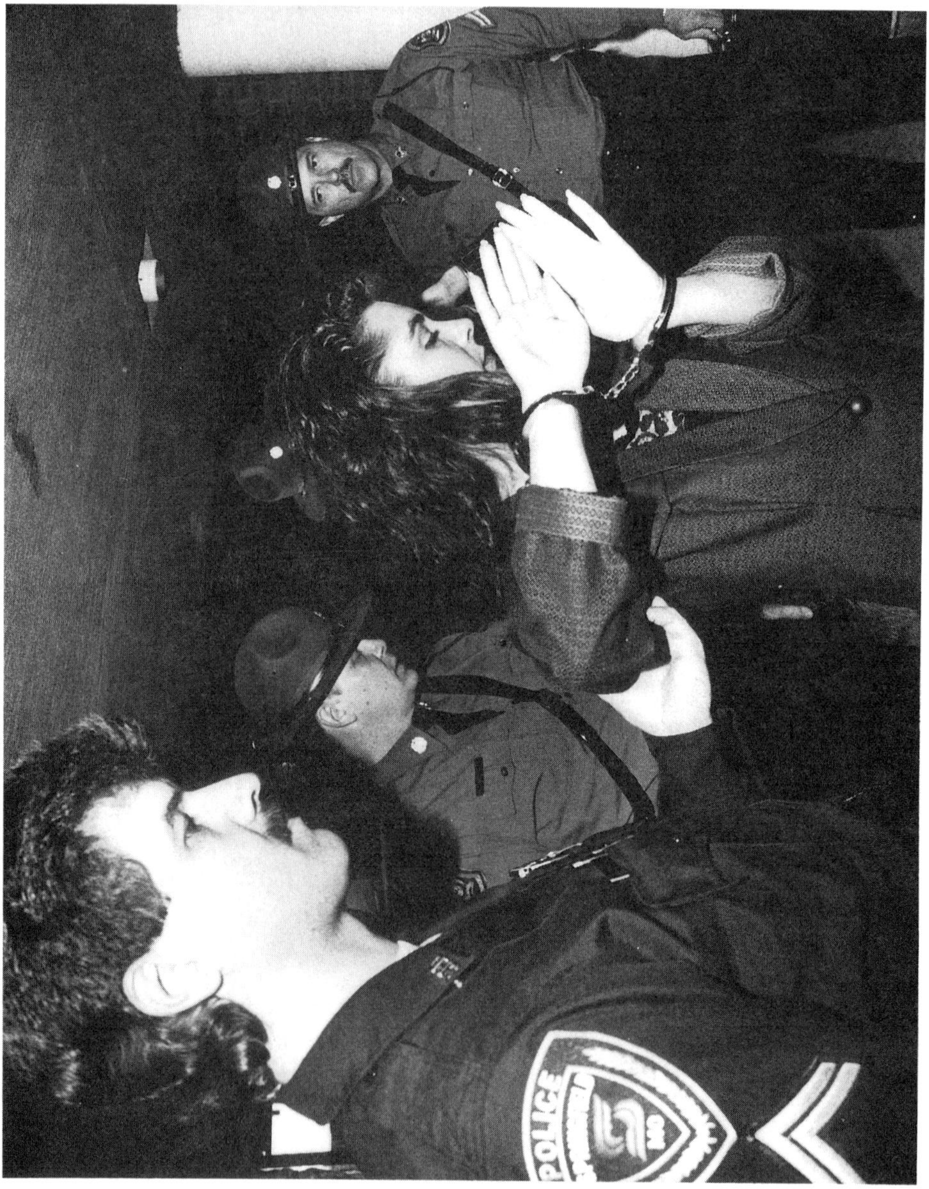
POLICE

Chapter 5

When Can I Be Arrested and Searched?

"There are seven million laws in this country, and I intend to break every one, including the law of gravity."

Abbie Hoffman

"There was the South National Bank looking as though it had been waiting for me."

Willie "The Actor" Sutton

"The right of the people to be secure in their persons, houses, papers, and effects, against unreasonable searches and seizures, shall not be violated, and no Warrants shall issue, but upon probable cause, supported by Oath or affirmation, and particularly describing the place to be searched, and the persons or thing to be seized."

Fourth Amendment,
United States Constitution

How to Act if Police Enter Your Home with a Search Warrant

The dreaded moment arrives. Police are knocking loudly on your front door, announcing their purpose to your neighbors, demanding entrance to serve a Search Warrant.

1. Don't panic. Once you open the door, supply them your name and identification. Sit down calmly and watch everything they do. If you have a tape recorder, turn it on. If you have a video camera, record the proceedings.
2. They have the right to search your entire house. You are not required to assist them. Resist the temptation to give them a guided tour, telling them where money, guns, drugs, contraband, or other items are kept.
3. Demand they leave a copy of the *Complaint for Search Warrant* and *Affidavit in Support* of Search Warrant. They probably won't. The law requires them to leave the Search Warrant and the Inventory (Receipt of Seized Property) in a conspicuous place. Demand a copy of the application and Affidavit as this is the most important document and may tell you who the informants are.
4. Police do not have the right to search you or others in the house. If they do, your lawyer can later file a Motion to Suppress. Do not make any sudden or suspicious movements.
5. If they're looking for large stolen items they do not have the right to look in tiny drawers or small spaces. If they are looking for drugs, paraphernalia, or other small pieces of evidence, they have the right to search small areas.
6. If they tear up your house, obtain a flash camera with color film and with a complete roll of film take photographs of every room.

RULE: RESIST THE TEMPTATION TO ASSIST THE POLICE IN SEARCHING YOUR HOME. THEY ARE LOOKING FOR EVIDENCE TO SEND YOU TO JAIL. DO NOTHING, SAY NOTHING, AND MAKE AN IMMEDIATE REPORT TO YOUR ATTORNEY.

So You've Been Arrested

Once you are under arrest, you are nervous and upset. You can barely remember your name. A thousand thoughts run through your head. You are wondering what is to become of you and your future. The officer reads you your rights, but you do not hear them.

You feel a compulsion to speak in order to get your guilt off your chest. No longer able to keep it inside, you feel that by telling all it will cleanse your soul. The truth is, you're digging your grave deeper.

The most common reason you talk is the misguided belief that you can talk yourself out of a situation that you have created. The practical affect is just the opposite. Instead of extracting yourself, you implicate yourself.

> **RULE: ANYTHING YOU SAY OR DO AFTER THE TIME YOU ARE ARRESTED, ASIDE FROM BEING RESPECTFUL TO THE OFFICER'S AUTHORITY, WILL CONTRIBUTE TO YOUR CONVICTION. DON'T GIVE INTO INTIMIDATION. KEEP YOUR MOUTH SHUT! THE POLICE MAY HAVE A CASE AGAINST YOU. IF SO, THEY WILL HAVE A CHANCE TO PROVE IT. IF NOT, KEEP YOUR MOUTH SHUT.**

You can be held no more than 20 hours in jail, then must either be released or the Prosecutor must file formal legal charges. You have the right to be taken before a Judge as soon as possible after the formal filing of charges and bail set.

RULES:

1. **IF YOU ARE CLEARLY INNOCENT AND IT IS A CASE OF MISTAKEN IDENTITY, YOU SHOULD COOPERATE WITH THE POLICE, AND AS EARLY AS POSSIBLE GIVE A COMPLETE AND FULL STATEMENT.**
2. **IF YOU ARE GUILTY, OR HAVE GUILTY KNOWLEDGE OF A CRIME FOR WHICH YOU HAVE BEEN ARRESTED, YOU MAY INVOKE YOUR "RIGHT TO COUNSEL" TO SEE AN ATTORNEY BEFORE BEING QUESTIONED FURTHER AND TO SEEK THE ADVICE OF A LAWYER.**
3. **DON'T EVER RESIST THE EXERCISE OF LAWFUL AUTHORITY. EVEN IF YOU ARE OPPOSED TO THE POLICE OFFICERS' ACTIONS, GO AHEAD AND CONSENT TO THEIR AUTHORITY.**
4. **BE CAREFUL ABOUT DISCUSSING YOUR CASE WITH FRIENDS AND NEIGHBORS. ANYTHING YOU SAY CAN AND WILL BE USED AGAINST YOU IF A PERSON TESTIFIES IN COURT.**

If it is possible for your case to be settled or plea bargained in court, listen carefully to the advice of your lawyer. He is skilled and has been through many previous cases. You may not like his advice, but you should carefully listen to it before making your own judgment.

Some citizens have a bad opinion of the criminal justice system. They believe police are unfair, judges are weak, Prosecutors are not vigorous, or criminal defense lawyers are dishonest. The fact is that most who work in the criminal justice system are hardworking, honest individuals who are trying to see that justice is done—even though their notions of what is or is not just in a case may be at opposite ends. You can depend upon the jury to attempt to be fair and depend on the criminal justice system with the utmost faith.

The whole process can be costly and time consuming both to the state as well as to the individual defendant. Bail bonds, attorney fees, and litigation expenses can be extremely high. The heartache, stress and embarrassment of family can also be great.

> **RULE: IT IS MUCH CHEAPER TO STAY OUT OF TROUBLE IN THE FIRST INSTANCE THAN TO GET INTO TROUBLE AND LATER PAY THE HIGH COSTS THAT MAY BE INCURRED.**

As a criminal attorney, I highly recommend parents take their children to the nearest courthouse and jail at the next available opportunity. Let impressionable young people and teenagers view a criminal trial and tour the jail. If *you* take your children to court and jail *before* they are 17, *they* will make it *their* goal to stay out of court and jail *after they reach 17.*

The Patrolman's Gun

The *Glock 17* is a partly plastic semi-automatic weapon, popular with drug dealers, but is now used by the F.B.I., and more than 4,000 federal, state and local law agencies. The barrel and slide are made of steel, the handle frame and magazine are made of non-metallic polymer. The gun comes in four different bore sizes (calibers), is lightweight, has a high velocity and near pin-point accuracy, particularly the 9 mm. It has a 17 or 19 round magazine and some extended magazines are able to fire up to 32 rounds and is extremely durable.

A police officer never displays his service revolver unless absolutely necessary.

> **RULE: WHETHER YOU ARE BEING ARRESTED BY POLICE, OR BEING ACCOSTED BY AN ARMED ROBBER, *NEVER ARGUE WITH A GUN.***

Arrest

The Fourth Amendment requires that all arrests, searches, and seizures be *reasonable.*

An *arrest* is the taking of a person into custody to answer for a crime and involves 3 elements: authority to arrest; assertion of that authority with intention to arrest; and restraint of the person arrested.

An arrest need not be made with a written arrest warrant but may be made upon probable cause of police that a crime has been or is being committed.

It makes no difference if the officer's arrest later turns out to be erroneous (if, for example, the officer arrested for felony stealing and the crime ended up being a misdemeanor). The officer is not expected to be a legal technician and his actions are tested by all the facts known to him at the time.

Delayed Arrest

A delayed arrest is permitted. Police may back off and let you incriminate yourself such as where a tape recording is being made of conversation. There is no duty to immediately arrest and as soon as probable cause is apparent; the officer can wait, giving you rope to hang yourself further.

Summons

A summons is a mandatory invitation to appear at a stated time and place to answer to a criminal charge and is a substitute for arrest.

If you refuse to sign a traffic ticket promising to voluntarily appear, you can be taken to jail, arraigned, and bail set. *Always set the traffic ticket.*

Arrest Warrant

Missouri requires the finding of probable cause before the issuance of an arrest warrant, since warrants can only be issued on probable cause.

Enough information is presented to the Judge so he knows the charges are not capricious.

Formal rules of evidence do not apply and it is sufficient that the officer have reliable hearsay information.

RULE: IN PRACTICE, THE JUDGE OR HIS CLERK REVIEWS THE PROSECUTOR'S PROPOSED CRIMINAL

CHARGE AND USES A RUBBER STAMP WHICH RECITES THAT PROBABLE CAUSE HAS BEEN DETERMINED TO EXIST. A WARRANT IS THEN DELIVERED TO THE SHERIFF OR POLICE WHO ARRIVE AT YOUR FRONT DOOR. WITHOUT FURTHER ADIEU YOU ARE TRANSPORTED TO JAIL.

Physical Force

An arrest does not require actual physical force, touching of your body, or even formal declaration of arrest. It is sufficient if you understand you're arrested and submit.

Police may use whatever force is reasonably believed necessary. Missouri allows the use of deadly force in *felony* arrests, or if a suspect is attempting to escape by use of a deadly weapon, or if life may be endangered or serious injury inflicted unless arrested without delay.

An arrest occurs by the hand, taping the shoulder, or mere gesture. As long as the police officer can reasonably expect from his conduct that *you believe yourself* to be under arrest.

The arrest is made by you *submitting to the custody* of the officer. The controlling fact is *substantial interference with your will to move for any appreciable time.*

Words

The law does not require any particular words be used or any words at all, and the choice of words is significant only for the purpose of determining that there was an actual restraint. If the officer does arrest, he should make it clear that you are under arrest and state the grounds and the facts whenever possible.

Using Discretion in Deciding Not to Arrest

There are many situations where good police practice requires no formal arrest:

1. Minor traffic offenses
2. Situations where an arrest might cause disturbance or lead to a riot
3. Minor domestic disputes
4. The handling of an intoxicated person creating no danger to the public, who might simply be assisted in getting home.

The policeman's primary job is to protect the public. When an arrest might cause greater risk or harm to the public or merely cause embarrassment to a person posing no real threat to the community, proper police practice may call for a decision not to arrest.

Such occurrences may call for using best judgment or, at other times, maybe controlled by local departmental policy. Not all situations in which an arrest *may* be made are situations in which an arrest *should* be made.

Citizen's Arrest

It is the right of any citizen, when someone has committed or is in the act of committing a crime, to arrest the offender without waiting for police.

The power of a citizen to make an arrest is closely limited. Citizens may make an arrest upon probable cause in a felony only if the felony *in fact* occurred.

It is required that the felony shall have been committed. The arresting citizen subjects himself to possible civil lawsuit for false arrest or false imprisonment.

Citizens can arrest for misdemeanors if committed in their presence, and involves a breach of the peace. A citizen may arrest a suspect whom he observes maliciously destroying a citizen's property. Missouri gives merchants and shoplifting detectives power to detain possible shoplifters where *reasonable grounds exist* to believe the crime has been committed, and holds the arrestor *immune* from prosecution for false arrest.

Sheriffs may request citizen help in making arrests especially in riot or emergency situations, such persons then becoming known as *posse comitatus*.

Hot Pursuit

You can be pursued across city, county, or state lines, whether or not the arresting officer has an actual warrant, when it is clear you are fleeing police. *Hot pursuit* is the immediate chase of a person fleeing to avoid arrest.

The Uniform Law of Fresh Pursuit permits an out-of-state officer to enter this state if the officer believes you have committed a felony in his state. Once captured, you must be taken to the nearest local jail, subject to extradition proceedings, to return to the original state.

The doctrine has also been applied if you are standing in the doorway of your home or front yard, and run into the house to hide. The fact that hot pursuit may end almost as soon as it begins does not render it any less a hot pursuit sufficient to justify the warrantless entry into the house. Police should enter houses with caution—only if they are sure of your identity and delay would result in destruction of evidence.

If you are in an open place, visible to public view, speech, hearing, or possible touch, any reasonable expectation of privacy has been abandoned and the police can pursue.

Probable Cause

In order for an arrest or a search to be legal, it must have been based upon *probable cause*. Courts speak of "probable cause", "reasonable grounds", and "reasonable cause", but are treated the same and often become the crucial issue.

An arrest is illegal if not based upon probable cause. Information obtained as a result of an illegal arrest, such as the search of a person or premises and the discovery of contraband, or the interrogating of a suspect and obtaining of subsequent admissions or confession, is illegal. Under the exclusionary rule, a defense attorney can file a pre-trial Motion to Suppress to have the incriminating evidence declared illegal.

Anonymous Tipsters

Anonymous telephone calls to police will provide sufficient justification for police to initiate investigations, but the tip itself probably will not justify a warrantless arrest or search.

If the information appears reliable, police begin to investigate to establish the reliability of the tip.

The information may become a part of the probable cause needed for the issuance of a search warrant. If police do independent investigation they can verify the tip.

An important fact is whether the tip is from *personal knowledge* or whether the tipster speaks from *hearsay*.

Warrantless Home Entry

Absent emergency circumstances, police may not enter your home to make an arrest. The prosecution has a heavy burden to justify going into a home. Physical entry into a home is very chief evil which the Fourth Amendment prohibits.

A firm line is drawn at the entry of the threshold of a house and it may not be crossed without a warrant, and then only very carefully and under strict rules.

If police see you standing in the doorway or sitting in the front yard or porch and then run inside they make a good case for entering your house.

Police may not enter your home to make a warrantless arrest, absent consent, or some emergency circumstances under the following guidelines:

1. The gravity or violent nature of the offense
2. If the suspect is armed
3. The degree of probable cause
4. The degree of belief that the suspect is in the premises
5. The likelihood of the suspect's escape if not swiftly apprehended
6. The peaceful circumstances if not swiftly apprehended
7. The peaceful circumstances of the entry.

A different problem is presented when police attempt to enter the home of a *third person* to serve an arrest warrant. The best policy is to obtain a search warrant in order to make the arrest.

In serving a search warrant, there is no *knock and announce* law but the better practice is to do so. Police may then quickly break the door or window and enter. If they had sufficient time to get a search warrant, they are required to do so. The fact that there are persons present does not automatically mean police have the right to search them unless police have suspicion or probable cause to believe they are armed and dangerous.

Warrantless entries have been upheld where police believe it is reasonably required to prevent the destruction of evidence or to save a life.

The search is legal if:

1. An arrest is planned at your home or office, a search warrant is required for a preliminary look within the premises.
2. The immediate area is within easy reach or control.
3. A consent to search is obtained.
4. Other possible dangerous persons are present. Other rooms may be searched for weapons (protective sweep).
5. Items in plain view may be seized.

6. Other rooms, drawers, closets, suitcases, or garage may not be searched without a search warrant or consent.
7. Arrested outside your house, you may not be taken inside for the sole purpose of searching.

Stop and Frisk

The U.S. Supreme Court in *Terry vs. Ohio* (1969) held that circumstances falling short of probable cause for an arrest may justify a *temporary stop and frisk* of a suspect (temporary detention), where the officer can justify some suspicion or evidence of criminal activity. A reasonable detention is allowed for interrogation and a *brief stop* of a suspicious person to determine identity and to momentarily *maintain status quo* while obtaining more information.

If police observe conduct that a reasonably prudent man with police experience would view as suspicious, he may approach the suspect, identify himself and ask questions. The *reasonable suspicion* necessary can be provided by an informant or by the personal knowledge of the officer.

Stopping crime before it happens is just a beneficial to society as apprehending a criminal after the crime has been committed. Consequently, if the officer has reason to suspect that a crime *has been, is being,* or is *about to be* committed, he is acting within his authority by stopping and detaining a suspect, conducting a pat down search, and initiating limited interrogation.

Police cannot detain you to search for *mere physical evidence.* If the officer has reason to believe you are *armed,* he may pat you down for the protection of himself and others. If the frisk results in the finding of a weapon, it is to be admissible into evidence after you are arrested. If the item does not feel like a weapon it cannot be removed.

Justification for a frisk includes:

1. Gait and manner of the suspect
2. Demeanor of the suspect, such as nervousness
3. Officer's knowledge of suspect's background
4. Strange bulges in suspect's clothing
5. Time of night or day
6. Conversations overheard by officers
7. Any suspicious third persons present
8. The street or area of town involved
9. Any known criminal conduct recently in the area (high crime area)

10. Flight or attempted escape of suspect
11. Minority race
12. Other observations and investigation of officer.

If you refuse to stop, reasonable force may be used. If you are detained for a long time, it will be treated as an arrest and the court will require full blown probable cause. You may be questioned about an explanation for your actions. Identification will be requested. If the answers received are unsatisfactory, contradictory, or incredible, they may serve as elements for factors giving probable cause to arrest.

If, in legitimate search of what is believe to be a weapon, contraband or evidence of another crime is discovered, you may be arrested on probable cause. A frisk may not be used as a pretext to search for evidence. There must be reason to fear for the safety of the officer or the safety of others.

RULE: YOU MAY BE STOPPED AND FRISKED EVEN THOUGH THERE IS NOT SUFFICIENT PROBABLE CAUSE TO ARREST IF:

1. **YOU ARE OBSERVED ENGAGING IN UNUSUAL CONDUCT THAT REASONABLY LEADS ONE TO BELIEVE THAT CRIMINAL ACTIVITY IS OCCURRING AND THAT YOU ARE ARMED AND DANGEROUS;**
2. **THE POLICE OFFICER IDENTIFIES HIMSELF AND MAKES REASONABLE LIMITED INQUIRIES AS TO YOUR CONDUCT;**
3. **YOUR RESPONSE AND ACTIONS DO NOT RELIEVE THE SUSPICIONS AND FEAR OF DANGER TO THE OFFICER.**

RULE: IF YOU ARE APPROACHED BY POLICE AND DO NOT WISH TO BE QUESTIONED, IGNORE THE OFFICER AND WALK ON. MAKE HIM STOP YOU. COURTS MAY TREAT IT AS AN ARREST AND IF IT IS WITHOUT PROBABLE CAUSE, IT CAN BE SUPPRESSED.

Investigative Detention

If police approach you and ask a few limited questions without a show of force or making an obvious arrest, it is an *investigative detention* as long as it is temporary, non-instrusive, simply to verify or dispel an officer's suspicion.

It is based on reasonable suspicion in the officer's mind which is not as strong as probable cause.

If police detain you and question you at length, use their weapons, transport you to the police station, then it turns the investigative *detention* into a full blown *arrest* and police will have to prove it, under the Fourth Amendment, that they had probable cause to make the arrest.

Ignore Them and They'll Go Away

May a police officer approach you on the street, sidewalk, or while you are being seated on a bus, train or plane; temporarily blocking your exit or standing in front of you and question you? Yes!

If a policeman places you in tight quarters and you feel constrained and not free to leave, it is improper police practice. If a reasonable citizen would not feel free to leave, then it constitutes an illegal detention or "arrest".

Speaking to someone in a conversational tone, in a public place, does not constitute an arrest. The increasingly common drug-interdiction tactic where police officers board a passenger bus during a layover without any particularized suspicion whatsoever requesting travelers' consent to search their persons or luggage is legal.

> **RULE: IF POLICE ATTEMPT TO QUESTION YOU ON THE STREET OR IN YOUR CAR ABOUT MATTERS UNRELATED TO YOUR ORIGINAL STOP, SHUT UP! DON'T BE INTIMIDATED. TELL THE OFFICER YOU'RE LEAVING. MAKE HIM MAKE THE FIRST MOVE BY DETAINING YOU. YOU CAN CHALLENGE HIS ARREST IN COURT AND WIN.**

Citizen or Jerk

If you're ever stopped by the police, you have to show them that you're a citizen. If they conclude you're a jerk, you're in trouble.

How Not to Be a Jerk

When you're dealing with police, it's not just a matter of what you say, but how you say it. Recognize the officer's power and authority, and be polite. Use the words "officer" and "Sir" as much as possible.

Police don't like defiance. They interpret it as an assault upon their authority. Challenging their authority is a prescription for disaster.

Traffic Tickets

If you're pulled over in your car, sit perfectly still with your hands on the wheel. Don't reach for your wallet or into the glove compartment.

Wait for the police to approach you. Be polite and courteous. If you have friends in high places, don't mention it. Don't threaten or bluster. Only jerks threaten a cop. If you come on too strong you'll get a handful of tickets instead of one.

Police can be very creative. The can and will cite you for anything from a dirty license plate to a cracked windshield.

The key is truthfulness. The police are experts at detecting bull.

Never try to buy your way out of a ticket. You're unlikely to bribe the officer, and you'll risk being charged with attempted bribery.

Although you should freely offer your name and address, say nothing of any illegal drugs or volunteer anything until you speak with your lawyer.

One exception: If you have information that might clear you, let the officer know.

How to Handle a Problem

Can police officers be held accountable for their actions? Yes they can once the incident is over.

Do this discreetly and don't ask for a badge number if you don't have to. Police will construe this as a challenge.

If you're contemplating a civil suit, never plead guilty to the offense. If you admit to wrongdoing, your case will be seriously weakened.

Talking Your Way out of a Traffic Ticket

When you're sitting at the curb and the policeman approaches you from his car, what is your frame of mind?

1. It could be anger if you're in a hurry and don't want to be delayed.
2. It could be an injustice to feel you've done nothing wrong.
3. It could be fear that you've never been stopped before and don't know what to expect.
4. It could be apathy if you really don't care.

5. It could be contempt if this is the tenth time you've been stopped.
6. It could be total surprise if you know you've done nothing wrong (but your tail light is out).

The responsibility for maintaining a good attitude is on you! Depending upon the officer's personality and frame of mind, if there is a way to talk your way out of a ticket it is dependent totally upon your attitude.

Keep your composure, be friendly and polite, and convey to the officer the following:

> "I'm not sure if I know exactly what I've done wrong, but I know you have a good reason for stopping me. I'm at your mercy. Are you willing to discuss the situation for a moment?"

Do's

1. Pull over as soon as possible when you see the red lights. Cooperation is essential.
2. Roll your window down, turn your radio off.
3. Keep your driver's license and proof of insurance card easily accessible.
4. Stay in your car unless the officer asks you step out. Police prefer you remain in the vehicle as it is safer for everyone.
5. Keep your hands where the officer can see them—at all times! He gets nervous if he can't see your hands.
6. Be cool, calm and collected, and always polite.
7. Politely inquire why you were stopped, "Have I done something wrong, officer?" or "I'm sorry I didn't realize I was going that fast. I guess my mind was on where I was going. Will you excuse me this time?"

   It's better to ask an innocent question than make a specific statement:

1. "How can I fix my car so that it will be legal?"
2. "I'm normally a very safe driver but for a second my attention was elsewhere. I promise to do better."
3. "Car insurance for a person my age is quite high so I've been trying to keep my record clean. Can you trust me not to make the same mistake again?"
4. "I have a perfect driving record. If you will give me a warning this time I'll do my best to keep it that way."

5. "I know this is my fault. Can you excuse me this time? I promise you won't have to stop me again."
6. "It's been a long drive. You've just made me realize I need to stop and get some coffee."
7. "I'm sorry. I should be paying closer attention. My boyfriend just broke up with me and it's hard to concentrate. I promise to be more careful."
8. "Officer, is there something I can do or say that will make a decision not to write a ticket this time and give me a warning?"
9. "I'm new to this area. I guess I need to pay closer attention to my driving."

RULE: IF YOU LIE, RATIONALIZE, OR BECOME SARCASTIC OR IN ANY WAY INSINUATE THE OFFICER IS LYING, YOU WILL PROBABLY GET THE TICKET. THE LESS SAID BY YOU THE BETTER OFF YOU'LL BE.

Don'ts

1. When signalled to pull over, don't pull into the center divider section.
2. Don't hand the officer your wallet as he does not wish to be accused of stealing money.
3. Don't ever say, "You can't write me a ticket—I haven't done anything wrong." Don't challenge the officer.
4. Never say, "I've had five tickets. If you write me one more I'll lose my license."
5. Don't cry, it rarely works. Cops don't trust women who cry over traffic tickets.
6. Even if you intend to take the matter to court, never tell the officer. He will remember your name and be better prepared to beat you by taking good notes. If you graciously accept the ticket, he may not make any notes and forget you.
7. Don't beg to be let off. It will probably cause the officer to want to write you a ticket even more.
8. Never threaten such as, "I'll see you in court," or "I'll get your wife and kids," or "I'll get you off duty." These never work, plus new criminal charges may be filed against you.
9. Never refuse to sign the ticket. You're not admitting guilt, only promising to appear in court. If you refuse to sign the ticket, he can take you to jail and make you post bond.

10. Never argue about the violation. It's alright to tell your side of the story, but don't argue.
11. Don't try to use titles or name drop. If you're close friends with a Congressman, lawyer, editor, mayor, or publisher, it probably will not influence the officer.

RULE: IF YOU DO GET TICKETED, DON'T FORGET TO SHOW UP IN COURT OR CLEAR THE TICKET THROUGH THE MAIL. IF YOU FAIL TO DO SO, A WARRANT WILL BE ISSUED FOR YOUR ARREST.

Radar

In order to beat a radar ticket in court, you're going to have to do some research. You need to know what type of radar is being used. Radar determines the speed of a moving object and is accurate. It uses the Doppler effect, but radar can be fooled by certain objects and may be clocking the wrong vehicle. Some radar is confused by aluminum foil which is stuffed in the nose of a vehicle. Radar may not be accurate in picking up fiberglass materials. Radar is always subject to malfunction or failure.

Radar may be affected by changes in temperature or outside interferences from electrical sources. It must be calibrated by tuning forks. In turn, the tuning fork must be calibrated. Each operator must make sure his unit is clocking the correct vehicle. Proof that a unit was tested recently is required.

Fuzz Busters

The purpose of radar detectors is to alert you to the use of radar by detecting electrical impulses given off by police radar units. Usually you are alerted in enough time to slow down to avoid being *clocked* by police radar.

They are totally ineffective against Instant On Radar, the type that does not send out a constant signal.

RULE: THE ONLY SURE FIRE WAY TO BEAT A RADAR TICKET IS TO STAY WITHIN THE SPEED LIMIT.

Drinking and Driving

Nothing I say should be construed as a guarantee of freedom from arrest or an endorsement to drink and drive. If you've made the wrong decision and decided to drink and drive, what is the best way to avoid getting killed or killing someone else?

If you're behind the wheel and have had a couple of drinks and feel a slight "buzz" by the alcohol, do this:

1. Roll down a window, don't turn on the heater and it will be easier to stay awake.
2. Drive in as straight a line as you possibly can. Keep your vehicle entirely within your own lane.
3. Don't drive slower or faster than the posted speed limit.
4. Concentrate on stop signs and red lights since your reactions are slower than you think.
5. Don't play soft music on the radio as it will lull you to sleep.
6. Be extra cautious after drinking any amount of alcohol because reflexes are numbed.
7. If you feel drowsy, stop, get coffee, and stretch your legs. Pull over to a safe place off the road and sleep for a while. Getting home late is better than not getting home at all.
8. If there is any question as to whether you should drive exercise these options:

    a. Walk to a bus stop and ride
    b. Walk home
    c. Call a friend or a relative
    d. Call a taxi
    e. Sleep in your car
    f. Walk to a motel and take a room
    g. Try anything, but don't make a live bomb out of your car.

When the Siren Comes On

Suppose you are being pulled over and you've been drinking. Popping breath mints, dousing your mouth with pocket breath spray, or smoking cigarettes, will tip the cop you feel you have something to hide.

Don't be stupid enough to be caught with an open container that can be seen anywhere inside your car.

You will be asked to exit your vehicle and walk to a safe location. The officer will want you to give a balance test, finger-to-nose test, ABC test, and will be filling out a *Alcoholic Influence Report Form*. where you're graded on how you react, as well as your breath, actions, eyes, clothing, and attitude.

RULE: BE AS COOL AND CALM AS YOU CAN. DON'T JOKE AROUND AND BE FUNNY, OR YOU'LL BE

CONSIDERED DRUNK. WAIT FOR THE OFFICER TO TELL YOU STEP BY STEP WHAT TO DO. DON'T VOLUNTEER CONVERSATION. FOLLOWING HIS INSTRUCTIONS IS PART OF THE TEST.

Quick Test Before Driving

If you want to test your own abilities prior to getting behind the wheel after a few drinks:

1. Recite the alphabet quickly, smoothly, and without hesitating.
2. Walk a straight line for about 10 steps, heel against toe. Turn briskly and repeat in the opposite direction. You can't stagger, space you steps, or stumble while turning.
3. With head level, eyes open and ahead, raise your left foot six inches off the floor and hold for 10 seconds. Now do the right foot.
4. Stand at attention, arms down, head tilted back, eyes closed. You should be able to stand still without swaying back and forth.

What Will Get You Arrested

Just because you've been drinking doesn't mean you'll automatically go to jail–it's your ability to operate a vehicle that is important. The cop's decision will be based on the following:

1. Your driving, breath odor, speech, eyes, and balance.
2. Your attitude–is it belligerent? Over cooperative? Combative? Sudden change in attitude from one extreme to the other?
3. Your physical appearance, hair, food spilled on your clothing, no shoes, fly open?
4. The officer's personal expertise in detecting subtle characteristics of a person who has been drinking.

RULE: IF YOU HAVE BEEN TICKETED ANYWAY, DON'T BE DISCOURAGED. LOOK ON THE POSITIVE SIDE AS GETTING A TICKET CAN BE FUN:

1. You'll meet new people, have a new friend on the police force, get to meet the clerks at the courthouse and maybe even the Prosecuting Attorney or a defense lawyer.
2. At the courthouse you can look around, acquaint yourself with the offices, and find new people to talk to.
3. If you're guilty, you should be satisfied that the system works. Pay your fine and court costs and resolve not to break the law again.

RULE: THE TRAFFIC OFFICER IS MERELY ENFORCING LAWS THAT CITIZENS HAVE DEMANDED. WE ALL WANT TO REACH OUR DESTINATIONS WITH A MINIMUM OF DELAYS OR INJURIES IN AN OVERCROWDED WORLD. THE POLICEMAN IS JUST ANOTHER CITIZEN YOU ARE PAYING TO PROTECT YOU FROM IRRESPONSIBLE AND MALICIOUS ACTS OF OTHERS. TRAFFIC LAWS ARE FOR YOUR OWN GOOD.

In representing DWI clients, I make no apologies for trying to even up the odds to give my client a fair shake and the chance of a fair trial. By the time clients come to me they have "sobered up," they're scared and in crisis. It's a perfect opportunity for me to help them help themselves.

If You Have a Car Accident

No one expects to be in a crash, but these steps could prepare you should one happen:

1. Keep a first aid kit in your car and know first aid.
2. Carry warning devices, flashlight, flares, or fluorescent plastic triangle.
3. Keep identification, paper, and pencil handy including your insurance I.D. card.
4. Survey the scene before you take action. Check for injuries, spilled gasoline, and determine your safety and whether you are in jeopardy.
5. Check for injuries. Get to a phone or call 911 or ask another motorist to do it as most people have CB's or mobile telephones.
6. Record all police officers' names and badge numbers. Request a copy of the police report and get a file number so that you can get a copy later.
7. Move your car out of traffic if possible if it's creating a hazard or blocking traffic. But if a passenger is injured put out warning devices and turn on your emergency flashers.
8. Jot down details concerning weather, visibility, road conditions, and how the accident happened, and make a sketch.
9. Admit nothing. Comments such as, "It was all my fault," or "Don't worry, I'm fine," can come back to haunt you in insurance claims or later in court.

10. Call your insurance agent or attorney immediately. All matters concerning the crash should be handled only by them. Refer all phone calls to them. Don't answer questions yourself.

Your Fourth Amendment Rights

The Fourth Amendment protects your reasonable expectation of privacy from unreasonable invasions of the police.

> **"We are not dealing with formalities. The presence of a search warrant services a high function. Absent some grave emergency, the Fourth Amendment has interposed a magistrate between the citizen and the police. This was not done to shield criminals nor to make the home a safe haven for illegal activities. It was done so that an objective mind might weigh the need to invade that privacy in order to enforce the law. The right of privacy was deemed too precious to entrust to the discretion of those whose job is the detection of a crime and the arrest of criminals."**
>
> Chimel vs. California,
> U.S. Supreme Court, 1969

If the evidence is obtained in violation of the Fourth Amendment will be held inadmissible and excluded from evidence.

With the possible exception of cases where private property must be entered to make an arrest, there is not constitutional requirement that an arrest warrant be obtained. A warrantless arrest occurs where it is "reasonable under the circumstance, and the arresting officer has probable cause to believe the accused is committing or has committed a crime."

> ...while probable cause implies that the information which has come either directly or indirectly to the arresting officer's knowledge must rise above *mere suspicion* of criminal activity, it at the same time need not be tantamount to that quantum of proof that would sustain a conviction of guilt.

Although you may be later acquitted, it is enough that under the circumstances you appeared to be guilty.

The court will look to see if the officer acted on the basis of facts known at the time of the arrest and actions of their parties present.

More than just good faith is required determined by what a *prudent man* reasonably knew, observed, heard, smelled, felt, and/or tasted, and the courts have allowed the officer special knowledge to give him an advantage over the ordinary citizen.

Police are permitted to draw inferences from known facts, but the inferences must be reasonable.

Examples:

1. Defendant dropping small white packages into open motor of parked car allows search of motor.
2. Downward motion of driver following officer's observance of marijuana allows search of car interior.
3. The knowledge of one officer is imputed to the other arrests based upon radio transmission.
4. Police reports supply probable cause even if they later turn out to be false.
5. Odors and sounds.
6. Flight.
7. Giving a contradictory explanation.
8. Tip of a reliable informer. An informer is not reliable simply because he has in the past supplied accurate information—the reliability of the informer and his tip.
   a. *Good citizen informants–the law presumes the reliability* of a good citizen informant who simply is doing his duty, or where the informant is the victim. It is not required to check into the informer's actual reliability.
   b. *Paid or habitual informers*—the tip from the snitch who mingles with the criminal element is far more vulnerable to attack. His identity may have to be kept a secret and it will *have to be established that he's reliable* and that he saw enough to justify his belief that a crime was committed.
   c. *Confidential police informant*—sometimes called an automatic informant, because information is given to police outside of official channels, and the police officer automatically reports useful information to interested police units.
9. Messages from law enforcement agencies.
10. Reputation. The known reputation of a suspect or of his frequenting with criminals is alone insufficient but is a circumstance to be considered.
11. Racial factors. The fact that the suspect may be of a minority race may be considered.

12. Bad reputation of associates.
13. Furtive or fidgety movements (coupled with prior reliable information or with actual observation of contraband).
14. Special expertise of officer, such as special training or work experience, (narcotics detail, shoplifting duties, etc.)
15. Information from NCIC, MULES, and the DOR.

Detention Officer Ernie Wells, Springfield Police Officers Ron Presley and Sgt. Bruce Headley corral a suspect in a reverse sting drug buy.

Saline County Sheriff Wally George runs narcotic detection dog "Alex" through a daily training exercise.

Kansas City Police Department Bomb Disposal Unit check a suspicious package (Bill Forbes, Arson Bomb Squad KCPD).

A new "Eagle" model headset has a bone vibrator that transfers incoming radio signals through the bones, leaving both ears completely open for hearing danger. The electronic microphone transmits voices, even whispers with great precision.

Missouri State Highway Patrol Officers checking a vehicle at a roadblock to contain a fugitive during a manhunt.

Springfield Crisis Action Team (CAT) officer Jack Van Matrey (L) and officer Don Fuhr (R) secure a suspect while serving a residential search warrant.

Springfield Police Officer Darryl Rader conducting a stop and frisk street encounter.

SWAT team enters a Springfield home on a search warrant bust (L to R, Brian Atkins, Mike Owen, Don Fuhr, Ron Hartman, Sgt. Steve Ijames).

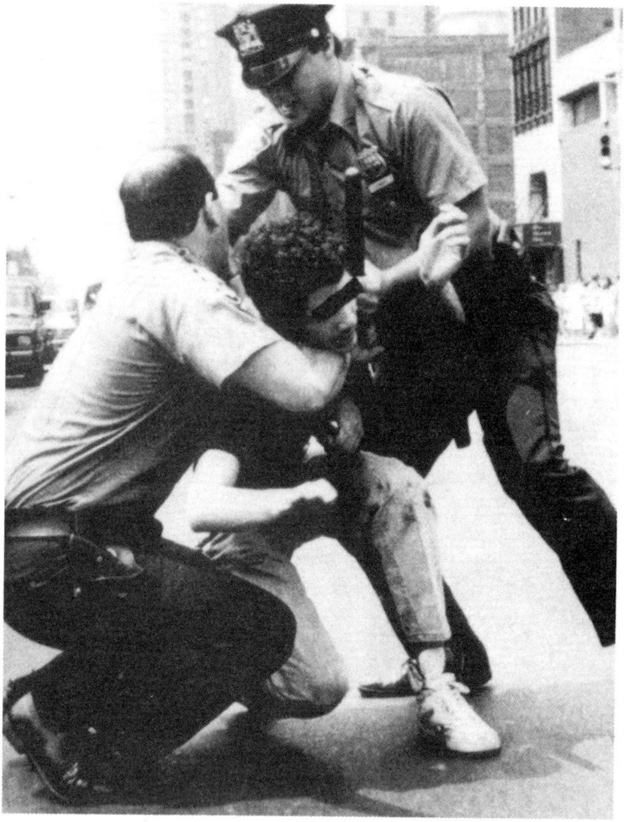

Poplar Bluff Police Officers Tony Wallace, Gary Greenlee and Steve James wait for suspects to come out of a house and is ordered to "hit the dirt".

The Glock 17 is a 9-mm semi-automatic hammerless weapon 7" x 5", 21 ounces with up to 19 round magazine. It is the weapon choice of many police departments.

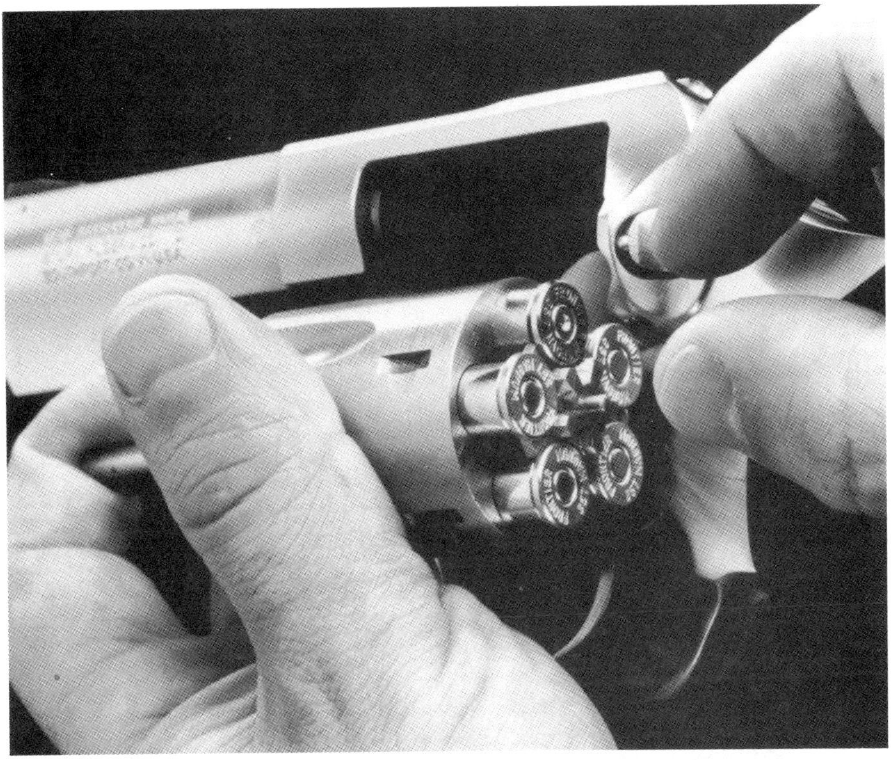

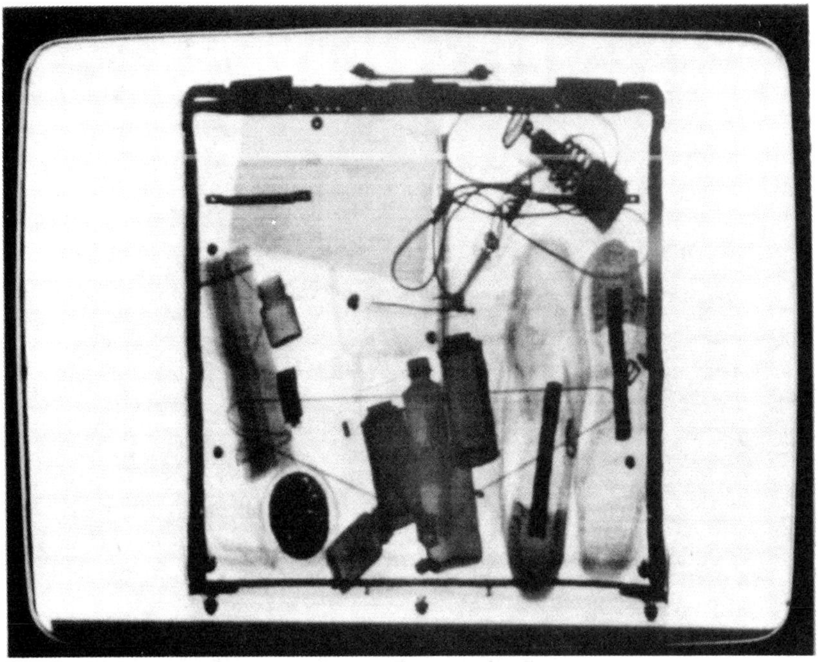

Notice the detail of the simulated bomb above.

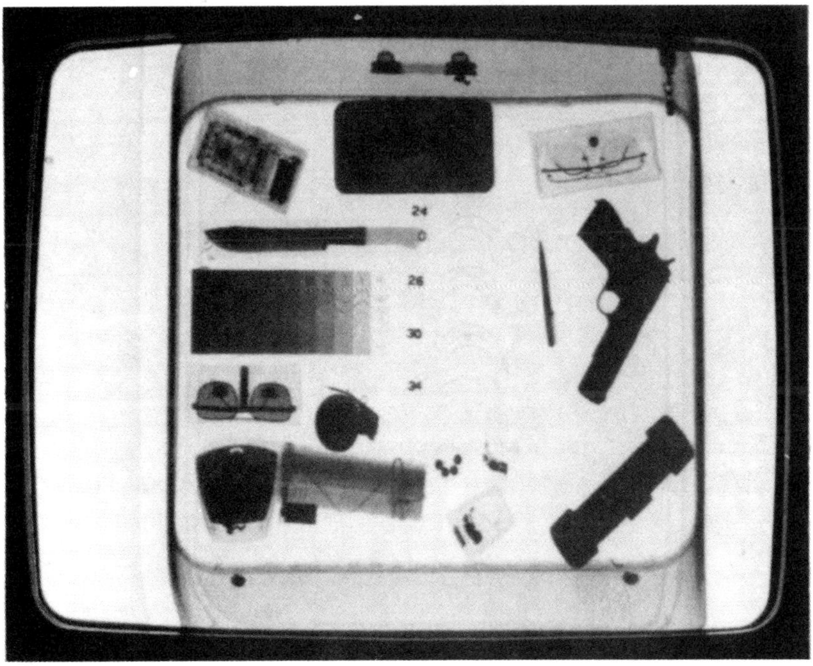

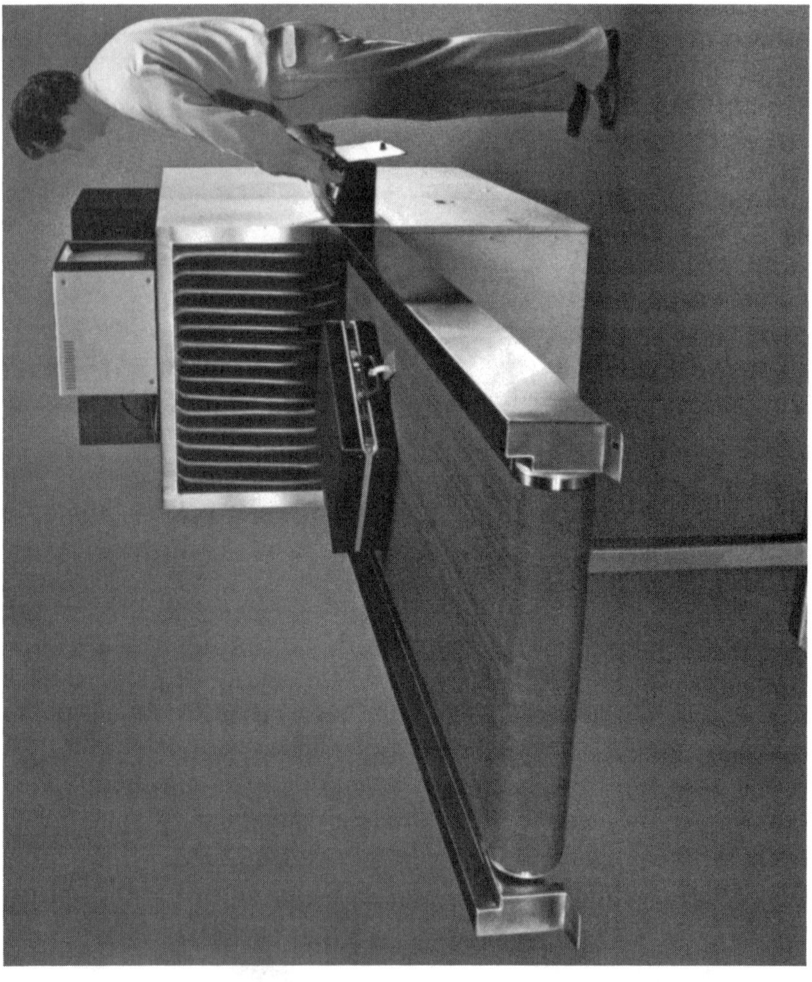

Line Scan is modern, high speed x-ray security screening, slicing a narrow x-ray beam through luggage. Fine wire, .38 gauge, can easily be discerned as well as 14 shades of gray, light plastics to heavy metallic objects can easily be seen.

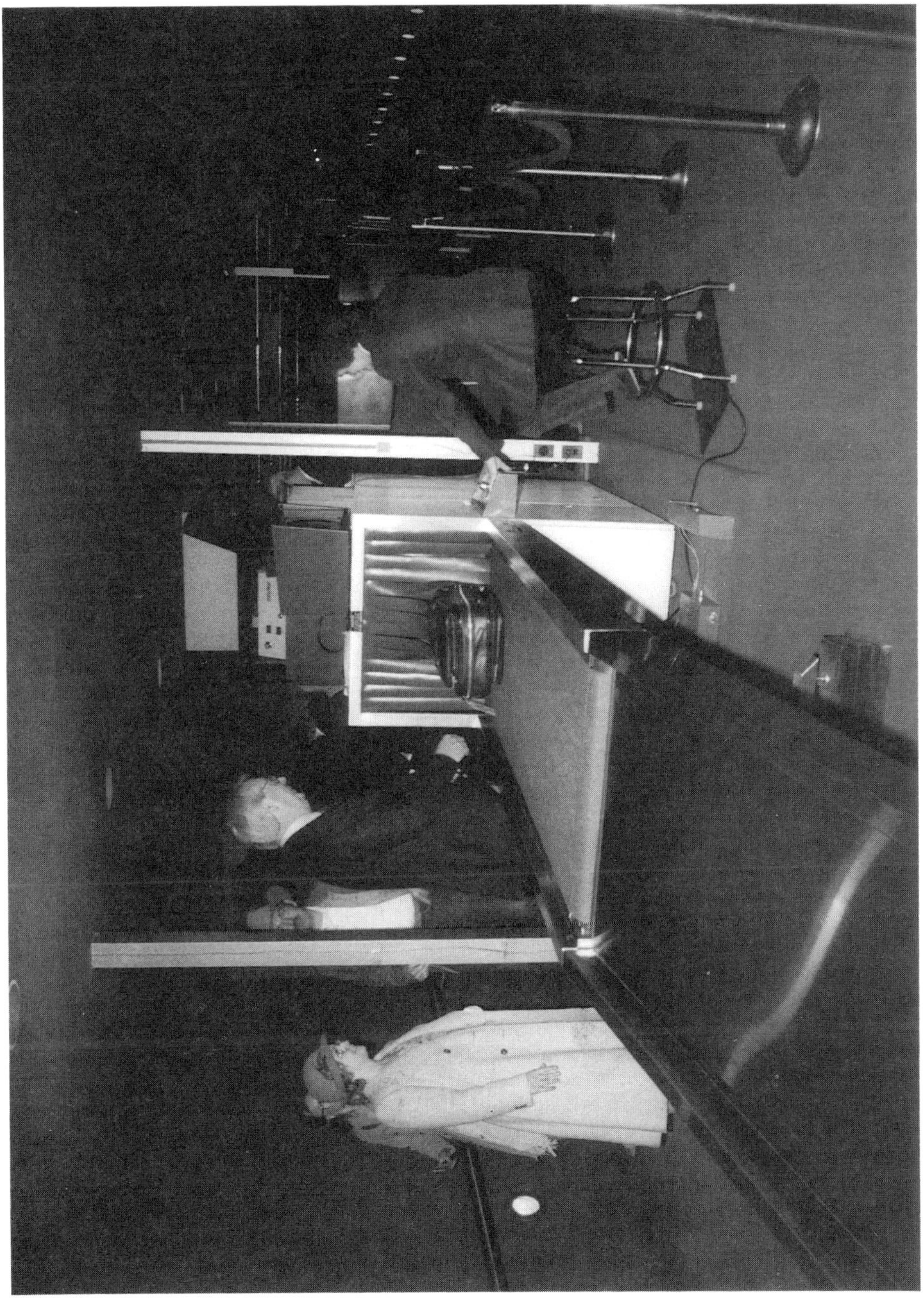

Chapter 6

How Far Can They Search Without a Warrant?

"For good or for ill, our government teaches the whole people by its example."

U.S. Supreme Court Justice Brandeis (1928)

Search and Seizure: What Police Can and Cannot Do

"The genius of the Constitution is that it sides with the citizen against the government."

The people's laws adopted by the new republic (the United States of America) were the Bill of Rights. Most Americans don't know what these rights are, and if they see them out of context usually consider them to be overall radical.

Police have no right to make *unreasonable* searches and seizures of citizens and their property. When a search is planned by police, a search warrant must be issued by a Judge. But most searches are not planned and, therefore, are warrantless. To be legal they must fall within specified categories of areas where there are *exceptions to the warrant requirement.*

1. What is a search? A search takes place whenever a citizen's privacy is invaded in the course of a criminal investigation

looking into books, papers, and things in a person's home or business.
2. What is an unreasonable search? Your right to be protected from an unreasonable search is open to various interpretations depending upon the facts of each case.
3. When can there be a search without a warrant? There need not be a warrant if the search is for things which are otherwise seen in plain view, or if you consent to the search, or if there is special emergency circumstances, or if the search is incident to a lawful arrest.
4. If the police are in hot pursuit, or are conducting an inventory search in order to check contents of your vehicle to prevent loss at a later time, or if you are engaged in suspicious activity you may be stopped and frisked on the street, police may legally make a search.

In a man's home, he is not required to retreat or run away since he has no place to go. A man's home is intrusion even to the point of taking the intruder's life.

A police officer may be an unlawful intruder if he enters the home of another when he is not under the protection of due process of law. The limits of his authority becomes questionable if decisions are made in a hurry.

There is little room in law enforcement for the trial and error method. If police don't know what to do, they shouldn't do it!

Search of Your Person

A search of a person occurs in the following instances:

1. A pat-down or frisk.
2. Entrance into a private home, office, building, or other area to seek evidence.
3. Electronic interception of communications.
4. Extracting body fluids from a suspect.
5. Prying into hidden places.
6. Examination of private papers (letters, documents, or checkbooks).
7. Examination of personal effects (clothing, bed sheets, suitcases, wallets, purses, lockers, luggage and mail).
8. Taking specimens of hair, tissue, breath, or fingerprints.
9. Observation of objects or detection of odors when the officer does not have a lawful right to be in the position necessary to receive such sensory perceptions.

Persons, Papers, and Effects Generally Not Protected

The protection of the Fourth Amendment is not required for the following:

1. Open fields
2. Grounds around a house (curtilage)
3. Objects accidentally discovered at a car accident
4. Items voluntarily shown to police
5. Items found during a lawful inventory
6. Conversations overheard without electronic aids
7. Recovering of items from dead persons
8. Public places
9. Looking through windows where objects are in plain view
10. Vacated premises
11. Jails and prisons
12. Objects in areas within plain view
13. Common areas accessible to the public
14. Public records
15. Abandoned articles
16 Fire escapes
17. Border crossings

Reasonableness of Search

The Constitution only prohibits *unreasonable searches and seizures.*

There is no clear cut means of ascertaining whether a search is *reasonable* but criteria include the following:

1. Was a warrant obtained?
2. Was there time to obtain a warrant?
3. Was the search conducted during the day or night?
4. What was the place subjected to the search?
5. What was the scope of the search?
6. Was force or coercion employed?
7. What was the purpose of the search?
8. What was the crime under investigation?

The Constitution does not define *unreasonable searches*. A judgment must be on a case-by-case basis.

Objects of Search

The scope of search must be justified by the circumstances which rendered it permissible.

When searching under the authority of a warrant, the objects of the search must be specified. With or without a warrant, any search must be reasonably limited and justified by the initial reason. Thus, in a homicide investigation in which the search is for a weapon, one would not be justified in going through personal papers.

Legitimate objects of a search include:

1. Weapons
2. Evidence of crime
3. Fruits of crime
4. Instrumentalities of crime
5. Contraband.

These items coming within plain view during a lawful search may be legally seized even if not listed on a search warrant.

Incident to a Lawful Arrest

The exception to the requirement of a search warrant is the search incidental to a lawful arrest:

1. There must be an actual arrest.
2. The arrest must precede the search.
3. The arrest must be lawful.
4. The arrest must be made in good faith and not for the sole purpose of creating an excuse to search.
5. The search must be bona fide for articles connected with the arrest.
6. The search must be reasonable and proximate to the arrest in time and place.

Where there is probable cause to arrest, there is always the right to search the person to protect the officer and make the arrest a safe one, and later, during the booking process, to protect the suspects' property (custodial duties of the officer).

The U.S. Supreme Court case of *Chimel vs. California* limits searches to those areas into which the person might reach to destroy evidence or weapons. The constructive reach or lunge doctrine allows a search into areas which you might jump or grab a weapon or evidence, such as a desk, glove compartment, dresser, or closet.

The common police tactic of requiring identification and then searching either the drawer into which you reach or your wallet is permitted. It is permissible to allow you to walk into various rooms to get clothing, make telephone calls, use the bathrooms, and then for the officer to conduct a search of such areas within the home.

A common problem is the search of briefcases, handbags, or suitcases that are carried or are located nearby an arrested person. A search of items carried by a suspect or located nearby is allowed, as in the case where an arrestee makes a suspicious move toward a briefcase, even if handcuffed.

Some courts do not allow the search of luggage and other similar items where they can be easily secured and a search warrant later obtained. Searches are more easily allowed when an officer testifies that he *feared for his safety*.

The Schmerber Doctrine

In *Schmerber vs. California*, the U.S. Supreme Court considered a DWI suspect who was forced to submit to the withdrawal of a small blood sample for analysis and upheld the search, provided it was limited and done in accordance with medically accepted standards with due regard for health and safety. The search does not violate the right of the suspect against self-incrimination.

As long as the physical intrusion is not a substantial one, does not endanger life or limb, or is not enough to shock the conscience or be offensive to one's senses of justice, the following intrusions have been held legal:

1. Fingernail scrapings.
2. Giving voice or handwriting sample.
3. Swabbing of hand and giving of paraffin test.
4. Palm prints and fingerprints.
5. Use of fluorescent lights.
6. Surgical procedures. Courts will allow the removal of a bullet from a suspect if:
   a. There is no other way to obtain the evidence,
   b. A presurgery hearing is held
   c. A qualified surgeon performs the operation.
7. Use of a solution compelling the suspect to regurgitate.
8. Use of reasonable blood tests.
9. Requiring a urine sample.
10. Waiting a reasonable time for a bowel movement.

The Booking Search

Once you are arrested and taken into police custody your clothing and property may be taken, searched, and inventoried for safekeeping.

Should the arrest later be held to be illegal (not based on probable cause) then the booking search is likewise illegal. This is a part of the routine booking process.

While under lawful arrest, whether or not during the booking process, but so long as the person is being lawfully detained. You may also be made to:

1. Be photographed.
2. Be recorded by motion pictures.
3. Be fingerprinted.
4. Speak.
5. Disrobe and have clothes taken as evidence.
6. Allow blood to be medically withdrawn.
7. Participate in a line-up.
8. Put on specific clothing.
9. Take Benzidine test for recent weapons firing.
10. Exhibit body, display scars or birthmarks.
11. Undress in interrogation room and have clothing inspected.
12. Have hair samples plucked.
13. Place hands under ultra-violet light.
14. Shave or alter appearance.
15. Give saliva or urine specimens.
16. Take breath test.

Once admitted to jail you retain *little expectation of privacy*. Anything you do or say which is observed by a jailer or other prisoners is legally admissible in court.

Search of Homes and Business

The search of your house without a search warrant is permissible only if you were arrested inside. Only the area from which you may gain possession of a weapon, destroy evidence, or the area into which you might reach can be lawful search. Another person on the premises may also be searched.

This burden of proof is on police to show that the item seized was with your *immediate control* and exceptions are carefully drawn. Courts allow police to expand the searchable area by directing you to get dressed and allowing you to walk into various rooms, and does have a right to create a situation which gives him a pretext for searching beyond your area of the immediate control.

Items seized should be connected with the arrest–items such as weapons, fruit of a crime, contraband, instruments used in committing the crime, or even items unrelated to the particular crime.

A dwelling is any place used as a home, apartment, or hotel, and the *curtilage* is the open space surrounding the dwelling that the average person would consider a part of the dwelling. The curtilage is often the enclosed area that surrounds the dwelling and is generally the lived-in area surrounding and close to the dwelling. Areas outside home so business not within the curtilage may be searched under the open fields doctrine.

If there is doubt as to whether the place to be searched is within the curtilage, a search warrant should always be obtained.

> EXAMPLES: Places within the curtilage include a farmer's barn separated by a driveway approximately 70 yards from a house, a trash container under a back porch, and a closed cupboard in a common hallway leading to a suspect's apartment. Examples of places beyond the curtilage are an open field 100 yards from the defendant's residence, and a small concrete building 150 feet from a residence and separated from the residence by a fence and gate.

Observation of your house and its curtilage may be used without a warrant from any place outside the curtilage, and use of a telescope, binoculars, flashlight, or similar devices, as there is not physical trespass. Listening to conversations or other sounds occurring in a dwelling or its curtilage may be accomplished without a warrant if there is no actual physical trespass of electronic or mechanical devices used to hear the conversations or sounds (unless an informant or other consenting person is within the dwelling).

The Protective Sweep

An officer may protect himself while making an arrest inside a home or business in a *protective sweep* or quick search of other rooms for associates or dangerous companions.

Plain View

Evidence seen by police by the *naked eye in plain sight* is legal if the officer has the right to be there. If the officer is searching under a car seat for a weapon and finds drugs, he may seize the drugs.

It should be an inadvertent finding of unsuspected evidence.

Window peeping is not allowed but police may observe evidence through an open door, a glass door, or through a window with open blinds.

Plain Smell Doctrine

The odor of illegal drugs smelled by law officers familiar with the odor, or trained marijuana sniffing dogs, has been held to support probable cause for a further search.

Investigatory Searches

There are limited times when police can forcibly interfere with a person's liberty on less than probable cause:

1. A reasonable search for weapons for the protection of officer (stop and frisk)
2. A border patrol check point stop
3. Routine detention of residents in a house while it is being searched under a search warrant.

In these situations, courts engage in a balancing test to see whether the detention and search are lawful.

1. Weighing the public concerns served by the seizure
2. The degree the seizure advances the public interest
3. The severity of the interferences with individual liberty.

Emergency Searches

Police may conduct searches in emergency (exigent) situations where, in the absence of such emergency, the search might otherwise be invalid. Courts have carved out an exception, allowing police to conduct an immediate search where life or limb may be in danger.

Originally, exigency cases related only to where there was threat or danger to *life*. If police believe life is endangered, the breaking into a home by force is not illegal, if it is reasonable under the circumstances.

In addition to the *lifesaving exception*, the doctrine includes situations where police have reasonable grounds to believe that *evidence* might be destroyed.

Examples:

1. Putting out a trash fire where items were being destroyed.
2. Where there is a threat of destruction of drugs.

Courts insist upon good faith belief that a real emergency did exist. The emergency circumstances will vary and the necessities carefully reviewed.

Examples:

1. The degree of urgency involved and amount of time necessary to obtain a warrant.
2. Reasonable belief that the contraband is about to be destroyed.
3. The possibility of danger to police guarding the site while a search warrant is being obtained.
4. Information indicating the suspect was aware police were on their trail.
5. The ready destructibility of contraband and the knowledge that efforts to dispose of narcotics and to escape are characteristic behavior of those engaged in narcotics trafficking.

Impounding Premises

The U.S. Supreme Court carved out a small exception in a *few specifically established and well-delineated situations* where officers may make a warrantless search of a dwelling without a search warrant. A strong burden rests upon police to show the existence of an exceptional situation, excusing the necessity for a search warrant under *Chimel.*

When an arrest occurs inside a house, police may guard the door to prevent the destruction of evidence while obtaining a search warrant.

If there is insufficient time to secure a search warrant (where evidence is in the process of destruction–such as being burned or flushed down a stool, or if it is otherwise impracticable to obtain a search warrant, then, only in such situations, officers may proceed to search a residence without a warrant.

Inspection Searches

In certain limited administrative situations, city, county, or state laws may require the inspection of certain *licensees* who engaged in a government-related business or a business which requires a government permit or license (i.e., firearm salesman, restaurants, packing plants, bars, liquor stores).

Such searches may usually be by surprise but administrative officials conducting the search should:

1. Announce their purpose.

2. Search at reasonable hours (though not necessarily convenient to the licensee)
3. Search without force (unless a formal search warrant may also be obtained)
4. Be acting on their own and without police collusion.

If you refuse inspection, the inspector must obtain a search warrant, but such refusal could be the basis for revocation of the license or other sanctions provided by law.

Administrative inspection searches have been allowed in fire prevention, trash collection, agricultural plants, and gun license inspections (where the need for surprise is recognized as being apparent). Inspection searches are official conduct authorized by law and what minor invasion of privacy may occur is outweighed by the effectiveness of the inspection system and the overriding public interest in the inspection as a credible deterrent.

Airport Searches

Airports have been regarded as a *critical zone* where special considerations adjust and the compromise Fourth Amendment standards of *reasonableness*. The urgency of the air piracy and hijacking problems make security searches an exceptional circumstance.

Courts recognized in order to offset incidents of bomb threats, air piracy, extortion, and other schemes endangering commercial aviation—security measures at airports are essential.

Hijackers are deeply disturbed and highly unpredictable persons—often paranoid or suicidal schizophrenics with extreme tendencies toward violence. Hijacking has been used as a device for carrying out acts of political violence and terrorism.

Where airport personnel have observed passengers appearing nervous, paying for tickets in small bills, jumping from line to line, not carrying luggage, giving inconsistent answers for giving false names on tickets, searches have been allowed at airports (Drug Courier Profile).

Where suspects give untruthful replies to bomb threat investigations, lack identification, or make suspicious moves, they may fit the *Hijacker Profile*.

Search of Students

Street crime often spills over into the classroom, such as possession of narcotics, stolen property, guns, assault, and robbery.

Searches conducted on university campuses and dormitories are judged by different standards than those in secondary school. Since secondary school students are minors, they are subject to a greater degree of supervision than college students. Yet neither teachers nor students completely shed their Constitutional rights at the schoolhouse door.

The U.S. Supreme Court in *Katz vs. United States*, (1967), the reach of the Fourth Amendment is measured by a person's *reasonable expectation of privacy*. Court decisions hold that, a student does enjoy a reasonable expectation of privacy in his locker and personal property.

The Fourth Amendment applies only to *police searches* and is aimed at controlling arbitrary illegal conduct of *government agents*. If the school search is conducted by teachers where school officials act *in concert with police*, the search is legal but is governed by Fourth Amendment standards.

If the search is by school officials only, the U.S. Supreme Court in *New Jersey vs. TLO* (1985), applies a two part test: (1) Was the search legal at the start? (2) Was the search reasonable?

The Doctrine of Loco Parentis

Loco parentis is an ancient principle which places the government in role of a lawful parent. A teacher is given parental authority to carry out her duties. Courts invoke this doctrine to justify the reasonableness of a search. School officials must have latitude in controlling the school environment and in trying to balance the personal privacy of the student against the need to maintain order in the schools.

Where the student is aware that school officials possess duplicate locks or combinations for lockers, and perhaps because of the nonexclusive nature of a locker where the locker is shared with another student, the teacher is empowered to consent to the search by police officers.

Search by Private Citizens

The protection of the Fourth Amendment *does not apply to private persons* not acting pursuant to a request by police or acting under *color of law*.

Even though there may be an otherwise illegal restraint of a suspect, or a completely illegal search where entry is made without the consent or knowledge of the occupant, the evidence can be used in court.

The exclusionary rule of the Fourth Amendment is only applicable to prevent *government misconduct.*

> **RULE: THE POLICY UNDERLYING THE 4TH AND 14TH AMENDMENTS DOES NOT DISCOURAGE CITIZENS FROM AIDING, TO THE UTMOST OF THEIR ABILITY, IN THE APPREHENSION OF CRIMINALS.**

The only remedy the arrested suspect has is the right of civil lawsuit against those who wrongfully took such property, but, nonetheless, the evidence seized remains inadmissible in both state and federal courts.

Items searched for or seized by the following persons may be admissible into evidence:

1. Foreign border officials
2. Foreign officials
3. Private investigators
4. Insurance agents
5. Airline employees
6. Husbands or wives
7. Private persons
8. Garage or service station personnel
9. Motel or hotel owners
10. School teachers.

Body Searches

For police to make embarrassing body searches (anal or vaginal), the following rules must be followed:

1. There must be clear indication the intrusion will supply important evidence
2. Must be accomplished by a safe, reliable method, no more psychologically uncomfortable than reasonably necessary
3. The court must weigh the probable worth of the evidence against any alternative means for obtaining the evidence.

Strip searches are allowed of prisoners in jails, where you no longer have Constitutional rights to be *let alone* or any expectation of privacy.

Consent Searches

Even the broadest search is legal if police prove you voluntarily and intelligently consented to the search. You may always waive your Fourth Amendment right to be free from unreasonable searches whether you are under arrest or not. The consent must be given knowingly, voluntarily, unequivocally, uninduced by fraud, duress or coercion, whether direct or indirect.

Police have the burden of proof to show by *clear and convincing evidence* that consent was *freely given* and you were *aware* of your rights and *waived* them. Courts use the *totality of the circumstances test* to determine whether consent was given.

Judicial preferences for search warrants has led to Supreme Court to observe that searches conducted without prior judicial approval are *per se unreasonable*, but courts recognize a warrantless search by law officers (with the permission of a suspect) is an exception to the warrant requirement of the Fourth Amendment.

> EXAMPLE: A landlord cannot consent to the search of a tenant's apartment, or a desk clerk to the search of a hotel room, although a co-tenant can consent to a search even if the supposed co-tenant later turns out only to be a guest.

A wife or mistress may or may not be able to consent to the search of her partner's property, depending on whether or not she had joint access. She probably cannot consent to the search of her partner's sole possessions.

Search of Mail

When in Jail, your mail is opened. Prison guards and jailers intercept and read all mail unless it is marked *Attorney-Client*. You have no expectation of privacy.

> A tenant can consent to an apartment search regardless of the wishes of the guest.

> An employer can consent to a work area of an employee unless it is the employee's exclusive area. A parent can give consent to the search of premises occupied by their child.

> **RULE: IT IS THE POSSESSORY RIGHT TO USE THE PREMISES RATHER THAN *LEGAL OWNERSHIP* THAT IS THE DETERMINING FACTOR.**

Although Miranda warnings need to be given at a consent search, the better practice is to do so.

A valid consent search presumes to continue until all covered areas have been searched or unless the consent is revoked. Evidence seized prior to revocation of a consent is admissible. It is permissible for police, in requesting a consent search, to mention that, absent consent, the officer intends to obtain a search warrant. This is not coercion.

You assume the risk (foreseeable by you) that your landlord, tenant, relative, or roommate will consent to a search of jointly occupied property.

If a *wired informant* talks to you and it is transmitted by microphone to federal narcotics agents, who later testify as to the contents of the conversation. Courts hold the Fourth Amendment does not protect you from your discreet conversation with one you trust.

You do not possess any legitimate expectation of privacy or secrecy in your bank or telephone records.

Consent searches are popular with police for several reasons:

1. Property sought does not have to be particularly described
2. Search does not have to be connected with an arrest or upon probable cause
3. No restrictions exist on time and place of search
4. Scope of search is not limited
5. Police need not look for any particular item.

Facts weighing heavily against a finding of valid consent include:

1. The display of weapons
2. The time of night
3. The number of officers present
4. The aggressiveness of police
5. Trickery or misrepresentations used in obtaining consent
6. Threats to obtain a search warrant or impound a vehicle
7. Interrogation without Miranda warnings
8. Interrogation with Miranda warnings, but so intensive as to compulsively induce the consent
9. Threats against women to take their children and place them in foster homes.

Abandoned Property

If you discard items at some place outside your house or its immediate area (known as the *curtilage*) police may seize such property (even though it is then beyond the person's physical control) on the ground that it is *abandoned.*

There is no requirement you intended to get rid of the property permanently.

If the property is discarded within your house, hotel room, vehicle, taxicab or other place under your control, it cannot be considered abandoned.

> EXAMPLES:
>
> A package of heroin picked up from the street after a scuffle during an arrest, contraband goods, or drugs thrown from an automobile which land on the street, sidewalk, or other public property after being thrown by the driver of the automobile, or items being thrown out of an apartment window by a person under surveillance. If you drop an envelope in a police station, or to a sidewalk after being arrested or questioned, it is abandonment. (Known as *dropsy cases*.)
>
> Trash placed in your yard for pick up is not yet abandoned unless placed in the street or papers fully shredded. If it's in your trash can it is not abandoned unless placed in a common dumpster.
>
> **RULE: THE TEST WHETHER THERE HAS BEEN ABANDONMENT IS:**
>
> 1. **WHETHER YOU STILL HAVE A REASONABLE EXPECTATION OF PRIVACY.**
> 2. **SOCIETY IS PREPARED TO RECOGNIZE YOUR ACTS AS REASONABLE.**

The Inevitable Discovery Doctrine

The U.S. Supreme Court in *Nix vs. Williams* (1984) (the *Inevitable Discovery Rule*). If the evidence ultimately and *inevitably would have been discovered* by lawful means, even if initially discovered illegally, it is admissible at trial. Having juries receive probative evidence is in the public interest and is properly balanced by putting the police in the same, not a worse position, than they would have been if not police error or misconduct had occurred.

In this famous *Christian Burial Speech Case*, police were looking for a small girl's body and obtained information as to her whereabouts illegally, in clear violation of a Miranda warning given to the suspect. The suspect had an attorney and requested his right not to talk. The two officers talked to each other, lamenting that if they knew the girl's whereabouts, her parents could give her a Christian burial. With this indirect questioning, the accused spoke up and confessed. Since volunteer searchers were combing the shoulders of the highways, the court decided her body would have been *ultimately dicovered by legal means* and allowed the evidence and conviction of the defendant although his confession was disallowed.

RULE: IF THE POLICE COMMIT AN ILLEGAL SEARCH, IF THEY CONVINCE THE JUDGE THE EVIDENCE WOULD HAVE BEEN INEVITABLY DISCOVERED THROUGH LAWFUL MEANS, IT WILL BE ADMITTED IN COURT.

Independent Source Doctrine

The Independent Source Doctrine allows evidence even though it may have originally been found through illegal means if they can prove they had information from an independent source that would have led them to the same discovery. It is not exactly the same as the Inevitable Discovery Doctrine. The Independent Source Doctrine relates to a situation where police illegally enter property and learn of contraband, but then later obtain the necessary information that would have supported the valid issuance of a Search Warrant.

A similar example is an initial illegal search occurs and a confession is made. If the court believes the confession may be sufficiently removed or *purged* of the *taint* of the illegal arrest, the confession is valid.

Aerial Searches

Plane or helicopter over-flights of residential areas at a relatively low height in order to view, inspect and photograph are allowed.

Only if it can be said that you erected high fences, roofs, canopies or demonstrated your intent to an *expectation of privacy,* would the evidence be disallowed.

RULE: EVEN IF THE OVER-FLIGHTS ARE IN CLEAR VIOLATION OF FAA RULES POLICE SPOTTER PLANES CAN PHOTOGRAPH YOUR FENCED BACKYARD.

Chapter 7

How Far Can They Search with a Search Warrant?

"Missouri is known as the 'Show Me State'. In our state, police ask: Show me what's in your car. Show me what's in your house."

"Probable cause exists where the facts and circumstances within the arresting officers' knowledge and of which they had reasonable trustworthy information are sufficient in themselves to warrant a man of reasonable caution in the belief that an offense has been or is being committed."

Draper vs. U.S.,
U.S. Supreme Court (1959)

"Searches conducted outside the judicial process, without prior approval by judge or magistrate, are per se unreasonable under the Fourth Amendment–subject only to a few specifically established and well-delineated exceptions."

Katz vs. U.S.,
U.S. Supreme Court (1967)

Search Warrants

Police have a legal right to search your house if they have a Search Warrant issued by a Judge. It must be based on probable cause and be in writing:

1. The affidavit must contain facts establishing probable cause. Conclusions and suspicions alone are not enough.
2. The warrant may not be general but specifically directed to your home and specific things within your home.
3. Warrants allow the search of your residence, garage, or car.
4. Do the police have to announce themselves? Before entering a house, police must first *knock and announce* their authority and purpose. Sometimes it can be dispensed with if police show emergency circumstances that they believe someone was being harmed.

> **RULE: IT IS A GOOD POLICY TO BE DIPLOMATIC AND POLITE TO POLICE, EVEN WHEN THEY DON'T RECIPROCATE. NOTHING IS GAINED FROM BEING IMPOLITE, SARCASTIC, OR ABUSIVE. IF THEY ACT IMPROPERLY, THAT ISSUE IS LATER REVIEWABLE BY A JUDGE. THEY ARE IMPRESSED BY DEFENDANTS WHO MAINTAIN THEIR COMPOSURE AND MANNERS, EVEN IN THE FACE OF POLICE MISCONDUCT.**
>
> **IF CONFRONTED WITH MISCONDUCT, IDENTIFY BY BADGE NUMBER OR NAME THE POLICE OFFICER AND KEEP COOL. YOU ARE NOT REQUIRED TO SHOW POLICE ON A TOUR OF YOUR HOUSE OR MAKE ANY STATEMENT. KEEP YOUR MOUTH SHUT! THEY HAVE THE SEARCH WARRANT AND THE AUTHORITY. LET THEM EARN THEIR SALARY.**

The Supreme Court has made it clear: search without a warrant is presumptively unreasonable. The test is: "*Is it reasonable for police to have obtained a search warrant*?" If it was, and police fail to do so, the search will be held void and the evidence excluded.

A heavy burden is placed on police. When knowledge of illegal contraband comes to police and there is sufficient time to get a search warrant, the officer must do it! Courts reward police for getting search warrants. In close cases, courts rule that a search based on a warrant will be upheld, since at least the officer did take time to seek judicial approval of his search and will be *given the benefit of any doubt.*

A Search Warrant Application must:

1. Be in writing
2. State the time and date of the application
3. Name the people and places to be searched and the things sought
4. State the date of the facts relied on
5. Be directed to a peace officer
6. Show probable cause
7. Be verified and filed in court
8. Be recorded if the warrant is for obscene matter
9. Be signed by the Judge
10. Command that all things seized be brought before the Court and accounted for within 10 days.

Warrants which fail to specify the person, place, and thing to be searched are known as general warrants and are forbidden.

A search warrant may be issued for:

1. Stolen or embezzled property
2. Any weapon, tool, or thing used as a means for committing a felony
3. Property for which possession is an offense
4. Property used by owner as a raw material in manufacturing anything for which possession is an offense
5. A kidnapped person, deceased fetus or corpse
6. Obscene matter
7. Any person or moveable thing
8. Papers or private records.

Preparation of Search Warrant Application

Every police agency has search warrant forms from which they can quickly prepare warrants.

They have a set policy with the Prosecutor as to whether the attorney is to assist in the preparation of the application before it is given to a Judge. The police officer should prepare the search warrant and two copies for the Judge to sign.

The following rules apply:

1. It cannot be overbroad. An *exact description* and itemization of all articles and things sought should be listed on the search warrant application and not be left to the officer's discretion. A negligent misrepresentation by an officer does not void the warrant, but an intentional one does. The description must identify

the property with *sufficient clarity* that a mistake will not be made and the officer executing the warrant *can reasonably* find it.

2. A description or diagram of the place to be searched should be given as accurately as possible, sufficiently described so that the Judge can say the police knew with *sufficient particularity* the area to be searched. Description by street and number is sufficient; it is not legally necessary to name the owner, although it is a good practice. Minor errors are permitted if the officers themselves knew where they were going.
3. All reasons for wanting the search warrant must be listed in detail:
   a. *Personal Observation.* If he has personally seen the crimes, he should state how he happened to see them, the date, attach copies of his reports to the search warrant affidavit, refer to them within the affidavit, and include any personal expertise he may have.
   b. *Hearsay.* If hearsay information (even if double hearsay), it must include from whom the information was received. Probable cause may be based upon information received through an informant and *corroborated by other proof within the officer's knowledge.* Information from fellow officers is automatically considered reliable, as is information from ordinary citizens.
   c. *Reliable Confidential Informant.* An informant is not reliable simply because he had supplied information in the past; his information must be *corroborated.* His track record of reliable information must be stated. If possible, he should be made to sign an affidavit and attached to the officer's affidavit. Whenever possible by surveillance or investigation, police should verify an informant's information, which adds to the reliability, and may give probable cause where the tip was given by an anonymous informant. If the informant was a *witness* to the crime rather than a participant, his presence may be demanded at trial to show he is not guilty or to disprove entrapment. If reliability can be shown, his name need not be given. If reliability cannot be shown, other corroboration is sufficient, such as from another informant, or any sufficient detail to show it is more than a casual rumor.

It is vital that police include *all of the underlying circumstances in the application,* and attach the written affidavits of other officers. An application for a warrant is good or bad on its face and is not changed by conversation with the Judge. It must state facts from which probable cause can be reasonably inferred. Even if the affidavit contains some unlawfully obtained information, if the untainted information establishes probable cause, it is legal. (Known as "dissipating the taint.")

Once police take the application to a Judge, the Judge holds a non-adversary hearing to see if sufficient facts have been stated. Missouri does not allow the officer to supplement the written papers with oral testimony. A later reviewing court will only read the written affidavit.

Misstatements in the Affidavit

In *Delaware vs. Franks*, the U.S. Supreme Court allows a defendant to challenge the *truthfulness* of the affidavit. However, there must be proof of deliberate falsehood or reckless disregard for the truth.

It must be more than mere inaccurate information. There must be evidence that is was *intended to deceive* or mislead the Judge.

Who Signs the Search Warrant

Any Judge can issue a Search Warrant.

Often Judges are contacted on off-duty hours, are away from court, and time is of the essence and the officers cannot wait for the Judge's Clerk to type and prepare the actual warrant, which the Judge signs. The Judge must personally sign the warrant and cannot delegate the authority, although a Judge from another jurisdiction may act.

A Warrant Application must be sworn to and signed before the Judge. The warrant must state the time and date it was signed by the Judge.

The warrant must be executed with reasonable promptness as it expires in 10 days. A late return does not void the warrant unless it was intentional and deliberate.

Police may stay on the premises only during the time reasonably necessary to search and seize the described property. The search should be as brief as reasonably possible.

Search of Persons on Premises

Searches of persons on the property can be justified if:

1. The Search Warrant identifies those persons
2. The person consents
3. Police reasonably believe you are armed or dangerous
4. There are factual grounds for custodial arrest and incidental search.

The U.S. Supreme Court in *Ybarra vs. Illinois,* (1979) ruled the mere presence of a person does not alone give the right to search him, and a standard of probable cause is required for each person present. A Search Warrant for a residence *does not permit a search of all the persons present* during the search unless there is reason to suspect that such person is armed or carrying items which reasonably could be objects of the search warrant.

Upon completing the search, an officer should be assigned at the scene to make at least two copies of an inventory, listing in detail each item seized. Carbon paper and inventory sheets should be taken to the scene and a copy of the search warrant and inventory left with the person in charge, or if no one is present, in plain view.

All items seized must remain in the custody of the officer who signs the inventory until further written court order.

The Prosecuting Attorney should not accompany a sheriff in serving a search warrant in the absence of exceptional circumstance since he might become a witness and could not also act as Prosecutor.

Serving the Warrant

The officer should act in a reasonable manner. Officers should *knock and announce* their identity and purpose. Unannounced entry is permitted only in emergency situations where some person is in peril of bodily harm or evidence is being destroyed. All necessary force can be used to enter the place to be searched. Once entry is gained, the warrant should be read in its entirety to the person in charge. Other officers may be asked to assist as are deemed necessary, and may enter by other doors or windows but cannot enter the premises before the officer serving the warrant. The search need not be made in the accused's presence, or in the presence of any occupant.

A search warrant should be served during the daytime. ("Daytime" exists if there is enough light to recognize a man's features at ten yards.) If the search begins in the daytime it may extend into the night, provided the officers executing the warrant act reasonably and do not delay.

A nighttime warrant may be obtained but will be granted only if the affidavit states the affiant is *positive* that the property is in the place to be searched. The search warrant may state that the search "can take place at any time."

Taking Items Not Named in Warrant

While legally searching in good faith for the items described in the warrant, if evidence of a different unsuspected crime is discovered, it may be seized under the *Plain View Doctrine*, but the newly discovered goods must be readily identifiable as contraband. There must be a *nexus* between the items seized and the criminal behavior. Some Prosecutors prefer "piggy back" search warrants, leaving one officer in charge of the premises while other officers return to prepare an additional search warrant for newly discovered items.

Reasons that might justify some delay in searching are:

1. Waiting for occupants to return to develop a possessory offense
2. Fearing possible violence, officers wait for occupant to leave residence, or where it is believed that the occupant would destroy evidence
3. More officers are needed to search the premises, and time was needed to group them
4. Bad weather conditions.

Good Faith of Police Officer

Even evidence discovered in the course of serving an *illegal* search warrant will not excluded, irrespective of the actual validity of the warrant, if the officer was in *good faith* and acted in *objective reasonable reliance* on the warrant. This is known as the *Leon, "Good Faith" Doctrine* and has been politically controversial.

RULE: SMART COPS WILL ALWAYS CLAIM TYPOGRAPHICAL ERRORS AND INSIST THEY WERE ACTING IN THE BEST FAITH POSSIBLE. SEARCH WARRANTS ARE DIFFICULT TO SUPPRESS.

Chapter 8

When Can They Search My Car?

"Under the automobile exception to the Fourth Amendment requirement of a search warrant, police may conduct a warrantless search of a car as thoroughly as a judge could authorize it if an application was made for a search warrant."

U.S. vs Ross,
Supreme Court (1982)

"The officer prudently may prefer to ask the driver of the vehicle to step out of the car and off onto the shoulder of the road..."

Pennsylvania vs Mimms,
U.S. Supreme Court (1977)

"When vehicles are impounded, local police departments generally follow a routine practice of securing and inventorying the automobiles' contents. These procedures developed in response to three distinct needs: (1) the protection of the owner's property...(2) the protection of the police against claims or disputes over lost or stolen property...(3) the protection of the police from the potential danger."

South Dakota vs. Opperman,
U.S. Supreme Court (1976)

F.B.I. statistics show that 75% of all crimes include the use of an automobile, and courts relegate vehicles to a special class by themselves.

Because of their mobility, probable cause requirements have been eased, since vehicles can be driven easily to another jurisdiction where police have no authority.

Mobility of automobiles precludes the possibility of seeking search warrants. A lesser degree of reasonable grounds is necessary to search an automobile than is required to search a home. The *automobile exception to the search warrant requirement* does not exist under every conceivable circumstance and police must show some need for prompt search.

Courts go further in upholding a search if it was a *protective search* (the officer felt that his life might be in danger). Where the officer can testify to facts showing that he was in possible fear of his safety, courts are inclined to give police, safety and protection. (Thirty percent of all shootings of police officers occur when an officer approaches a person seated in a car during a traffic stop.)

A search for physical evidence can follow a mere passive nonculpable traffic offense only if there is reasonable belief that the contents offend against the law. A driver's person can always be searched when arrested, and although the search of the entire car on a purely exploratory fishing adventure is not allowed it is allowed if the driver reaches into the interior of the car and obtains a weapon (where a weapon could be obtained).

Automobile stops may be made for:

1. Giving a summons or making a traffic arrest
2. Routine traffic investigation
3. Probable cause to believe a crime has been committed
4. Investigative detention (stop and frisk)
5. Probable cause to believe the vehicle is stolen or there is other need to identify the vehicle
6. Road blocks, if searching for a particularly described vehicle or occupant
7. Checking of serial, engine number, driver's license, or license plates
8. Seizing an instrumentality of the crime
9. Safety inspection stops
10. Searches at borders.

Police may stop an automobile to make a routine check for an operator's license. The driver and passenger may be made to get out of the car. It is not a crime to fail to produce a driver's license, but failure is presumptive evidence that the person is unlicensed. Once stopped, if police develop cause to search for evidence, the interior of the car may be searched including the trunk, locked glove compartment, or under the back seat.

> **RULE: *THE VEHICLE SHOULD BE SEARCHED IN THE IMMEDIATE VICINITY OF THE ARREST.* EVEN IF YOU ARE HANDCUFFED, GUARDED, OR LYING ON THE GROUND, YOUR VEHICLE CAN STILL BE SEARCHED.**

Normally you are arrested in or near your car and it is within your immediate control or free access and is still mobile. The car can be towed to police headquarters and searched immediately for evidence or weapons. One exception would be if the officer has a good reason for removing the car to headquarters rather than searching immediately at the scene. Examples are that the search might have created a traffic hazard or congestion, or that an unruly crowd gathered and the officer feared a riot, or where it becomes too dark to see properly, or other urgent circumstances. The automobile is actual evidence itself of a crime, because the accused used it to commit the crime, as a means of escape, or transport contraband, and the vehicle can be seized and searched as if it were an item of evidence in the case.

When a car is stopped and police observe contraband in *plain view* it is admissible into evidence.

> **RULE: *THE SEARCH MUST BE CONTEMPORANEOUS WITH THE ARREST.* IF THE TIME LAPSE IS A SIGNIFICANT ONE, A SEARCH WARRANT SHOULD BE OBTAINED AND THE VEHICLE KEPT UNDER SURVEILLANCE TO AVOID THE LATER CONTENTION OF EVIDENCE PLANTING. THE TIME LAG SHOULD NOT BE AN UNREASONABLE ONE UNDER THE CIRCUMSTANCES.**

> **RULE: *THE ARREST MUST BE LAWFUL,* MUST BE BASED ON PROBABLE CAUSE AND WILL BE MEASURED BY THE FACTS AND CIRCUMSTANCES KNOWN AT THE TIME OF THE ARREST. IT CANNOT BE A CONVENIENT EXCUSE, SUBTERFUGE, OR PRETEXT FOR CONDUCTING A SEARCH.**

Courts allow searches:

1. Under the front seat
2. Behind the front seat

3. The front floorboard
4. Back seat
5. Glove compartment.

The automobile is not a magic word in whose presence the Fourth Amendment completely disappears, but police may make searches of cars within the above rules, without need of a search warrant.

Vehicles Other Than Autos

Mobile homes and camper trailers are treated like all vehicles unless located in a trailer park, in which case a search warrant must be obtained.

Truck trailers, when connected to a cab or parked and U-Haul trailers are treated the same as automobile trunks. If parked without a cab, or where trailers are parked overnight or longer, a search warrant is needed.

Public passenger vehicles, buses, planes, trains, and boats may be halted to arrest a suspect and a limited search of the area under his control.

Privately owned boats and planes may be searched without a warrant and are treated like mobile homes.

> **RULE: POLICE STOP RENTAL VEHICLES FROM *SOURCE* (DRUG) STATES, RENTED BY THIRD PERSONS WITH SPANISH NAMES. THEY LOOK FOR AIR FRESHENERS, MAPS, U-HAUL TAPED BOXES, LITTLE OR NO LUGGAGE, INCONSISTENT STORIES BETWEEN DRIVER AND PASSENGER, TO EMPLOY THE *DRUG COURIER PROFILE* TO JUSTIFY A FULL BLOWN SEARCH OF YOUR VEHICLE.**

Stop and Frisk of Automobiles

Courts allow police the right to stop a motor vehicle on reasonable suspicion not amounting to probable cause.

Using the same line of reasoning in *Terry vs. Ohio* (a stop and frisk on a *sidewalk*), can stop a car, or reach into a stopped car (if he believes that criminal activity may be occurring. There is no difference in principle between detention on a sidewalk and stopping a car on a street. The officer must identify himself, initiate limited questioning, require you to identify yourself, and make reasonable inquiries concerning your activity, without being adjudged to have made a formal arrest. In the course of such temporary investigative detention, if contraband evidence is seen in plain view or other evidence of a crime is discovered, it is admissible at trial.

> EXAMPLE: Two police officers generally patrolled a large parking lot where there had been several recent cases of stolen cars. They observed a parked car with two occupants, and as they approached the car and headlights came on and the car proceeded out of the parking lot at a fast speed. They follow the vehicle down an alley, around a corner and see one of the occupants bend over the front seat, stop the car, ask for identification and observe a weapon lying on the front floorboard. The weapon was proved to have been used in an earlier murder and was charged with murder.
>
> ANSWER: The stop was not an arrest, but a lawful temporary detention. The pistol was not searched for, but was observed in plain view. The weapon was properly admitted into evidence.

Police are not permitted to stop every car that passes. They must:

1. Believe a crime may have been committed
2. Have a reasonable ground for such belief
3. Absolute necessity for immediate investigatory activity.

Such situations include:

1. Officer observes item within car believed to be stolen
2. Car left hurriedly from store believe to have been burglarized
3. Car matching description of auto observed earlier at burglary
4. Officers instructed by radio to arrest for stealing
5. Driver's evasive action (furtive movements) and police observance of suspicious article in car
6. Existence of suspicious facts leading officer to believe trunk contains contraband
7. Suspicious collection of clothing, burglary tools, stolen revolver, or items believed stolen
8. Emergency circumstances.

A search of the entire automobile after a mere traffic violation will not, standing by itself, provide reasonable cause for the officer to believe that the contents of the automobile offend the law. The search cannot be justified by what is actually found.

Search of Trunks

A search of a trunk is justified under the same conditions as search of a car. If the officer is searching because of the need to seize weapons or where there is probable cause to believe the car contains evidence of a crime, all parts of the car may be searched.

Inventory Search

The U.S. Supreme Court in *South Dakota vs. Opperman* (1986), allowed police a lawful basis for acquiring custody of a vehicle. To avoid leaving an unattended vehicle on a public street, and to keep the vehicle and its contents safe, they may search the vehicle or locked containers. The officer's motive must be *protective* and not investigative and not a cover up merely to search for evidence of a crime.

Standard police procedures regarding inventory searches must be in writing (a department regulation).

> **RULE: TO SUCCESSFULLY ATTACK AN INVENTORY SEARCH YOU MUST PROVE THERE WAS A *REASONABLE ALTERNATIVE TO IMPOUNDMENT*, OR ANOTHER RESPONSIBLE PERSON TO DRIVE THE CAR HOME OR THAT POLICE DON'T ALWAYS IMPOUND AND SEARCH CARS IN SIMILAR CIRCUMSTANCES.**

If a vehicle is abandoned, it can be seized and searched without a warrant and without probable cause. Rights to possession are relinquished at the time of abandonment.

Stolen vehicles may be searched without a warrant. A car thief has no right (standing) to object to a search.

Impoundment of a vehicle is unnecessary:

1. Where other passengers could have taken charge of the auto
2. If a friend could have removed the car within a few hours
3. If the suspect would be absent only for a brief time to post bond
4 If police could have driven the car to a nearby parking area where it would be reasonably safe
5. If police don't usually compound and search
6. If police have no written standard policy.

Search of Closed Containers Found in Car

The search of closed or locked containers can be justified and is allowed under the moving vehicle exception to the Fourth Amendment's warrant requirement.

A closed box, luggage, sack, knapsack, or other container may be opened and searched without a search warrant so long as the police have probable cause to believe that contraband is within the container.

Search and Destroy

For the past decade the U.S. Supreme Court has been hammering down the coffin lid containing the remains of your right to privacy in your car. The Fourth Amendment is explicit about your freedom from unreasonable searches, guaranteeing your right to be *left alone.* Police must first appear before a Judge and under oath state their reasons for suspecting criminal activity. If the Judge accepts their arguments he will issue a Search Warrant, and thereafter the search is legal.

There are a number of exceptions to the Fourth Amendment, developed in court interpretations over the past 200 years. Police do not need a warrant to conduct a search if:

1. They are in *hot pursuit* of a fleeing suspect.
2. They have strong reason to believe a serious crime is about to be committed (*Stop and Frisk*).
3. They see *contraband* in plain view.
4. You freely *consent* to a police request "to have a look around".
5. Police are in the process of making an arrest and may search within the suspect's *grabbing distance* if the crime is serious enough to allow them to take you into custody.
6. Police have *probable cause* in their own mind, but without having to convince a Judge beforehand to believe that a car is transporting contraband (the Automobile Exception of *Carroll vs U.S.*, (1924)).

The *Automobile Exception* to the search warrant requirement receives the most attention and is intended to ensure that police would not be suddenly confronted with dangerous weapons or the destruction of evidence. Recent decisions have established a double standard with regard to your car. Police are not permitted to search your home or anything in it without first getting a warrant, but take your suitcase from your home and put it in the trunk for a drive to the airport, and suddenly you have a lesser expectation of privacy.

The Fourth Amendment's protection requires those inferences be drawn by a *neutral and detached judge* instead of police engaged in the competitive enterprise of ferreting out crime. The potential for police abuse is clear.

What Are Your Rights?

What should you do if stopped by the police when keeping company with contraband? Even though the U.S. Supreme Court has empowered police to search pretty much at will, you can improve your chances, so presence of mind is called for.

1. Make sure nothing illicit is in plain view where it could be lead to a search.
2. Police always prefer to search under the *Consent Exception* which allows them to scratch the itch without an arrest procedure if you consent and waive your Fourth Amendment rights. Most people are so terrified when stopped with contraband they'll go along to appear innocent. When asked, "If you mind opening your trunk?" respond: "Officer, is that really necessary?" Be respectful, but try not to assist in your own bust.
3. If you are pulled over for an arrestable offense, police have the right to search the interior of your car. He may chose not to do so, however, so be gracious in accepting whatever citation he wants to give you. It may lessen the likelihood of a search. Don't argue. If you're carrying contraband: "You're right, Officer. Sorry".
4. If contraband is found, keep quiet. Don't add to your own problems. Ask for an attorney. You still have a chance to be acquitted. Your silence cannot be used against you.

RULE: YOU HAVE LITTLE RIGHT OF PRIVACY IN YOUR CAR. SITTING IN YOUR CAR GIVES YOU ABOUT THE SAME CLAIM TO PRIVACY AS SITTING ON A BENCH IN A PUBLIC PARK. IF YOU TRANSPORT CONTRABAND WHAT CAN YOU DO TO AVOID OPEN SEASON ON AUTO SEARCHES? YOU'D BETTER WALK!

Reasonable Expectation of Privacy

Although you have privacy in your own home what about open curtains, garages, or doors seen from the street? At some point an area becomes so shared with other people that one simply cannot reasonably expect seclusion.

A search is a governmental trespass of a constitutionally protected area. The Fourth Amendment is designed to protect *people, not places.*

Courts look to your *legitimacy of expectation of privacy* as to whether the government's intrusion infringes upon personal and societal values protected by the Fourth Amendment.

Should dogs be allowed to sniff your luggage for drugs? Should planes be allowed to fly over your fenced backyard and take photographs?

The doctrine of *Katz vs. U.S.* requires the court to suppress evidence and declare the search illegal if your *zone of privacy* is violated.

Lt. Hal Smith and Cpl. Don Clark, Springfield P.D., having probable cause to suspect contraband, have the complete right to open and search boxes in the locked trunk.

Chapter 9

When Can I Be Questioned?

"My client has no intention of leaving the country and looks forward to the opportunity of clearing his name."

"Nor shall any person be compelled in any criminal case to be a witness against himself."

Fifth Amendment, United States Constitution

"Many link frequently compose the chain of testimony which is necessary to convict any individual of a crime. It appears to the court to be the true sense of the rule, that no witness is compellable to furnish any one of them against himself. And the court ought never to complete a witness to give an answer which discloses a fact that would form a necessary and essential part of a crime which is punishable by the laws."

Chief Justice Marshall,
United States Supreme Court, 1807

In 1966, in *Miranda vs. Arizona*, the U.S. Supreme Court ruled *all suspects in custody being interrogated by police* must be advised of specific constitutional rights prior to the interrogation. Once the investigation ceases to be general and begins to *focus* on an accused, statements made are not admissible unless he has been advised of his rights.

The courts will consider:

1. *Arrests.* If you are arrested or taken into custody, Miranda warnings must be given. Contrary to popular belief, *Miranda warnings are not technically required* after an arrest and do not affect the arrest.
2. *At the time of transport.* If you are transported to headquarters, you are in custody. It is not uncommon for booking or transporting officers to find a talkative accused. No warnings are required merely to listen, but if questioning occurs, warnings are required.
3. *Jailhouse questioning.* Prisoners questioned about other crimes should be re-advised of their rights.
4. *No arrest.* If a suspect is not under arrest, the place of questioning is an important factor in determining whether custody has attached, requiring Miranda warnings.
   a. *Police stations.* Questioning at a police station is often held to be custodial even if the questions weren't intended to yield damaging information (or if the person came voluntarily to the station and police knew him to be lying.)
   b. *Police cars.* If questioning is undertaken to obtain incriminating statements, warnings should be given and waivers obtained.
   c. *Street encounters.* A street encounter is custodial where a suspect is stopped at gun point, handcuffed, or questioned about a specific crime. Otherwise, no warnings are required. A policeman may approach you on the street, in a store, on a bus, train, or plane and question you. A *street encounter* does not require Miranda warnings.
   d. *Crime scenes.* Miranda was not intended to hamper police in investigating crime and general on-the-scene questioning.
   e. *Homes.* Lateness of the hour, number of officers, directness of questions, and whether officers were invited or not, may necessitate the warnings be *custodial interrogation,* even though a suspect is in the familiar surroundings of his own home and not under arrest.
   f. *Places of employment.* If the crime occurred at the place of employment, it is a *crime scene* interview. If police are investigating a crime which occurred somewhere else but there is still a *coercive atmosphere* during questioning, it is recommended police give warnings to all employees suspected of criminal activity when there is more than routine questioning.

g. *Search warrant locations*. The legality of a search is not dependent upon Miranda warnings and if police have arrest warrants or intend to arrest Miranda is not required. If officers question bystanders or during the search incriminating evidence is discovered, Miranda warnings should be given.

The *Miranda warnings* are:

1. You do not have to make a statement and you have the right to remain silent.
2. Anything you say can and will be used against you in a court of law.
3. You are entitled to consult with an attorney before interrogation and to have an attorney present at the time of interrogation.
4. If you cannot afford an attorney, one will be appointed for you.

Custodial Interrogation

When police are merely investigating, such as in a typical auto accident, (Where an officer arrives on the scene and questions bystanders), or in a traffic stop, or regular booking procedures, Miranda does not apply. If statements are volunteered, they are admissible if you are not in custody. If you are the prime suspect the Miranda warnings should precede further questioning. Courts look at the facts known to the officer to determine his intent, as well as whether you might reasonably think you are custody.

Any actions by police intended to elicit comments are illegal tactics, and does not *scrupulously honor* rights. Any confessions obtained as a result will be suppressed. Sometimes police encourage spontaneous statements and silently encourage people to speak. Once a person has been placed in a patrol car, taken to the station, and removed from his home (or even questioned in his own bedroom), courts rule this is *custodial interrogation.*

In you are in custody on another unrelated charge and questioned by different officers about a *different* crime, you should still be given Miranda warnings. The warnings should be given even if a freed suspect later approaches officers voluntarily to visit.

Miranda warnings must be given when:

1. You are in custody
2. Deprived of your freedom in a significant way
3. Under formal arrest

4. The police officer is unwilling to let you go
5. The officer believes you have committed a crime
6. The officer's actions lead you to believe you are not free to go.

If you volunteer information before interrogation begins and before an opportunity to advise you of your rights, any statements may be used against you at trial.

Police carry a Miranda warning card. The Miranda card is admissible into evidence and is shown to the jury. Many police fail to read both sides of the card (the reverse side recites your waiver of rights).

Waiver of Rights

> I have read the Warning Statement advising me of my legal and Constitutional rights and I understand what my rights are. I have been given the opportunity to use the telephone to call an attorney or a member of my own family. I am willing to answer questions and make a Statement. I do this voluntarily and of my own free will. I understand and know what I am doing. I do not want to call or consult with a lawyer and I do not want a lawyer to be present to advise me of my rights and with whom I can consult. No promise of immunity or other promises of any kind have been made to me and no physical force or pressure of any kind has been used against me to cause me to make a Statement.

No precise words need be used. A number of variations are available, but police will strictly adhere to the four warnings.

Reciting the Miranda warnings, standing alone, *does not constitute compliance* with *Miranda vs. Arizona* unless you voluntarily and intentionally *waive* your Fifth Amendment rights.

The following rules should be kept in mind:

1. *An oral waiver is good.* if you make an oral confession. If the confession is written, a written waiver should be obtained.
2. *Continuing questioning* after you request a lawyer or express a desire to remain silent *is prohibited.* You cannot be persuaded to waive your constitutional rights.
3. *Silence* can never be used as an admission of guilt.
4. The warnings should be renewed every time you are requestioned and after delays. Police must stop whenever you wish to stop.
5. If you refuse to talk and later change your mind and wish to make a statement, police must obtain a clear indication of your understanding of your rights and willingness to talk.

6. If you have a lawyer you may still waive your rights. Police must obtain a clear waiver from you unpersuaded by police.
7. If you express the desire to talk with some person other than a lawyer (friend, relative, or employer) you have not asserted your Miranda rights.
8. If you answer some but not all questions, it is not a refusal in the Miranda sense and police need not cease their interrogation.

If the accused has low intelligence, limited education, is a juvenile, has some physical pain, or is wounded, great care should be taken and courts will consider these factors. If the accused has been held incommunicado, physically abused, promised leniency, given false promises, is emotionally upset, threatened, the confession is illegal. The fact that a suspect may be intoxicated or under the influence of drugs may be considered in deciding whether the statement was voluntarily made but does not void the confession if the accused understood what he was doing.

Legality of Confessions

Deception, artifice, and trickery ordinarily will not, of themselves, nullify a confession. The court will look to see if the deception was of such a nature as to *prompt untrue statements* and whether the statements were still reliable.

Confessions overheard by a cellmate are legal even if the cellmate is a government informant or if a confession is overheard by the jailer. A jailed prisoner has no reasonable expectation of privacy.

Once you refuse to answer or request a lawyer, *all questioning must cease*, and neither the Prosecutor nor the police can comment on silence although the Prosecutor can argue to the jury your failure to present evidence (but not your failure to testify). If you are not under arrest and under circumstances where only a guilty person would remain silent, such silence "(tacit admission rule)" may be shown.

You can request a hearing to determine the voluntariness of your confession. The Judge must decide whether the confession is legally admissible to the jury. If so, the jury gives whatever weight or credibility that it deems proper to the confession. They evaluate the circumstances in which it was given.

Videotapes or secret recordings of confessions are permissible. There is no requirement that you be told statements are being recorded.

Where statements have been spontaneously uttered, occasioned by excitement surrounding a crime or auto accident, such statements are a part of the *res gestae*, and are known as the *excited utterance exception* to the hearsay rule without the Miranda warnings.

Small mistakes given in the Miranda warnings are allowed if they are harmless. If the mistakes give rise to confusion, the confession must be suppressed.

Exculpatory statements are statements made by a defendant which tend to show his *innocence. Inculpatory statements* are those which tend to incriminate or show *guilt*.

The rule that "silence does not mean a waiver" is not an absolute rule. Your failure as a defendant to make any affirmative waiver does not mean you waive your rights and courts refuse to find an automatic waiver.

Courts look for any clear manifestation of a desire to waive— showing a knowing intent which could be combined with words, acts, and all the evidence of the surrounding facts and circumstances. It is not required that you expressly state a waiver of your rights.

Traffic Offenses

The Miranda warnings do not have to be given to a motorist who is stopped for a minor traffic offense, in the following situations:

1. To examine the driver's license and registration of a motorist stopped for speeding,
2. A motorist detained while police check out the possibility of a stolen car,
3. A motorist stopped for weaving across a double center line and volunteers that he has been taking drugs,
4. A motorist asked by officers why his plates are expired,
5. A passenger in a motor vehicle who is stopped for a traffic offense is not subjected to custodial interrogation,
6. A motorist volunteers statements after a routine traffic stop,
7. After stopping a vehicle for driving without lights at night, officers ask a general question about the contents of the trunk,
8. Police ask a driver if he has been drinking,
9. Officers ask general questions pertaining to destination and permission to drive the vehicle,
10. Police officers request a driver to show his license and registration, and

11. A motorist volunteers information while an officer is writing out a speeding ticket.

No Need for Miranda

You always have the option of waiving your constitutional rights. If approached by police at your home, business, or on a street corner, the questioning is noncustodial, (you are not under arrest) any statement you make is a *voluntary statement*. If it is incriminating, it can be used against you and the officer will testify against you in court.

If you are in an automobile accident and your words were *spontaneously uttered*, occasioned by the excitement of the events, it is admissible (the *excited utterance rule*).

If words are spoken by third persons that normally *call for a response*, such as your wife's making a heated remark during an assault, police officers can testify to what the third person said and your *lack of response*. (The tacit admission rule). The failure to contradict such a factual assertion constitutes an admission or damaging evidence against you.

If you have claimed your Miranda warning rights you still can be questioned on *unrelated crimes*.

Defenses to Keep Out Your Incriminating Statement

Once it is clear that you are the target of an investigation, you may claim your Fifth Amendment rights by insisting upon *having an attorney present. Your request must be scrupulously honored by the police*. Some police will negligently or intentionally violate your Constitutional rights by continuing to pester you with further questioning.

If you do confess to the crime or make otherwise incriminating remarks, you can file a pretrial motion to suppress (a Jackson-Denno Hearing) and request the Judge to hear evidence to exclude your statement on the following grounds:

1. That you were not properly read all of your Miranda rights,
2. That you did not *waive* those Constitutional rights and voluntarily speak with police,
3. Due to alcohol, drugs, fatigue, medication, physical injury or limited intelligence you *did not fully understand* your Constitutional rights,
4. That police used duress, threats, and coercion to overcome your will and forced you to talk.

SOBRIETY
CHECKPOINT
AHEAD

Missouri Highway Patrol Trooper S.K. Munden talks with a motorist during a traffic stop.

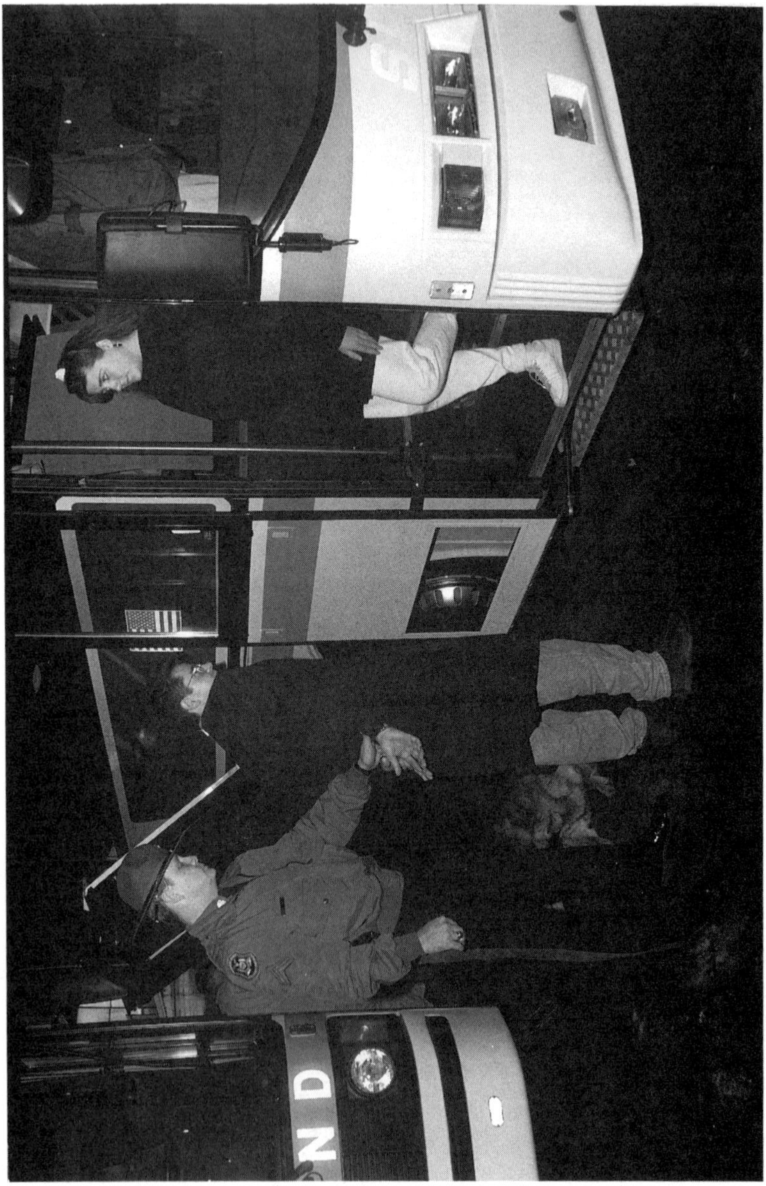

Cpl. David A. Henson detains a questioned drug courier under the U.S. Supreme Court decision in Florida vs. Bostic.

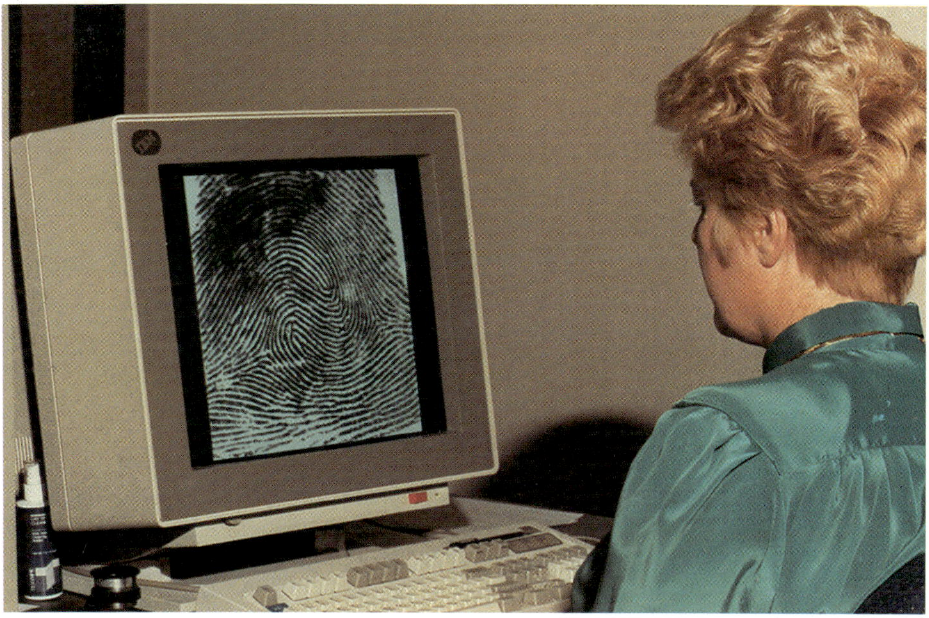

Latent Fingerprint Technician Carma Wegman of the Missouri State Highway Patrol's Criminal Records Division in Jefferson City manually enhances a fingerprint from a tenprint card as part of quality control for entry into the Automated Fingerprint Identification System (AFIS).

The primary function of a state patrolman is the safety of those traveling our public roads. This trooper directs traffic around a burning vehicle near Taos, MO.

Federal prisoners are housed in approved local county jails until sentenced and sent to federal penitentiaries. (L to R: Deputy U.S. Marshal Anthony Hambrick, Chief Jailer Joy Jones, Suspect Tom Snow, Supervisory Desk Deputy Marshal, and Chris Whitcomb, Special Agent FBI (Photo courtesy *Springfield News Leader*).

SWAT Team member takes aim with a Mossberg shotgun.

Jefferson City Police make regular use of dogs for night security checks inside a local hardware store where a burglar alarm has sounded.

Pour patterns found at a residence fire prove "incendiary origin" in a Jasper Co. arson case. (Sheriff, W.J. Pierce and Lt. Stephen Weston).

Taney Co. Major Crime Investigator Chip Mason obtained numerous fingerprints at this burglary scene. (Courtesy of Chip Mason, Major Crime Investigator, Taney Co Sheriff's Office).

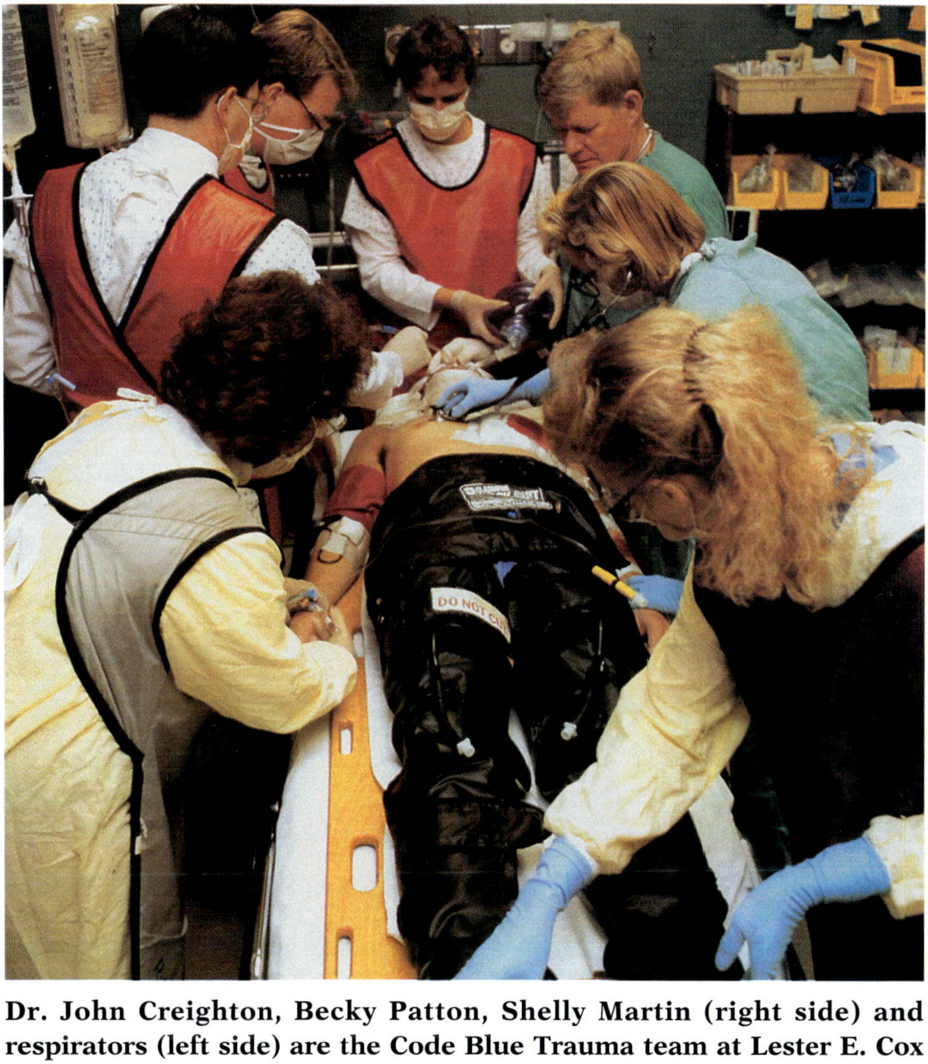

Dr. John Creighton, Becky Patton, Shelly Martin (right side) and respirators (left side) are the Code Blue Trauma team at Lester E. Cox Medical Center in Springfield.

Missouri Highway Patrol Corporal T.R. Selvey taking measurements to evidence left on the roadway, during his investigation of a motor vehicle accident.

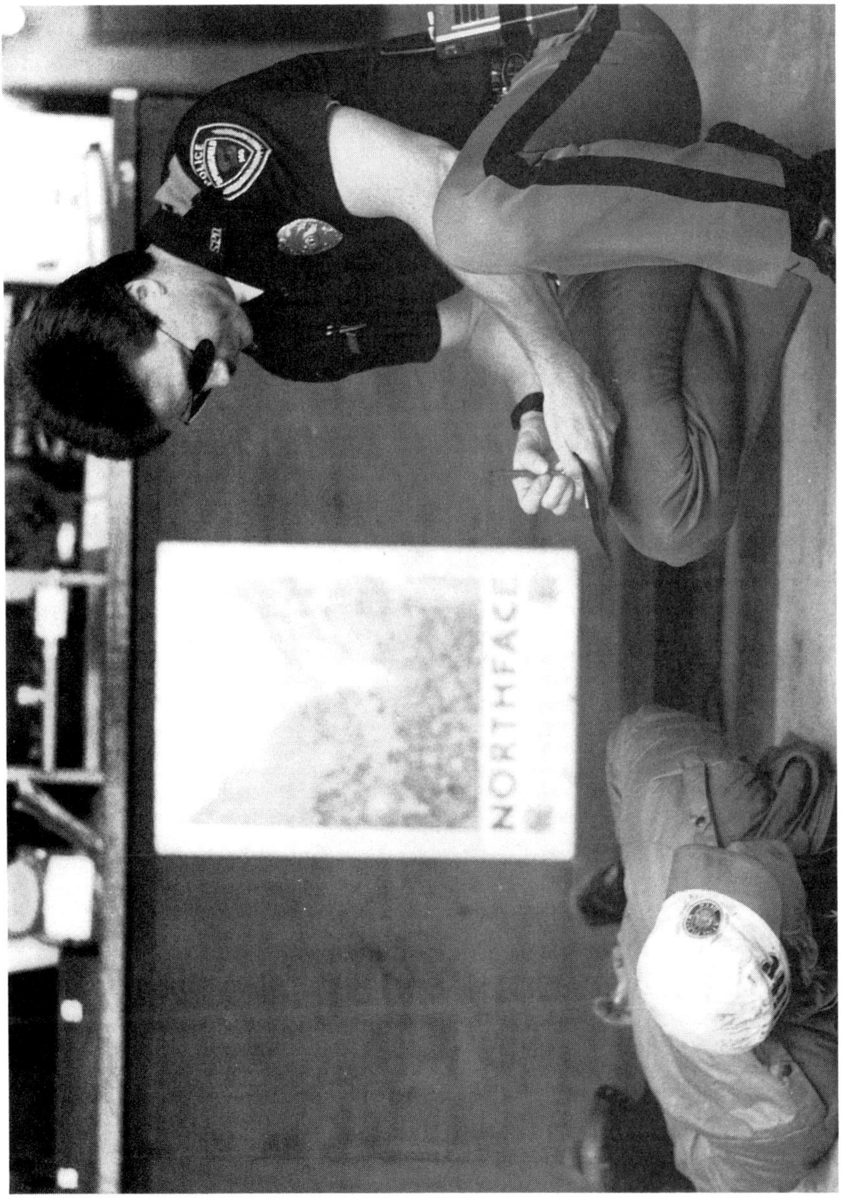

Springfield Police Officer Don F. Fuhr, Jr. after reading Miranda warnings, obtains a waiver and consent to interrogate.

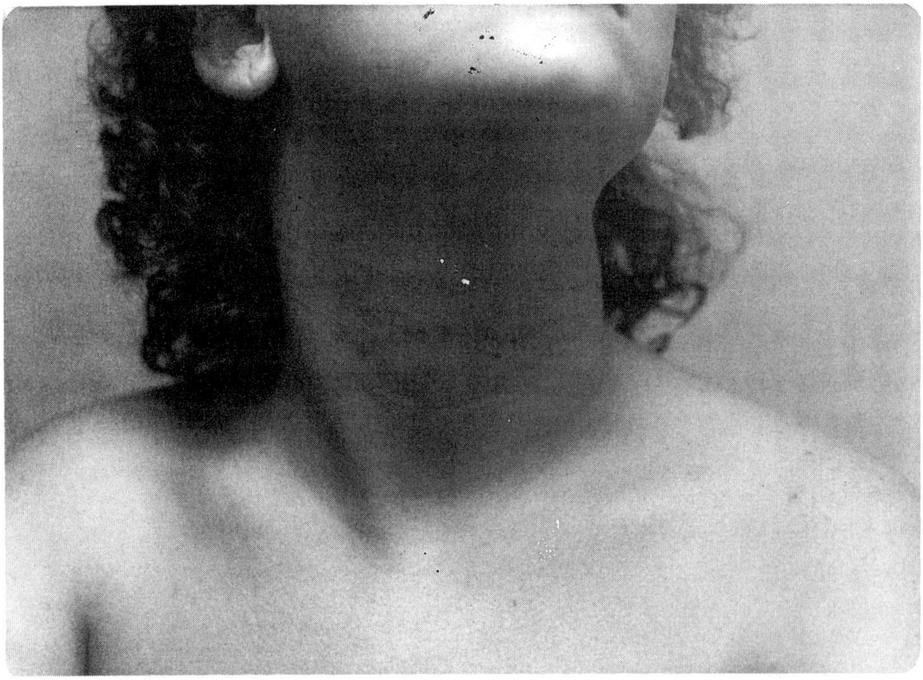

Scatches inflicted on assault victim. (Jasper Co. Sheriff, W. J. Pierce and Inv. Stephen D. Weston).

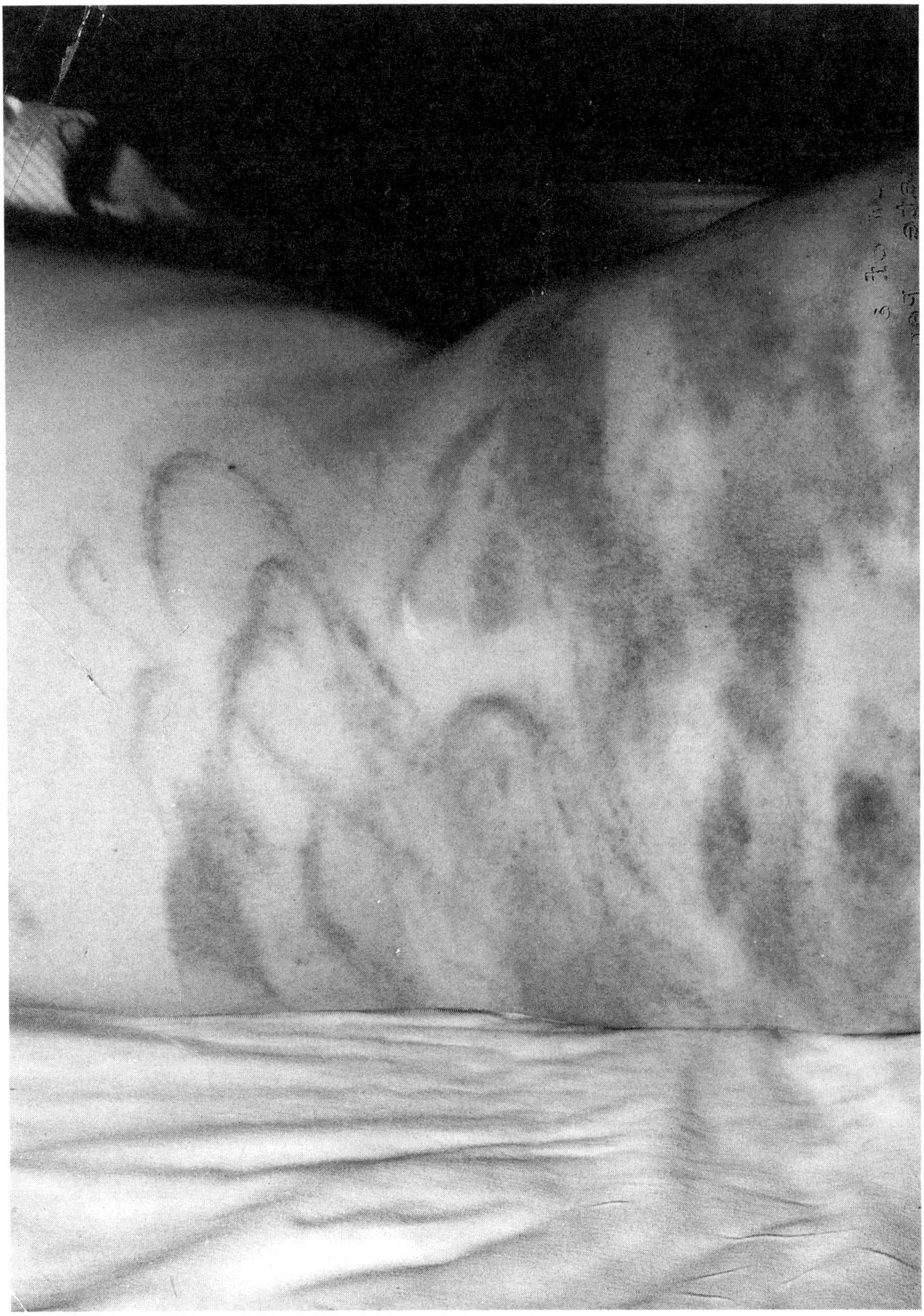

Child beating photograph shows leather strap marks (St. Louis County).

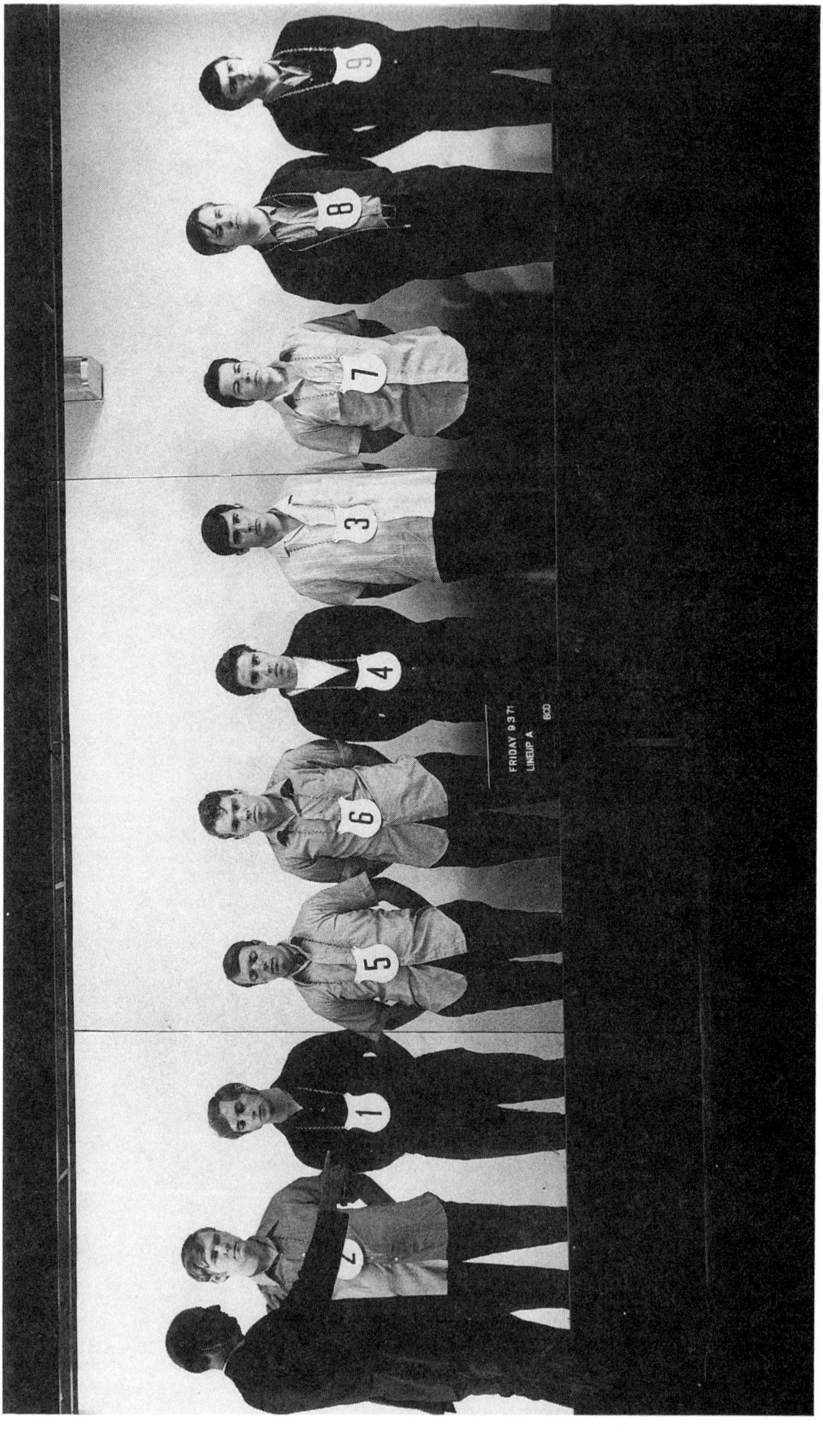

Washington D.C. Police Department conducts a line up with one suspect and police officers.

Chapter 10

When Can I Be Placed in a Lineup?

A lineup is a legally arranged confrontation between an accused and the victim.

The U.S. Supreme Court in *United States vs. Wade* and *Gilbert vs. California* (1967) held that any lineup conducted after the filing of formal charges is a *critical stage* in the criminal proceeding, requiring the presence of a lawyer. If a witness has identified the accused at an illegal lineup, the witness cannot testify to the lineup or identify the accused until a separate hearing is held and established by clear and convincing evidence that the in-court identification had an *independent source* and is based upon observations of the suspect at the scene of the crime and is purged (free) of any primary taint from the illegal lineup.

Some states require a lawyer even at pre-indictment lineups, Missouri only requires counsel after the filing of formal charges.

If a defense attorney appears, his reasonable suggestions should be given consideration but he is present only as a mere observer. The names of all people present are noted and may later be subpoenaed as state witnesses (including the lawyer). If the suspect has a lawyer appear, the state will have an easier burden of proof to show the lineup was fair.

Five or six persons of approximately the same age, weight, height, complexion, race and manner of dress as the accused are carefully selected. Once the lineup is assembled, a photograph is taken of each witness allowed a separate view. The exact words of the witness is noted and nothing is suggested to the witness encouraging identification.

It is permissible to have lineup participants move in any direction, walk, move arms or leg, remove glasses, shave, reveal tattoos, put on different costumes, wear a hat, or speak non-testimonial statements such "This is a stick up," "Give me your money," or "I'll blow your head off." The accused's voice may be an identifiable physical characteristic.

A lineup card is given the witness, who view the lineup separately, and circle the proper number corresponding to the person identified. The card is dated, signed by the witness, and retained by police.

A bad lineup does not automatically stop an in-court identification, but there is a heavy burden on the state to prove the witness' in-court identification was not affected by the lineup. Witnesses are under obligation to swear their in-court identification is based *solely from observation* of the suspect at the time of the crime.

An accused has no right to refuse to submit to a lineup. Reasonable force may be used to compel participation. If the accused absolutely refuses to stand or participate in lineup, his refusal can be commented upon at trial.

Emergency Identification: Confrontations and One-Man

A suspect may be returned to the scene of a crime for immediate identification.

The *Wade-Gilbert* rule of *right of counsel* does not apply to on-the-scene confrontation between the suspect and witness if there is an imperative need under the circumstances for conducting the confrontation.

1. *Mental State of the Witness*. Police should avoid giving the witness the idea that they have captured the suspect. Police should tell the witness, "We have a person who may know something about this case or who may be a witness in this case," without saying anything further. The witness should volunteer his identification.
2. *Avoid Custodial Appearances*. Once the suspect is brought before the witness, he should not appear in handcuffs or surrounded by officers.
3. *Avoid Delay*. On-the-spot confrontations must be conducted within minutes after the crime, at or near the crime scene. If a long delay occurs, the officer should conduct a regular lineup.

Emergency identifications are sometimes necessitated by the severity of the victim's injuries.

Examples:

> Suspects may be brought to the scene of the crime for identification by witnesses. A store owner is called to the site of the arrest. A victim is asked to view the suspect by the side of a seized truck. Two victims may identify the suspect together ten minutes after holdup at the scene of the crime (although it is best to have the witness identify the suspect individually). A witness may view a suspect at home minutes after seeing the suspect with the stolen goods. A suspected bank robber may returned to the bank minutes after the robbery for the purpose of on-the-scene identification after having been continuously pursued by a bank employee. A suspect may be identified while sitting in a police cruiser near the scene of the crime.

Mug Shot Lineups

When a suspect is not in custody but his mug shot is available, it is possible to conduct a mug shot lineup by placing the suspect's picture, along with other filler pictures, before a witness. The *Wade-Gilbert* rule requires the lineup must be *fair.* (Not suggestive.)

Exact identification of the facial features should be first obtained from the witness, so comparable mug shots can be secured demonstrating those particular features. The mug shots should be marked in order, placed in a separate envelope, and preserved as evidence.

The witness is shown a number of photographs of the accused (not just a single photograph of the accused); the mug shots should not be referred to as "mug shots" or show the prison numbers.

Lineup Guidelines

In order to successfully combat defense charges of a suggestive lineup, police do the following:

1. Obtain a signed waiver of counsel and consent to have the lineup.
2. Record the name of the suspect's attorney if he is present.
3. Record the name, age, date of birth, height, weight, and position of each person that participates in the lineup.
4. Record the names of all police officers present.

5. Record the date, time, and location of the lineup.
6. Write brief notes about what happened at the lineup.
7. Arrange for the lineup participants, insofar as possible, to be of the same general age and race, have similar physical characteristics, and wear similar clothing.
8. Take a color photograph of the lineup.
9. Require any physical movements or verbal statements performed uniformly but once, by all lineup participants, except for requested repetition by the witness.
10. Do not have the suspect appear to be in custody or in handcuffs or indicate his identity to the witness in any manner.
11. Do not permit more than one witness at a lineup in the lineup room.
12. Do not allow witnesses to talk with each other.
13. Do not permit witnesses to view photographs of the suspect prior to lineup identification.
14. Do not draw any special attention to the suspect.
15. Do not engage in unnecessary conversation with witnesses or permit unneeded persons in the lineup room.
16. Record comments made by witnesses.
17. Furnish each witness with a lineup identification form.

Lineup Warnings

Prior to a lineup the following warnings be given:

1. Although you do not have a right to refuse to appear in a lineup, you do have a right to have a lawyer present when the witness views the lineup.
2. If you are unable to pay for a lawyer, a lawyer will be appointed to represent you during the lineup free of any cost to you.
3. Where voice identification is desired the police officer should say, "You and the other participants in the lineup will be asked to repeat certain words, phrases, or sentences spoken by the person who committed the crime.

RULE: MISSOURI GUARDS AGAINST THE, *SUBSTANTIAL LIKELIHOOD OF IRREPARABLE MISIDENTIFICATION* AND USES A THREE-PART TEST TO DECIDE IF A PRIOR IMPROPER LINEUP SHOULD VOID THE IN-COURT IDENTIFICATION.

1. THE PRESENCE OF AN INDEPENDENT BASIS FOR IDENTIFICATION

2. THE ABSENCE OF ANY SUGGESTIVE INFLUENCE BY OTHERS

3. POSITIVE COURTROOM IDENTIFICATION.

The purpose of a lineup is not only to identify the guilty, but to clear the innocent.

RULE: IF YOU ARE REQUESTED TO STAND IN A LINEUP, YOU HAVE NO CHOICE. DEMAND YOUR RIGHTS TO SPEAK WITH AN ATTORNEY IMMEDIATELY UPON ARREST.

Now you understand court procedures and your rights upon being arrested, searched and questioned. There are set rules of evidence that apply in every case. Understanding them will help to limit the Prosecutor's case and will aid you in presenting your defense.

Chapter 11

Understanding Rules of Evidence

Law Professor:	**"Every law has its exceptions. There is nothing on earth that is certain."**
Student:	**"Are you sure?"**
Professor:	**"I am certain."**

"I ought to bust your butt down to traffic, or better yet, kick it off the force. You're a dinosaur, Callahan. Your ideas don't fit today."

Captain Briggs
to Inspector Harry Callahan
(Clint Eastwood) in *Dirty Harry*

"If the law supposes that, Mr. Bumble...the law is an ass."

Charles Dickens
from *Oliver Twist* (1937)

In a jury trial, there are thousands of possibilities of different pieces of evidence, as far as your imagination can stretch.

Jury trials are won by evidence!

Jurors are impressed by the *energy* and *impact* of evidence. Before walking in the courtroom, think of every conceivable exhibit that might be used to prove your case.

Photographs, motion pictures, slides, diagrams and many other items, are extremely helpful to juries who are impressed with the imagination and resourcefulness of the attorney. Other helpful items include city maps, charts, dummy torsos, mannequins with metal rods tracing bullet wounds, plaster casts, plastic skulls, reconstruction of bombs, models of houses, murder weapons, satellite photographs, and scientific exhibits.

In criminal investigations, the attorney always assumes his case will eventually be tried before a jury. An abundance of evidence should be gathered and labeled so the admissibility will not be questioned. He can present his theory of the case in a clear and more understandable manner by the use of physical evidence. It is more difficult to cross-examine than it is a live witness. In a jury trial, *there is no such thing as too much evidence*.

Evidence is the means by which triers of fact (the judge or jury) are satisfied of the truth of the criminal charges. To be admissible it must be *relevant, material, competent.*

Once evidence passes the test of admissibility, it has potential for influencing the outcome of the trial. Any piece of evidence, perhaps in combination with another piece, may be persuasive to the jury. This is the *impact energy* of an item of evidence.

Corroborative evidence is evidence that strengthens or confirms other evidence.

Prima facie evidence is evidence that, if not contradicted, is sufficient on its face to establish a fact.

Direct evidence proves a fact without any additional presumption.

Circumstantial evidence relates to a series of facts other than those at issue that tends by the use of an inference, to establish the fact at issue. This type of evidence is usually presented item by item in a chain of circumstances and is coupled with some direct evidence.

A *presumption* is a deduction which may logically or reasonably be drawn from a fact or group of facts.

Admissibility

There are many rules of evidence to test whether an item is relevant, material, and competent. Before admitting an item into evidence, it is necessary for the court to establish the qualifications of a witness, the existence of a proper chain of custody.

The fewer people who handle evidence, the easier to show a short chain of custody. A break in a chain goes to the weight given evidence by the Judge or jury and the test is whether there is enough proof of the chain of custody to establish a *reasonable assurance* that the item is the same as originally seized and in the same condition. If the item has been changed or altered, perhaps by a scientist performing a scientific test, then such alteration should be explained so that the jury is not misled.

The law does not require the chain of custody eliminate all possibility the evidence has been altered–it suffices the evidence establish it is *more probable than not* that the object is the one connected with the case.

In many cases, the uniqueness of an item may make the testimony easier with items such as a painting, an item of furniture, wearing apparel, or a unique weapon, there would be less requirement of proof of chain custody.

Chain of custody gaps cannot be filled by a presumption of proper performance by officials. If an item has been unintentionally lost, a replica may be introduced. The witness need not positively identify the item, only that it "looks like".

Great care should be taken to preserve all evidence, whether or not police believe the evidence will be used at trial. Even the unintentional destruction of evidence could be held to deny the accused due process, and result in an acquittal.

Photographs

A photographer or anyone having knowledge of a photograph (whether or not physically present when it was taken) can testify that the photograph is a *fair and accurate representation* of what it depicts at the time and place it was taken is sufficient to identify photographs.

Color photos of blood and gore, such as a stabbing victim at a morgue, may be gruesome and inflammatory, but does not affect the admissibility as long as the relevancy and probative value of the photographs assist the jury to better understand the theory of the case. Missouri allows photos at trial that throw *any relevant light* on the case.

Fingerprints

Fingerprints are unique to each person and are by themselves sufficient to support a conviction even without other evidence of guilt.

Fingerprints found at the scene of the crime and compared with known fingerprints of the suspect are crucial. The print is photographed and enlarged to be viewed by the jury.

Latent fingerprints (those found at the scene of the crime) are almost always poorer because of irregular surface or heavier pressure exerted by the fingers in picking up an object. The print area is dusted with powder, and a fine camel's hair brush is used to dust away the powder. Light surfaces require light powder, and dark surfaces a white powder. If large areas are to be dusted, police use a powder atomizer or spray.

All surfaces should be powdered and photographs of any latent fingerprints should be made immediately. Gloves insure that no new fingerprints are made.

The lifting of fingerprints is accomplished by covering the dusted fingerprint with a gummed *lifter* contrasting in color with the dusting powder, and the dusting impression of the print, upon removal, will adhere to the sticky surface. The impression can then be placed against a new background for photographing.

Motion Pictures, Video Recordings

Motion pictures are relevant and admissible into evidence if they represent a fair and accurate representation of what they depict.

Movies, video tapes, of confessions, auto accident scenes, booking procedures, or scenes of a crime are admissible even though they might be more sensation-creating.

Courts make a clear distinction between "*communications* from a defendant" and "*physical evidence* from a defendant." Where the film shows the accused speaking making oral communication, courts do not require the state to show he was informed of his Miranda rights.

Films are often taken of the accused during the booking process to show intoxication in drunk driving or manslaughter cases, where the accused is required to perform physical tests or illustrate his inability to walk the line, pick up an object, or perform the finger-to-nose test. (Field Sobriety Tests)

Diagrams

A scale diagram to depict a crime scene will help the jury better understand locations and distances. The diagram need not be to actual scale.

Attorneys have their own preferences on how diagrams are prepared, on large sheets of white cardboard clearly showing marked distances to scale, a direction guide and scale guide, name of the draftsman, and other information. Diagrams are overlaid with clear plastic sheets taped to the cardboard on which witnesses can draw, initial, and date with marking crayon during their testimony.

Experiments

Experiments and demonstrations are admissible in criminal trials. Objections to such experiments go to the *weight given* to the experiment, rather than the *legal admissibility* of such evidence.

1. The person making the experiment must be competent to do so.
2. The conditions surrounding the experiment must be substantially similar to those at time of occurrence.
3. The results must be relevant to an issue in the case.
4. The experiment must have been honestly and fairly done.

The Expert Witness

Juries are impressed by the testimony of the expert witnesses. Often such testimony can raise the reasonable doubt required for acquittal.

An expert is any person who, by reason of specialized experience or education, *possesses superior knowledge* respecting a subject about which persons having now particular training are incapable of forming an accurate opinion or of drawing correct conclusions. This expertise can be acquired by study, investigation, observation, practice, or experience.

Opinions generally are not allowed by lay witnesses since the *invade the province of the jury*. The duty of a jury is to hear all evidence, including opinion evidence, to weigh it, and decide the issues, and the expert witness helps because in many matters conclusions cannot be drawn from facts by inexperienced persons.

Examples of expert testimony include:

1. *Chemists* testify about serology (blood type), semen stains, narcotic tests, effects of drugs upon the human body, nitrate and paraffin tests regarding recent firing of guns, powder patterns, perspiration, saliva, paint chips, glass fragments, metal fragments, hair identification, tool mark comparisons, soil comparisons, and trace metal detections.
2. *Physicians* testify regarding force, angle, and depth of stab wounds, force and number of blows by blunt instruments, including X-ray reading, physical condition or capability, mental condition, or sanity.
3. *Police* testify that crowbars or screwdrivers could have been used to open certain doors or make certain marks.
4. *Ballistics experts* testify that bullets could have come from a certain shell casing or were fired from a gun.
5. *Pathologists* testify about cause and time of death.
6. Testimony is allowed regarding trained dogs tracking a suspect or sniffing drugs.
7. *Mechanics* testify as to the condition of brakes and other mechanical matters (based on the fallen debris from the vehicles).
8. *Accident reconstruction experts* testify about the exact point of impact, speed of a vehicle and breaking distance.
9. *Fingerprint experts* testify about fingerprint comparisons.
10. Experts testify about handwriting comparisons.
11. Fire investigators testify to the *incendiary* origin of an arson.
12. Police testify about human *footprints* or similarity of *tire tracks*.
13. *Bite marks* may be identified by physicians or veterinarians.

RULE: IF YOU CAN AFFORD THE COSTS, EXPLORE THE POSSIBILITY OF EMPLOYING AN EXPERT WITNESS. JURIES ARE MOST IMPRESSED AND IT WILL LIKELY MEAN THE DIFFERENCE IN YOUR VICTORY.

Polygraph (Lie Detector) Tests

Polygraph tests are not admissible in criminal or civil cases. Courts rule the admissibility of lie detector tests has not been shown to have reached scientific reliability necessary to be legally competent.

There is also a hidden fear that lie detectors will replace the jury system, taking the guilt-innocence fact-finding function away from the jury, or that the test will over-impress the jury. Traditional Anglo-Saxon notions of due process have always afforded the accused the right to a jury trial by his peers.

Allowing a scientific test to tell a jury the very thing they are sworn to decide is contrary to our notions of law.

A few courts have admitted polygraph tests, such as in a perjury case or parole violation hearing. Most courts refuse to admit polygraph evidence in pre-sentence reports or at the sentencing and also refuse mention of defendant's refusal to take the test.

> **RULE: SHOULD YOU TAKE A LIE DETECTOR TEST? THE ANSWER IS SIMPLE. IF YOU HAVE ANY GUILTY KNOWLEDGE WHATSOEVER THAT YOU COMMITTED THE CRIME, OR ASSISTED, OR HELPED COVER IT UP, OR HELP IN ANY WAY, DO NOT TAKE THE TEST. ONLY IF YOU ARE 1000% INNOCENT, WITH ABSOLUTELY NO GUILTY KNOWLEDGE, SHOULD YOU AGREE TO TAKE IT. DON'T TRY TO FOOL THE TEST OR CON THE EXAMINER.**

Any mention of a refusal to take a polygraph test is forbidden.

Evaluating Lie Detector Results

Polygraph (lie detector) accuracy levels exceed 90%. Key factors are (1) the examiner; (2) the suspect; (3) the investigation; and (4) proper conditions.

1. *The examiner* should be trained at a reputable polygraph school through a course accredited by the American Polygraph Association, in "numerical analysis" method of chart interpretation which promotes objection evaluations. Refresher training each year as an aid to retaining proficiency to recognized standards and procedures is important.

2. It is important the *suspect* have food and rest and not be under great emotional stress. Persons who are injured, physically fatigued, have recently undergone significant emotional shock, are not good candidates for examination. It is possible for the suspect to be honestly mistaken about what he believes and investigators must assess the likelihood that examinees accept their statements as truth.
3. Information developed during the *investigation* is important since erroneous information about the offense, the crime scene, evidence or the examinee's role in the case could actually cause the examiner to miss the mark. In a bank robbery investigation, for instance, if a person is found in possession of bait money, it is possible that the person came into the possession of the money through innocent means. A well-qualified examiner will consider including questions concerning "knowledge of the crime" or "participating in any way" and "evidence connecting" in the examination instead of just the obvious question, "Did you rob the bank?"
4. *Examination conditions* are important. No hint should be made as to the results that are expected or desired. The polygraph room should be designed to eliminate distractions, outside noises, and once started should not be interrupted. Any examination which takes place under crisis-like conditions can get out of control and result in less than optimum performance.

Confession During Polygraph Test

A suspect will often make incriminating statements *after* a polygraph test. Such incriminating statements *are admissible*, as long as there is no mention that statements were made in connection with the actual test.

The attorneys may enter into an express *written stipulation* where the defendant waives all rights and objections to the polygraph test and both sides agree the results will be admissible into evidence at trial.

If the suspect passes the test, the Prosecutor agrees to drop charges. If he fails it is agreed that at the trial the government may introduce such evidence for the jury to consider. Such agreements are valid in Missouri.

Merely because the government may choose to give a polygraph test to one defendant does not mean that other defendants have a constitutional right to a test. If the Prosecutor agrees to dismiss a criminal charge, it is a pledge of public faith, and the Prosecutor is required to do so.

The test helps determine whether a victim or witness is telling the truth and often is used on a government witness. Defense attorneys commonly use an initial *private* polygraph test to see how their client does.

> **RULE: THE TRICK IS NOT THE TEST. THE PRE-TEST AND POST-TESTS INTERVIEW ARE THE TRICK. ONCE IN THE PRE-TEST INTERVIEW YOU ARE ASKED YOUR LIFE STORY, TO GET PRIOR CRIMES OFF YOUR CONSCIENCE. AFTER THE TEST, IF YOU ARE FALSELY TOLD YOU FLUNKED, MANY SUSPECTS IMMEDIATELY CONFESS. THESE CONFESSIONS ARE ADMISSIBLE AGAINST YOU AT TRIAL. TAKE THE TEST IF YOU CHOSE. ONCE YOU FINISH, WALK OUT!**

Unless the state has entered into a prior written stipulation, there is little reason to administer a polygraph test to an accused, since it is inadmissible at trial.

Expert polygraph operators suggest that any person taking a test be carefully watched for 24 hours prior to the test so that he cannot have access to alcohol or drugs which might affect the test result.

Test questions are always drawn up and *agreed upon in advance,* the questions being divided into *relevant* (relating to the crime) and *irrelevant* (where the answer is known in advance to establish a normal response).

> **RULE: DON'T AGREE TO TAKE A TEST WITHOUT HELP FROM YOUR LAWYER. THE QUESTIONS SHOULD BE FRAMED CAREFULLY SO AS NOT TO BE TOO BROAD. DON'T GIVE IN TO INTIMIDATION IN AGREEING TO TAKE A TEST.**

The Autopsy

An autopsy is the medical study and removal of organs when a person dies suddenly or unexpectedly from trauma (injuries) in a suspected homicide, suicide, or accident, to determine the cause and time of death.

All observations are minutely and carefully made, measured, and accurately recorded, to determine all circumstances regarding the death. A pathologist cannot guess but will testify to the cause of death with *reasonable medical certainty.*

1. In *gunshot* murders, the pathologist views the entrance wound, a round hole with a small abrasion around the edge, and the exit

wound, which is often irregular. The contact wounds are powder staining and burning of the edges of a wound by the discharge of a gun and such unburned and partially burned granules of powder act as missiles for a short distance, penetrating the skin and leaving the area around the wound stippled with small satellite wounds.

2. In *stab* wounds, a pathologist can say that a wound is consistent or inconsistent with a certain type of knife, regarding the length of the wound and how long the victim might have lived.
3. *Blunt force* injuries committed with the fist, feet, or the use of a blunt instrument, may cause numerous fractures. Hammers, pipes, and blunt instruments leave certain pattern wounds.
4. *Battered children* are consistently and repeatedly damaged over a long period of time by one of the parents, where they are jumped on, kicked, beaten with fist, placed in boiling water, starved, and subjected to other horrors. In an autopsy of a battered child, it is important to record the numerous injuries and scars, often pattern scars, to show that the beatings have been repetitive, and the child should be X-rayed to reveal old, poorly healed or untreated fractures.

Ballistics

A ballistics expert can compare guns by determining the direction and twist and the amounts of lands and grooves of the test bullets. These ridges and valleys allows ballistic comparisons where the land and grooves are left in the bullet as it passes through the rifling of the bore of the firearm.

By use of the *comparison microscope*, the corresponding edges of lands compared to *signatures* engraved by the same firearm. *Congruence* is the coincidence of two adjacent elements seen through the comparison microscope.

The outer edge of the bullet wound entrance is often discolored and is called the abrasion collar. The location of the wound in the body and the physical appearance of the bullet wound entrance are the two most important factors.

Contact wounds are formed when the muzzle of the gun is pressed against the victim's body. The powder burns or powder "tattoos" can be cause by the muzzle blast or cylinder flash.

Shotgun wounds, rifle wounds, and handgun wounds will all cause different appearances in entry and exit wounds.

RULE: BALLISTICS TESTING IS A DEFINITE AND CERTAIN SCIENCE WHICH IMPRESSES JURIES EQUALLY AS MUCH AS FINGERPRINT EVIDENCE.

Neutron Activation Analysis

Neutron activation analysis utilizes a complicated device for comparing known samples with unknown ones.

The ability of this method to detect methods of elements in tiny samples enables it to solve identification problems that were previously considered hopeless. Material to be analyzed is made radioactive (charged to give off radiation gamma rays). This radioactive sample is then exposed to a crystal and every time a gamma ray interacts with the crystal, it emits a flash of light converted into an electrical pulse whose voltage is proportional to the energy of the gamma rays. An electronic device called a multi-challenge differential analyzer then sorts the electrical impulses into different energy groups and adds up the pulses in each group. The result is in the form of a graph shown on an oscilloscope screen which can then be transcribed onto magnetic tape for future reference.

No sample of material is too small to be analyzed. A single hair or small piece of automobile paint the size of a pin head can be analyzed and identified. If one thumbful of arsenic poison is diluted into ten tank cars of water, the exact amount of arsenic present could be determined. Another advantage is that the material tested can be preserved for presentation in court or saved for analysis by another method.

This new scientific device is not experimental but clearly demonstrable as a reliable piece of scientific evidence admissible in court.

The device is used to identify hair samples, gunshot residues, bomb and dynamite residues, paint, sand, concrete block samples, sewing thread, safe insulation, unidentified particles, moonshine, drugs, pipe fittings, wheat paste, gun metal, grease, and thousands of other items (except blood samples).

Additional crime lab instrumentation includes atomic absorption analysis, infrared and ultraviolet scpectrophotometer, pyrolysing gas chromophotography, mass spectogas chromophotography, X-ray diffraction.

RULE: CRIME LAB ANALYSIS IS THE MOST DIFFICULT EVIDENCE FOR A DEFENSE LAWYER TO EXPLAIN AWAY, MUCH MORE DIFFICULT FOR INSTANCE, THAN EYEWITNESS TESTIMONY. EXPERT SCIENTIFIC EVIDENCE DOESN'T LIE. UNLESS YOU CAN ATTACK THE SCIENTIST PERFORMING THE TEST, YOU MUST LIMIT THE EVIDENCE BY TRYING TO EXPLAIN IT AWAY.

Mere Presence

Mere presence at the scene of a crime, without more, is insufficient evidence to convict. It must be proved that you *affirmatively participated* in the criminal act. Companionship, opportunity to commit the crime, help in planning and preparation, or flight from the scene, are all circumstances from which your purpose may be inferred.

Telephone Company Surveillance

The telephone company can attach a pen register to a telephone which does not record a conversation but does record or *trap* the telephone number of the party making the call, making it possible to identify telephones which are being used for harassment.

Wiretapping of the actual conversation by the telephone company is illegal.

Domestic Relations Cases

It is common for distrusting husbands and wives involved in marital disputes and pending divorces to wiretap family or business telephones.

Courts do not allow a spouse to tap a phone being maintained in their home unless you are speaking on the phone at the time.

Some spouses will tap and record their phone and simply *use the information gained from the call.* If the husband agrees to meet his girlfriend at a certain motel, a wife can use this knowledge to hire a private detective to be present at the appointed time to take photographs which may be used in court.

Cordless and Cellular Telephones

Subscribers to cordless and cellular phones should exercise care when talking since the telephone is *wireless.*

The Electronic Communications Privacy Act makes it a crime to intentionally intercept a cellular call, disclose, or use the contents of the call.

There are monitoring scanner devices and the communications are not secure. The cellular industry is converting cellular telephones from analog to digital technology since scanners are not capable of intercepting and converting digital cellular signals. Customers concerned about the privacy of their communications should not use digital cellular phones.

Luminol

An ordinary spray bottle with adjustable tip can be used to spray Luminol (a chemical mixture). The finer the spray the better the results. Luminescence usually lasts about 30 seconds or so. Photographs can be taken of the blue glow that results, indicating the presence of blood.

There is often blood shed in a violent crime. Blood is the most commonly discovered evidence as a result of violence, a viscous fluid, thicker and more adhesive than water.

Because blood is highly visible and recognizable, a perpetrator will often attempt to remove blood from items or locations that could be incriminating. Police are confronted with potential crime scenes in which little or no blood is visible, or one where an attempt was made to hide blood stains.

The older the stain, the longer and more pronounced the luminescence. The aging process of blood forms *hematin* which reacts with the luminol.

DNA Analysis

In 1953, James Watson and Frances Crick made the most exciting discovery in the history of genetics, that genes are composed of a acid (DNA).

Before this we knew:

1. Genes were hereditary factors known to be associated with specific character traits.
2. The one gene-one enzyme theory was that genes controlled the structure of proteins.
3. Genes carry chromosomes.
4. The chromosomes consist of DNA and protein.

5. Bacterial cells from these genes can be transformed into cells that express a different phenotype and that transforming agent is DNA.

The basic information in DNA is familiar to anyone who has read a high school biology text or magazines or newspapers taking you back to the 1950's. But the discovery of the structure of DNA is new.

Most human cells contain a nucleus, which in turn contains 46 chromosomes that arrange themselves into pairs. Tightly coiled and packaged within these chromosomes are DNA strands consisting of two strands running in opposite directions.

A gene is a segment of DNA that determines physical characteristics such as hair, eye color, and genetic defects. There is a certain quantity of DNA which apparently provides no code for characteristics, and this is referred to as *space* or *junk* DNA. A DNA molecule contains more than 3 billion units, and although a human receives half of his DNA each from his mother and father, the final links of DNA are unique to each individual.

DNA fingerprinting process employs six steps: (1) extraction; (2) fragmentation; (3) electrophoresis; (4) southern blotting; (5) hybridization; (6) autoradiographic.

1. DNA is chemically extracted from a blood sample and purified.
2. The DNA molecule is cut into fragments at a precisely designated point by a restricting enzyme.
3. It's placed in a gel between two electrically charged poles to determine an orderly pattern of the fragments and parallel lines.
4. The DNA band pattern is then transferred to a nylon membrane (a sheet of heavy blotting paper) and DNA strands are unzipped from one another.
5. Radioactive tagged probes are introduced onto the nylon membrane which attach themselves.
6. The excess probes are washed away, the nylon membrane is placed next to a sheet of X-ray film and exposed for several days, the end result being a series of dark parallel bands resembling universal bar codes on labels commonly found in retail stores to identify merchandise. The result is an audiograph or an autorad, known as the *DNA fingerprint.*

When blood is taken and matched into a DNA pattern, a serologist can check it against *any body fluid* found at the crime scene. If a rapist leaves seminal fluid at the scene, he might as well be leaving his Social Security card.

DNA technology is a crystal ball for rape and homicide cases, and even more precise than fingerprinting or a polygraph. Shaped like a ladder, it can be extracted from blood, semen, urine, hair roots, or other tissues, and except for identical twins, no two people are known to share the same DNA pattern. Serology can rule out a high percentage of the population for an individual crime, and thus free a person who might otherwise have been suspect.

Once extracted scientists use a restrictive enzyme to "cut" a specific section of DNA and translate the pattern into what looks like a grocery store bar code.

With a series of green blips on a computer screen, the frequency and length of the bars are measured to minute detail. Scientists have used this analysis to determine paternity for many years, but police have only recently begun using "DNA fingerprinting".

The actual DNA analysis image, the bar code, can be saved and stored in computers with thousands of other DNA fingerprinting analysis from blood samples.

Best Evidence Rule

The Best Evidence Rule applies to writings, photographs, and recordings. Whenever possible, the original writing must be produced in court, and not a carbon or photocopy. The court wants to be satisfied the item being offered into evidence is not a fake or forgery. The purpose of the rule is to prevent fraud or the likelihood of mistake when proving the contents of a writing.

Business Records

In our business world there are thousands of different types of business records needed to prove a fact in a trial. *Business records are admitted to prove the truth* of notwithstanding the Hearsay Rule. Four things must be proved:

1. The business entry or record was made at or near the time of the particular transaction
2. The person testifying made the entry or was responsible for the document
3. The person must be a custodian of the record and
4. Be familiar with how the records are kept.

Hospital, police, and many other types of records are admissible. The records must be reliably proved.

The lawyer should be extremely careful because once a business record is received into evidence, the entire document is before jury.

There may be some harmful or derogative comments in the records unfavorable to you and the jury will read all the reports.

Res Gestae and Dying Declarations

Certain statements made by a person are presumed to be truthful and reliable. If an *excited utterance* is made at the scene of a crime or automobile accident, immediately and in response to the excitement of the act of his words are clothed with trustworthiness because the person did not have time to fabricate a lie. It is a part of the excitement or the *res gestae* rule!

If a person knows they are fatally injured and dying, statements made by a dying person are admissible as a *dying declaration.* The law assumes a person *knowing death is eminent* would not meet his Maker with a lie on his lips.

Hypnosis

Courts are reluctant to allow witnesses to testify who have previously been hypnotized and encouraged to recall identifications of faces, license plates, vehicle descriptions and other details. If the reliability of the hypnosis is established by expert testimony as to whether the hypnotized testimony is truthful, fantasy, or unduly suggested to the patient then it is admissible. Hypnosis is a dangerous and unreliable technique because it suggests to the witness to recall facts and might result in a miscarriage of justice with a high risk *induced testimony* thought to be *inherently unreliable.*

Many people may be susceptible to suggestions given them during hypnosis which fabricates events to fill in memory gaps. It also unfairly limits the defense lawyer's ability to cross-examine the witness.

Offer of Proof

If a lawyer requests permission to mark an exhibit or item of evidence and introduce it to the jury and if the court refuses the lawyer can ask for an out of court hearing to make a *offer of proof.*

The lawyer will put the witness on the witness stand and by narrative questions or by definite and specific questions demonstrate the admissibility and relevancy of the evidence. The purpose is to ensure the Judge and opposing lawyer understand what evidence is being offered and why.

Should you later lose the case, that issue is preserved for appeal and an appellate court may reverse the jury verdict and send the case back for an entirely new trial.

Now that you have a complete understanding of the court system and rules of evidence, you should consider carefully the exact criminal charges against you.

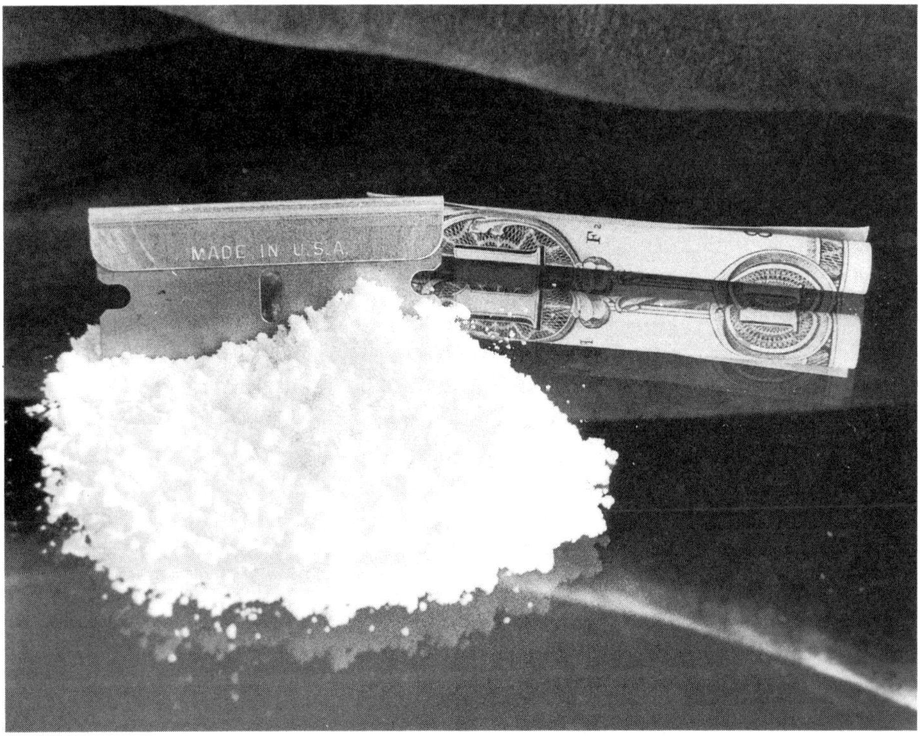

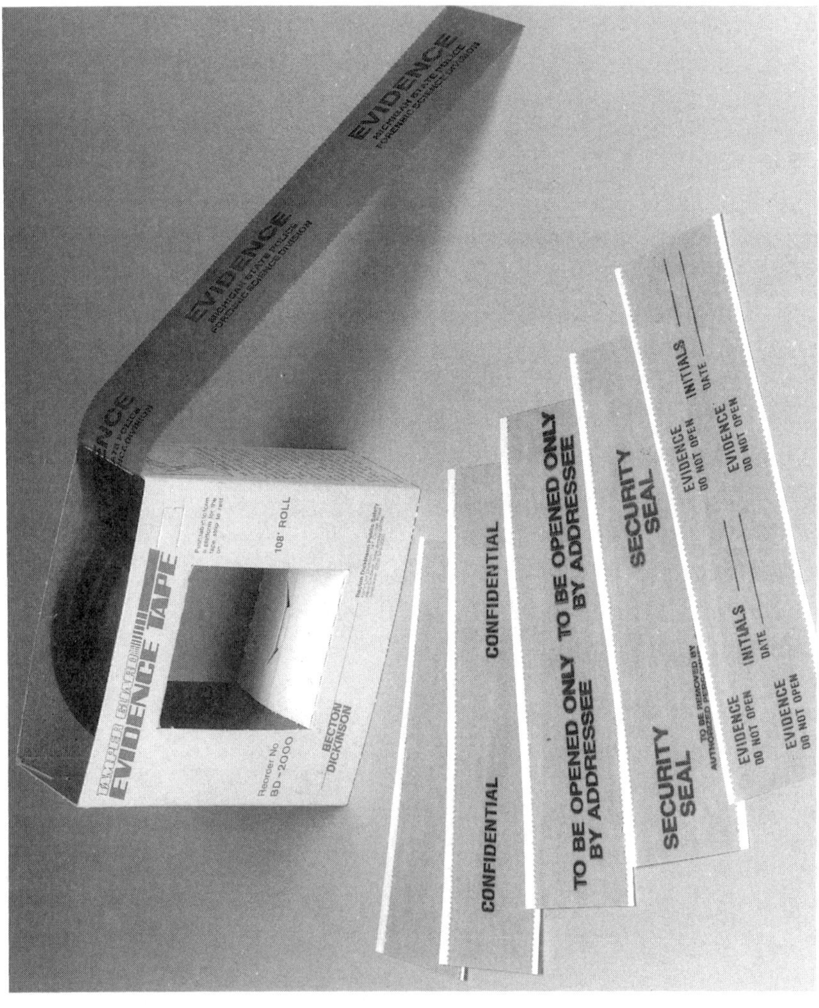

Special Tamper-proof evidence tape, *sticks* permanently to all evidence. It is initialed and dated by all police in the "chain of custody" so there are no breaks in the chain.

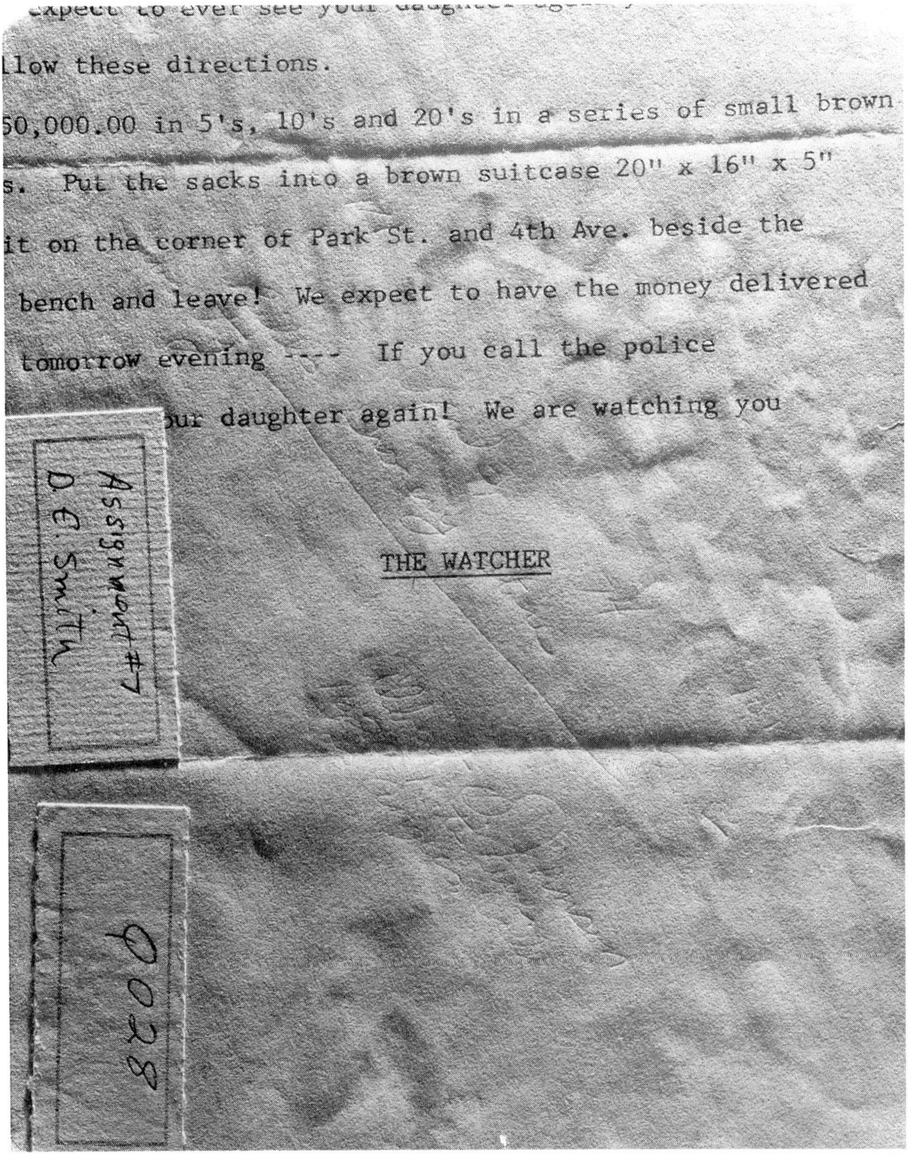

llow these directions.

50,000.00 in 5's, 10's and 20's in a series of small brown

s. Put the sacks into a brown suitcase 20" x 16" x 5"

it on the corner of Park St. and 4th Ave. beside the

bench and leave! We expect to have the money delivered

tomorrow evening ---- If you call the police

our daughter again! We are watching you

THE WATCHER

A ransom note over which a kidnapper had earlier written a personal check, made an indentation on the paper. *Incident Lighting* can enlarge the note and bring out the kidnapper's name using high contrast film.

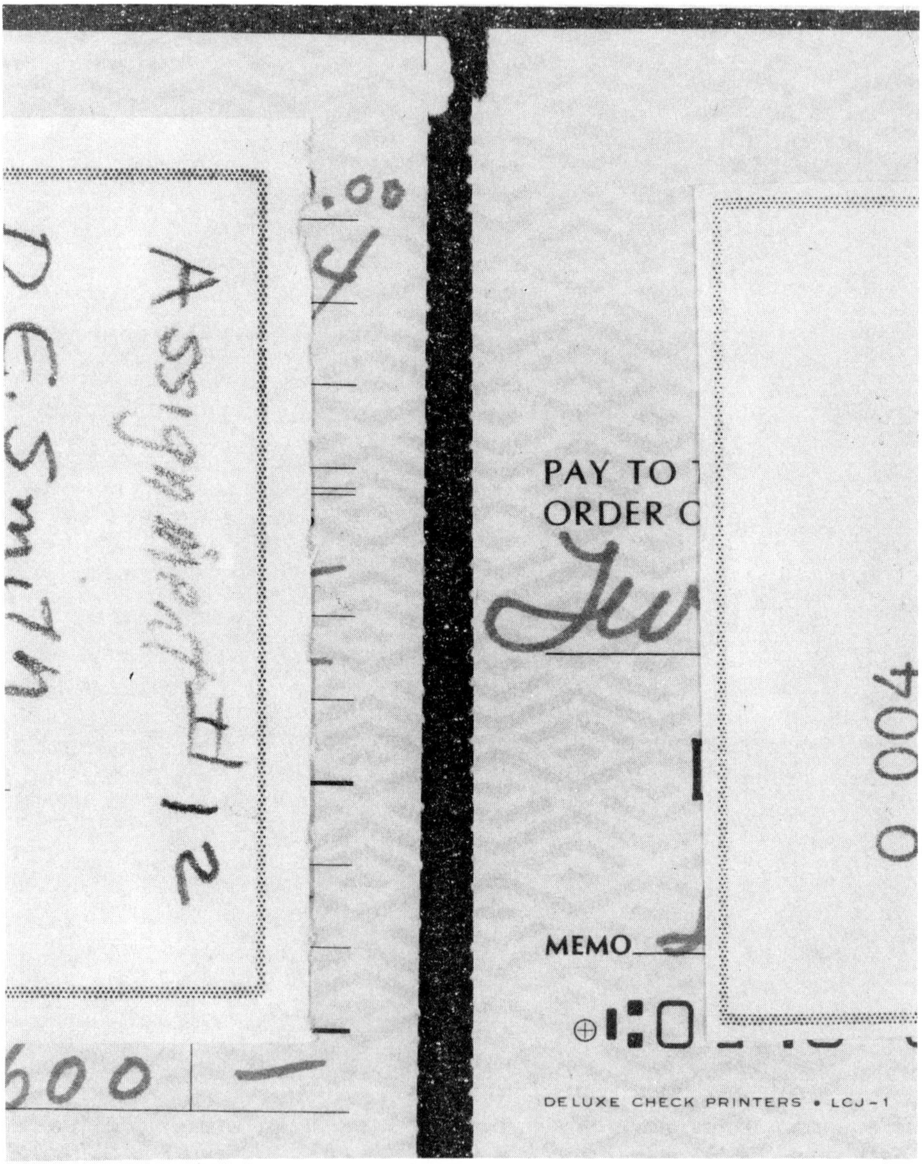
PAY TO T
ORDER C
MEMO
DELUXE CHECK PRINTERS • LCJ-1

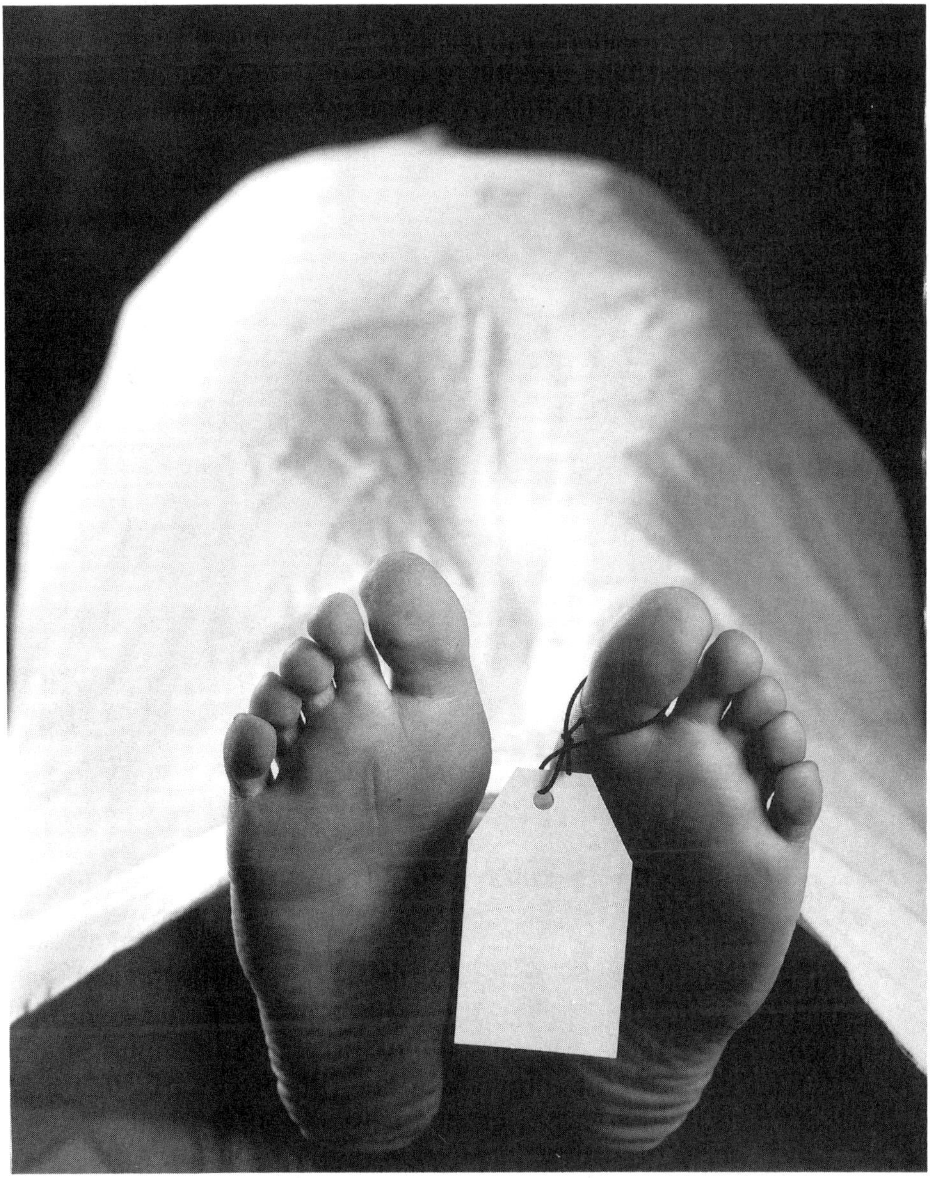

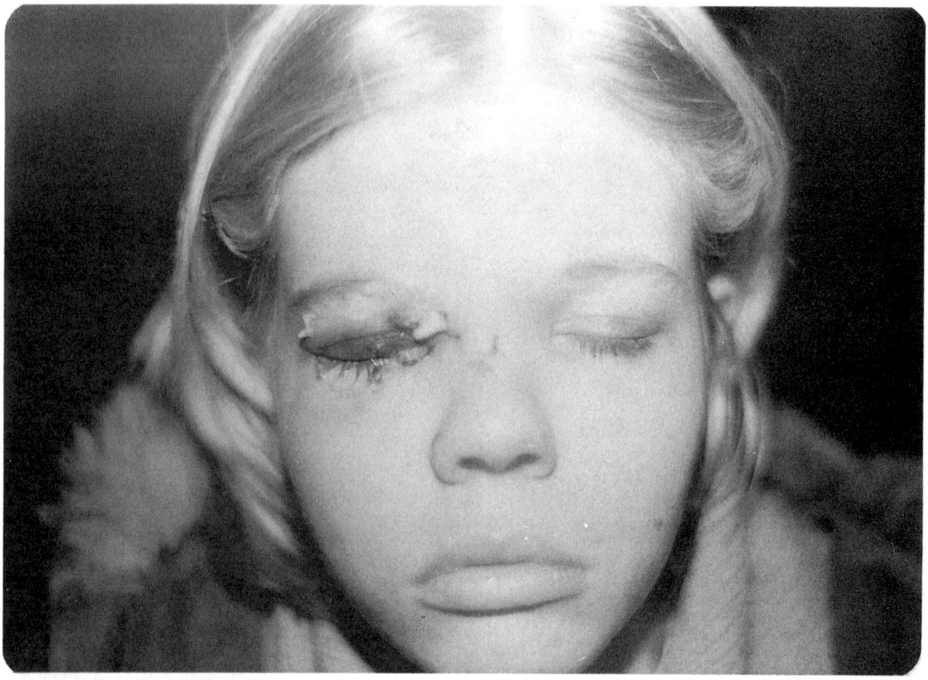

Assault victim showing bruises

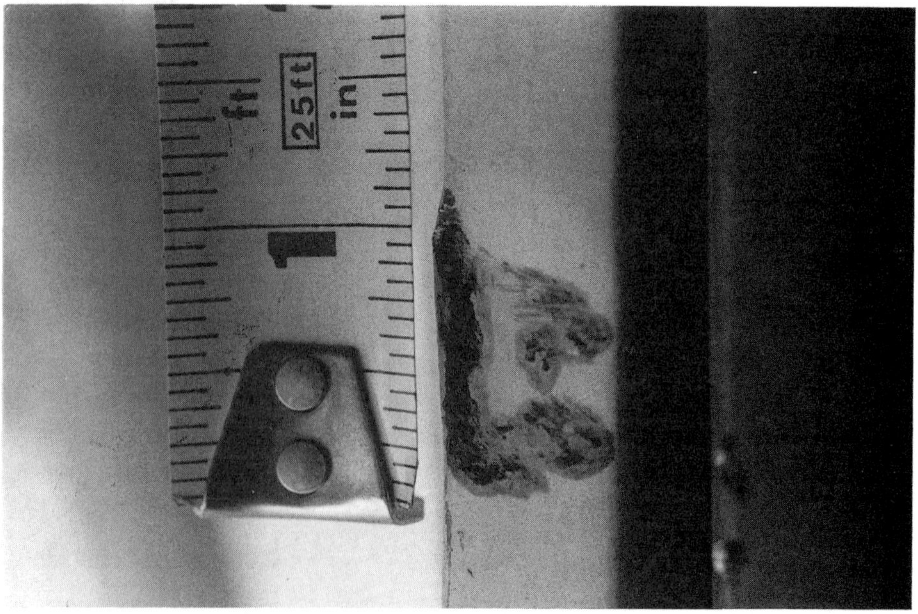

Photo of tool mark on door jam at a Taney Co. business can later be matched because of the marks and stuations on the pry bar and paint striations on the pry bar and paint samples to a pry bar found in defendent's posession (Chip Mason, Major crime Investigator Taney Co Sheriff's Office).

Many photographs should be taken of burglary scenes. Broken doors and glass are taken by police and marked for later evidence in court. All suspected areas are fingerprinted.

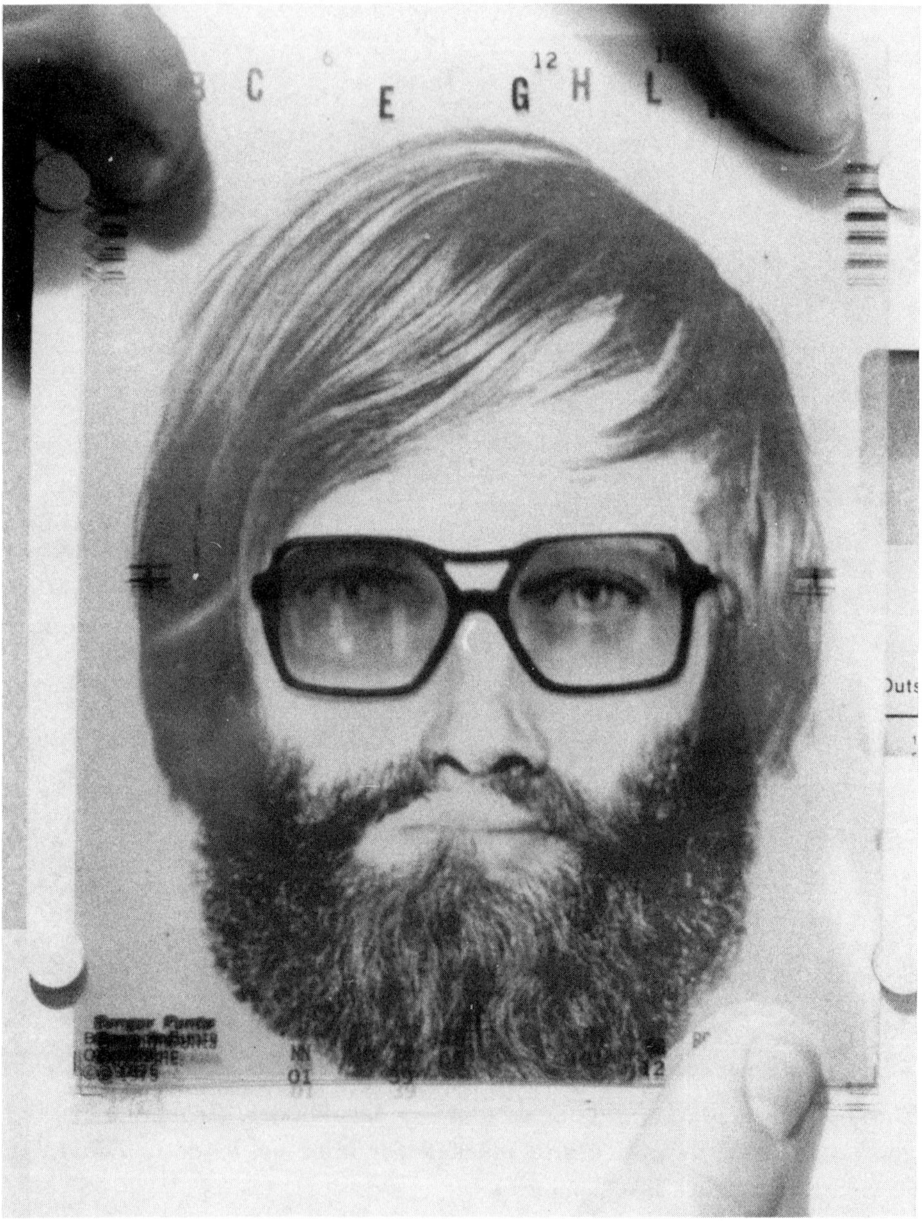

Police use transparent identification features to attempt to match a face to the victim's description given in an armed robbery case (St. Louis County).

An arson fatality victim leaving an impression on burned carpet (Det. LaVerne Williams, Carthage P.D.).

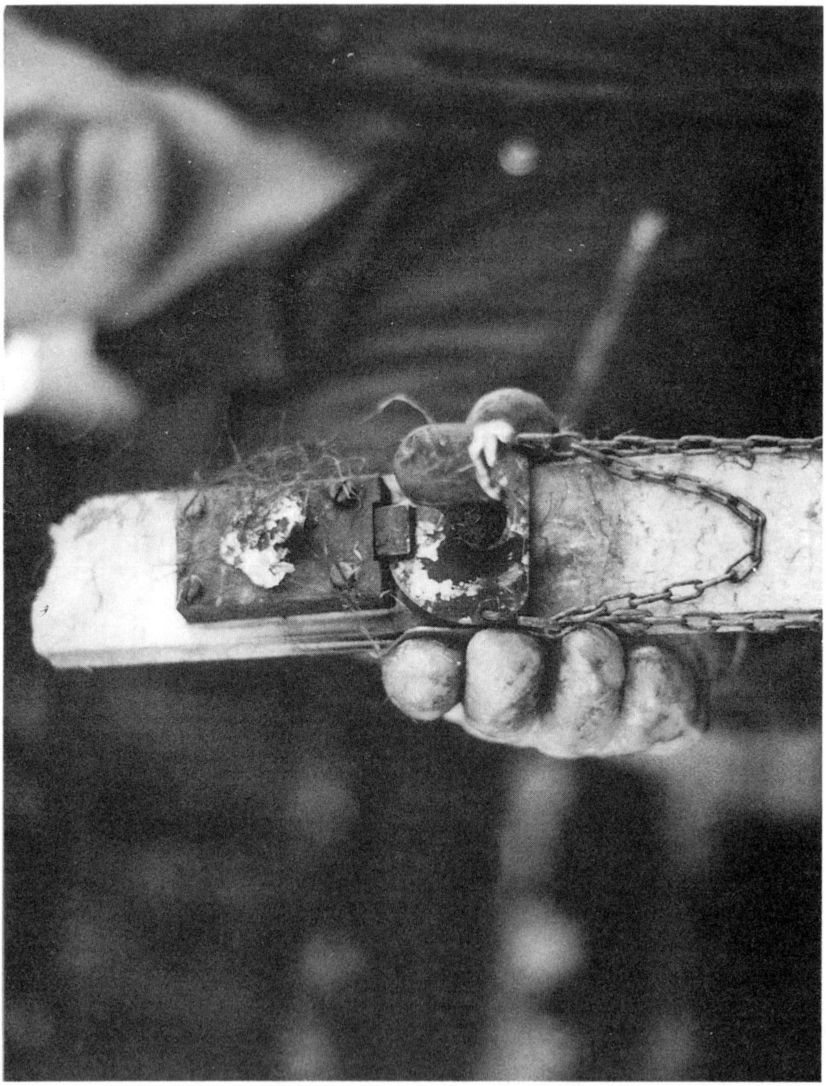

Overhead door lock showing it in locked position at time of arson fire (photo courtesy of Carthage P.D.).

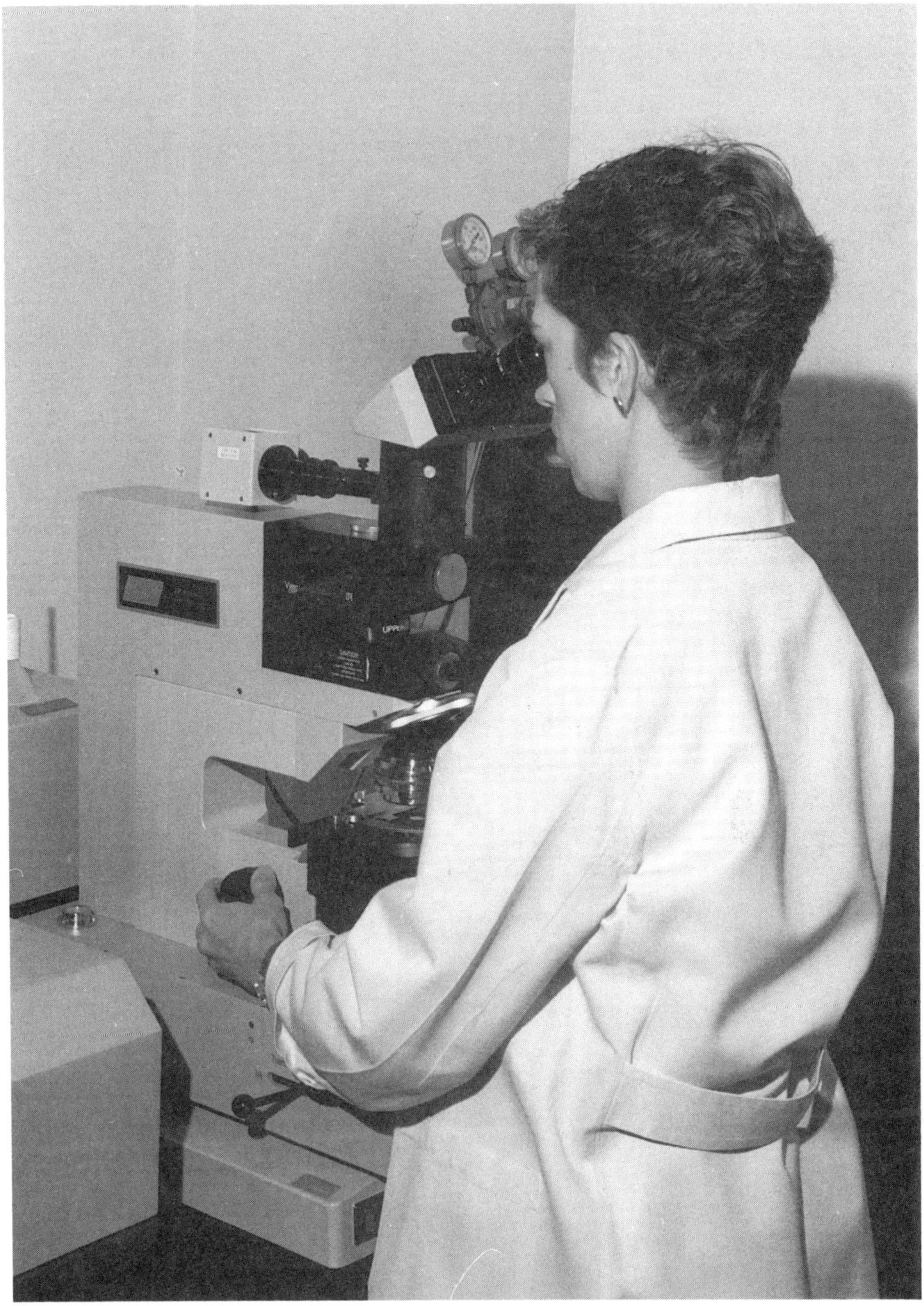

Forensic chemist Jenny Smith performs a microscope Fourier Transform Infrared Spectrophotometer analysis of trace substances at the Missouri State Highway Patrol Crime Laboratory in Jefferson City.

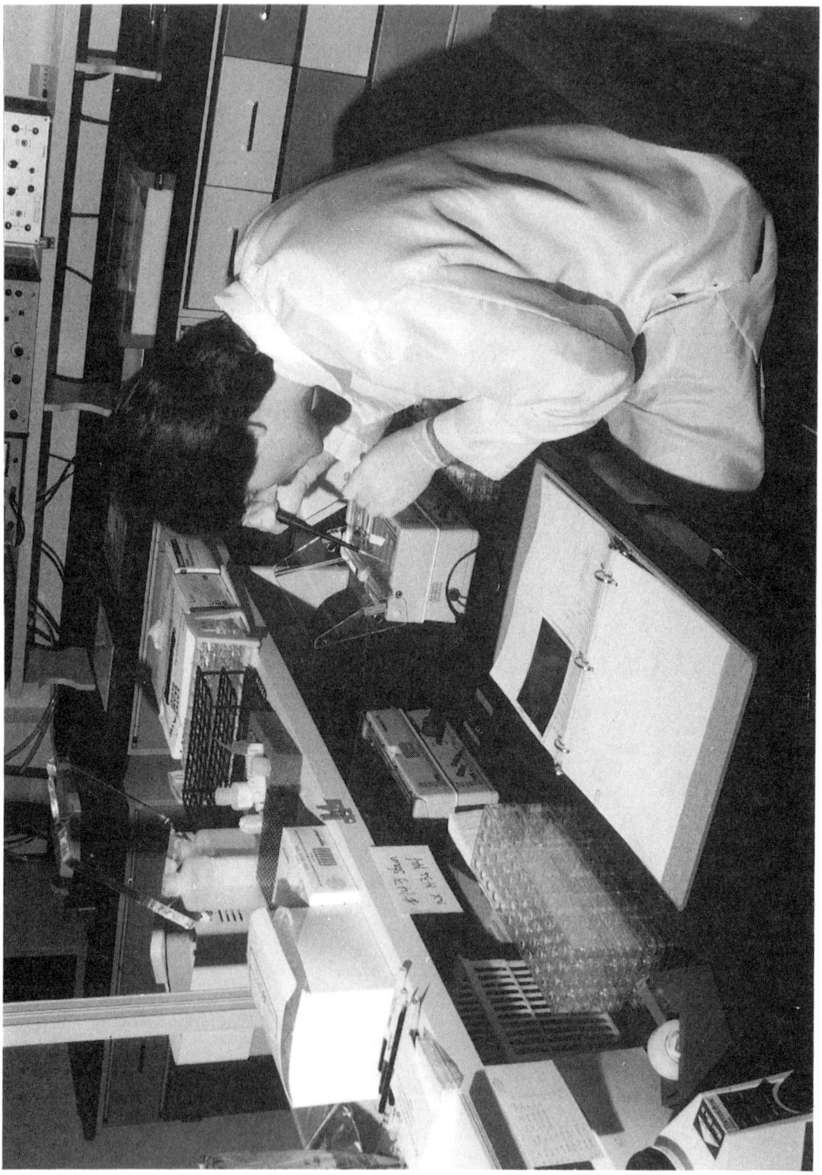

Forensic chemist Cary Maloney loading a test gel to determine the quantity of DNA at the Missouri State Highway Patrol Crime Laboratory in Jefferson City.

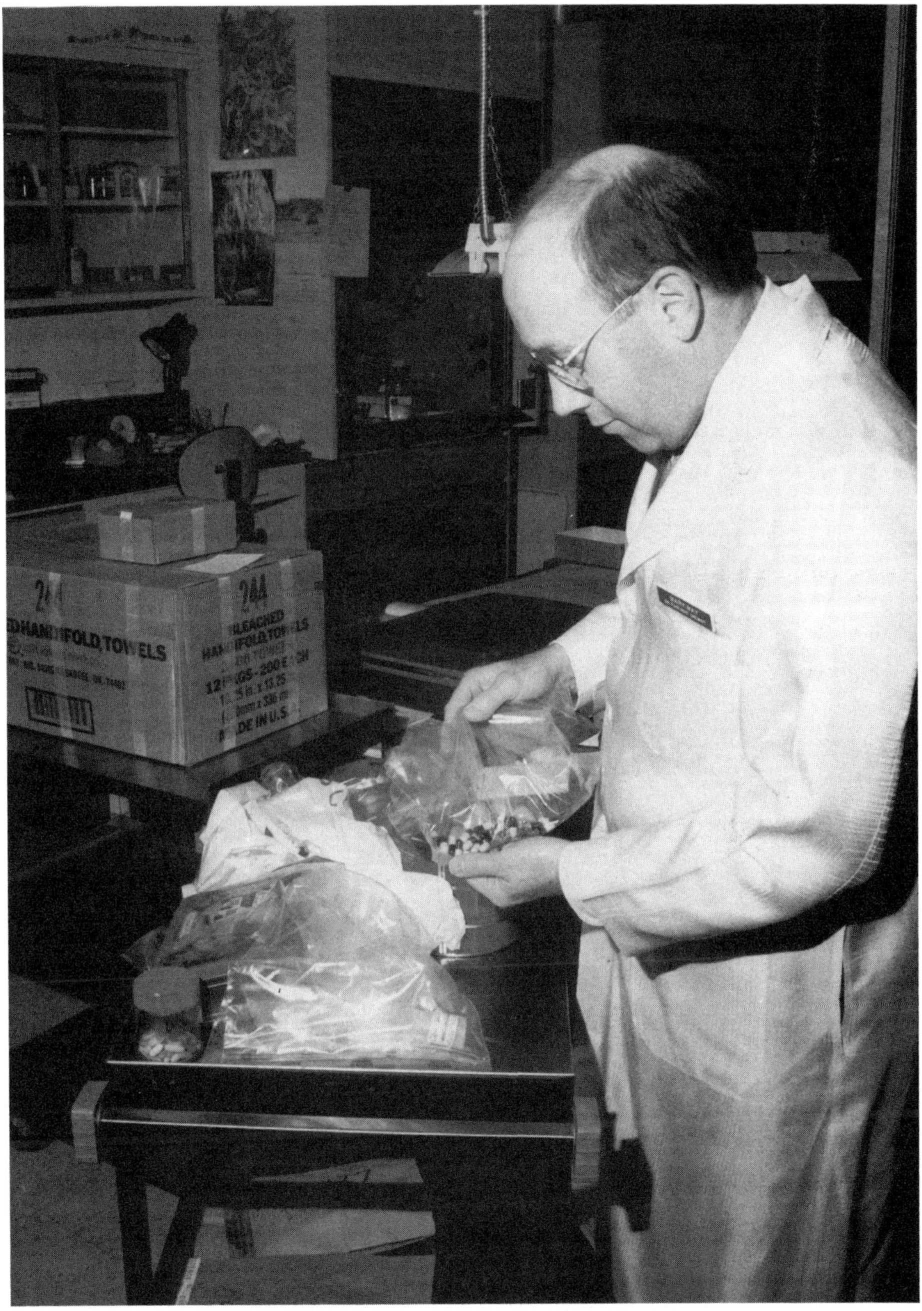

Senior Forensic chemist Everett Markway performs a preliminary examination of capsules for controlled substances at the Missouri State Highway Patrol Crime laboratory in Jefferson City.

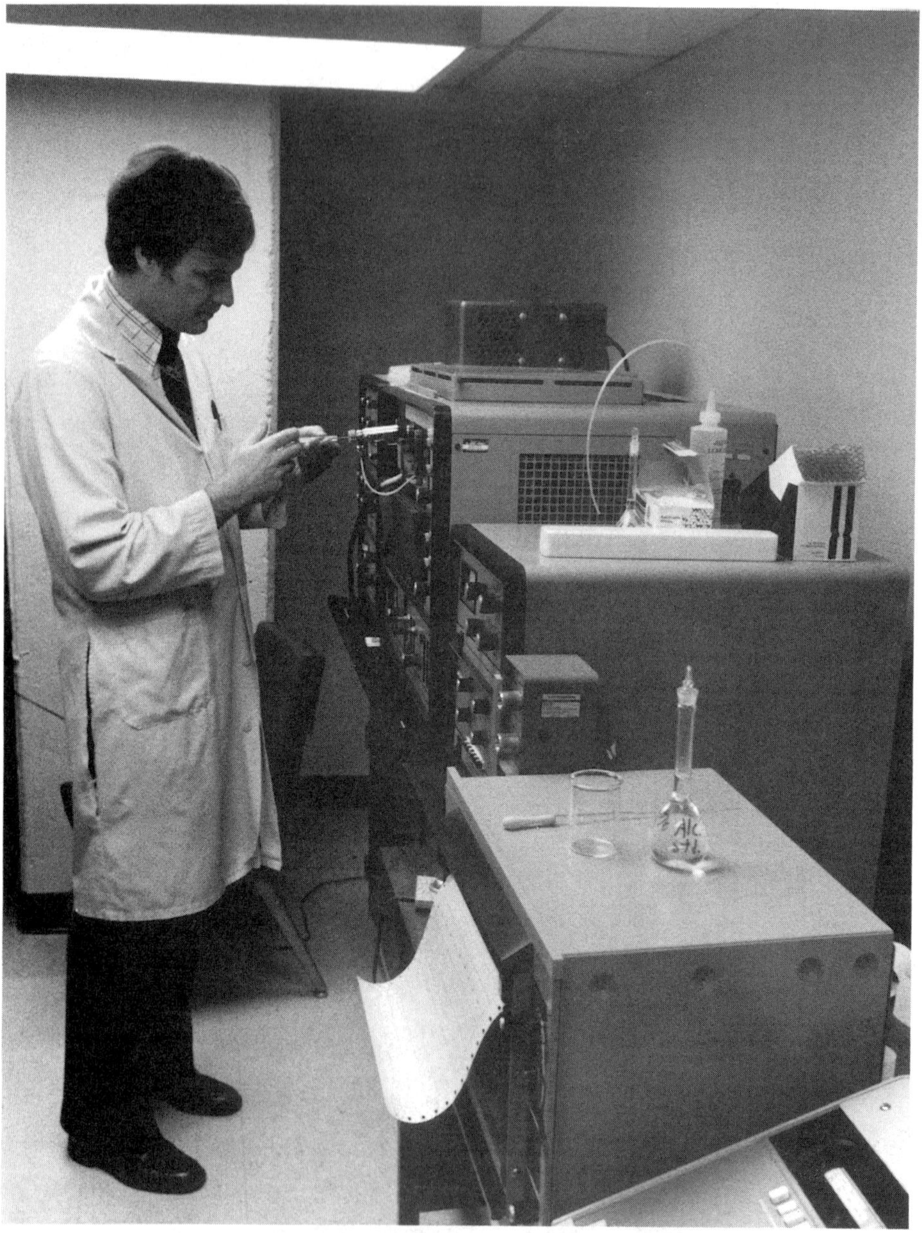

A chemist is shown injecting a sample in a gas chromograph for blood sample or drug analysis, using a Hamilton syringe into a pyrolis chamber to vaporize the sample and analyze the gases.

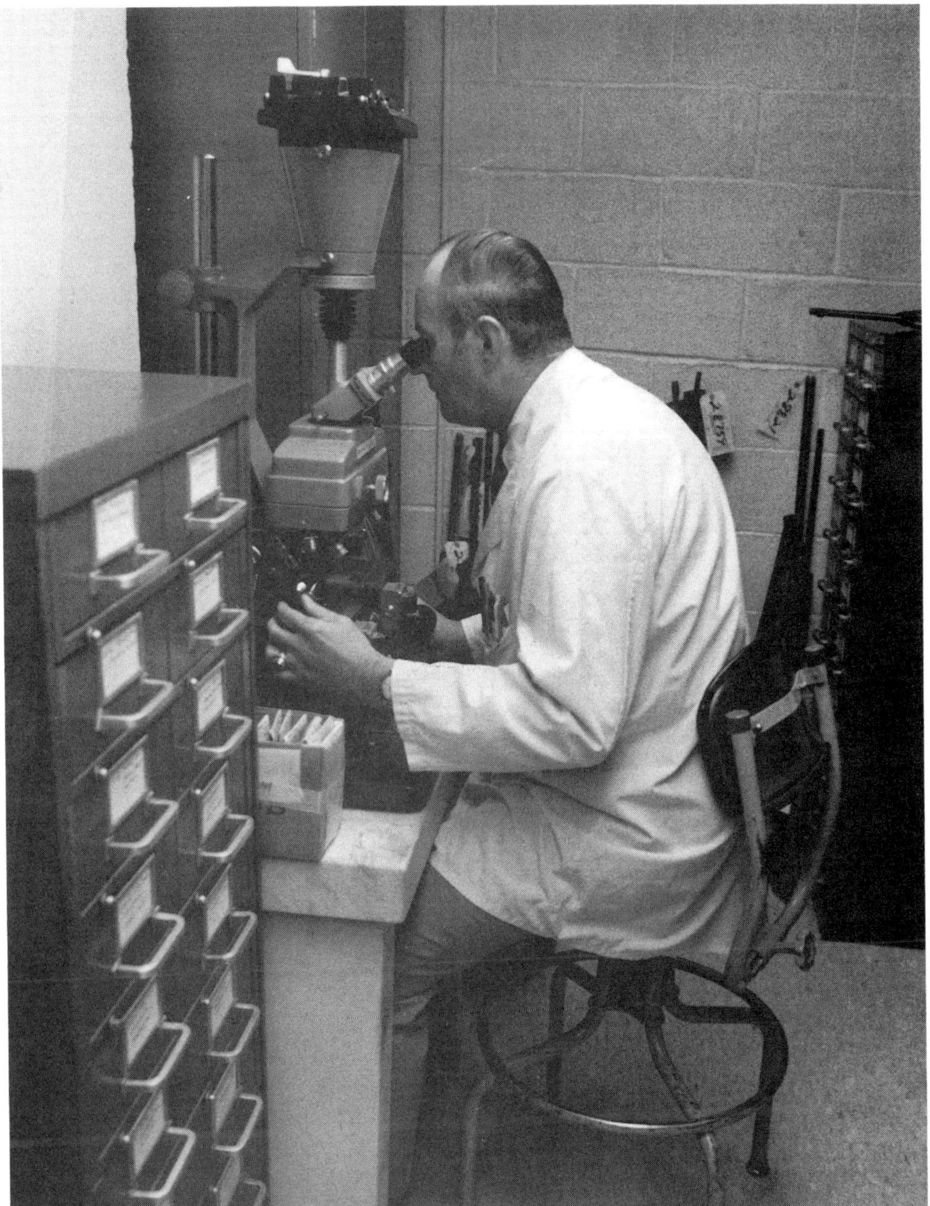

Crime Laboratory specialist at the St. Louis County Police Department attempts to match fingerprints on a comparison microscope.

NEC BIT IV FACSIMILE

ORIGINAL PRINT

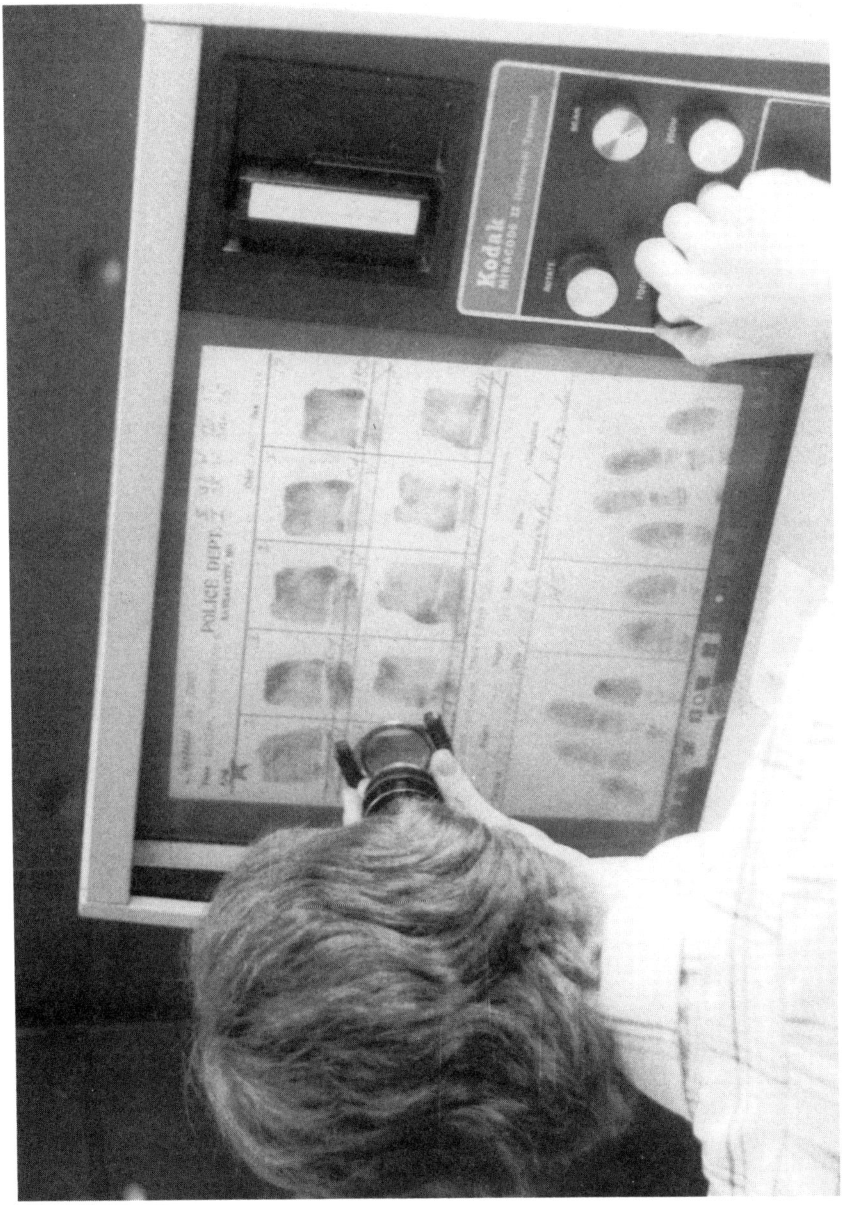

Kodak MIRACPODEII Retrieval Terminal, uses microfilm system when 10 finger-print cards are filmed and put into the system by use of a 3 digit coding system. Once crime scene cards are received, a search can be made of over 26,000 suspect cards in an attempt to identify the suspect.

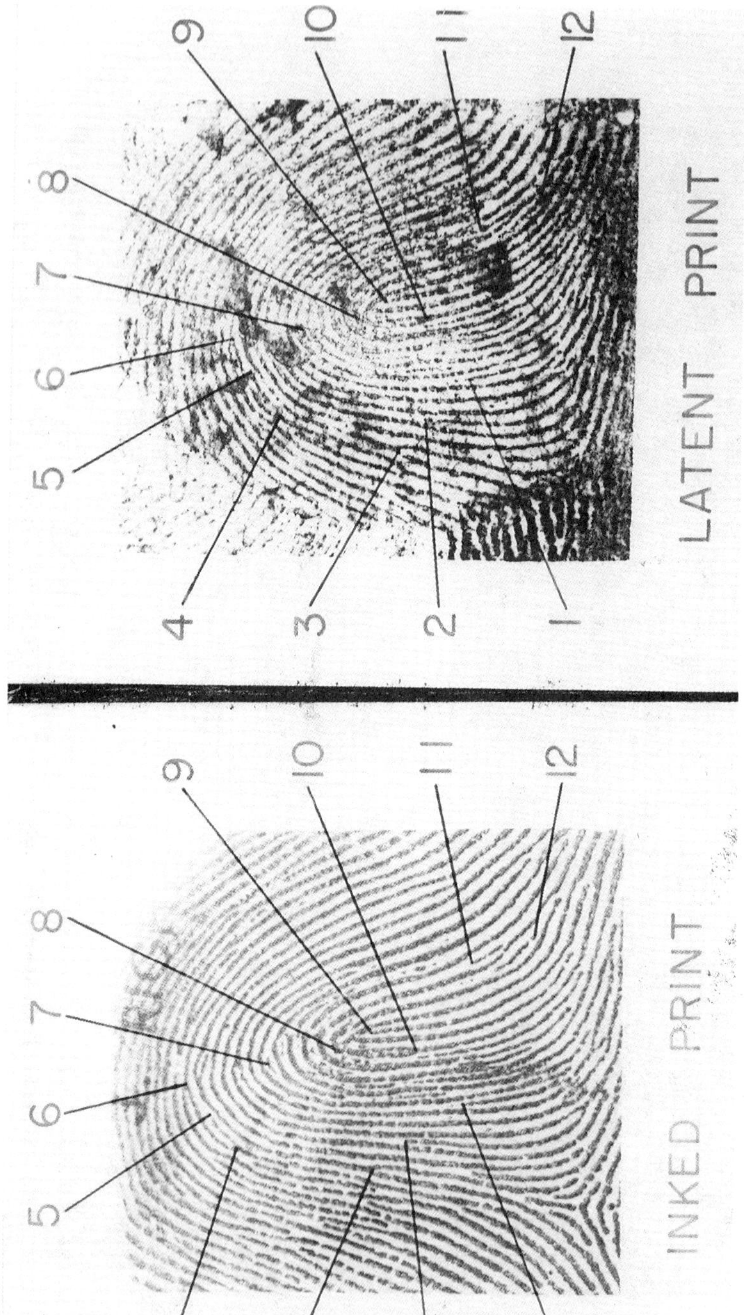

This fingerprint comparison, almost by itself resulted in a major criminal conviction.

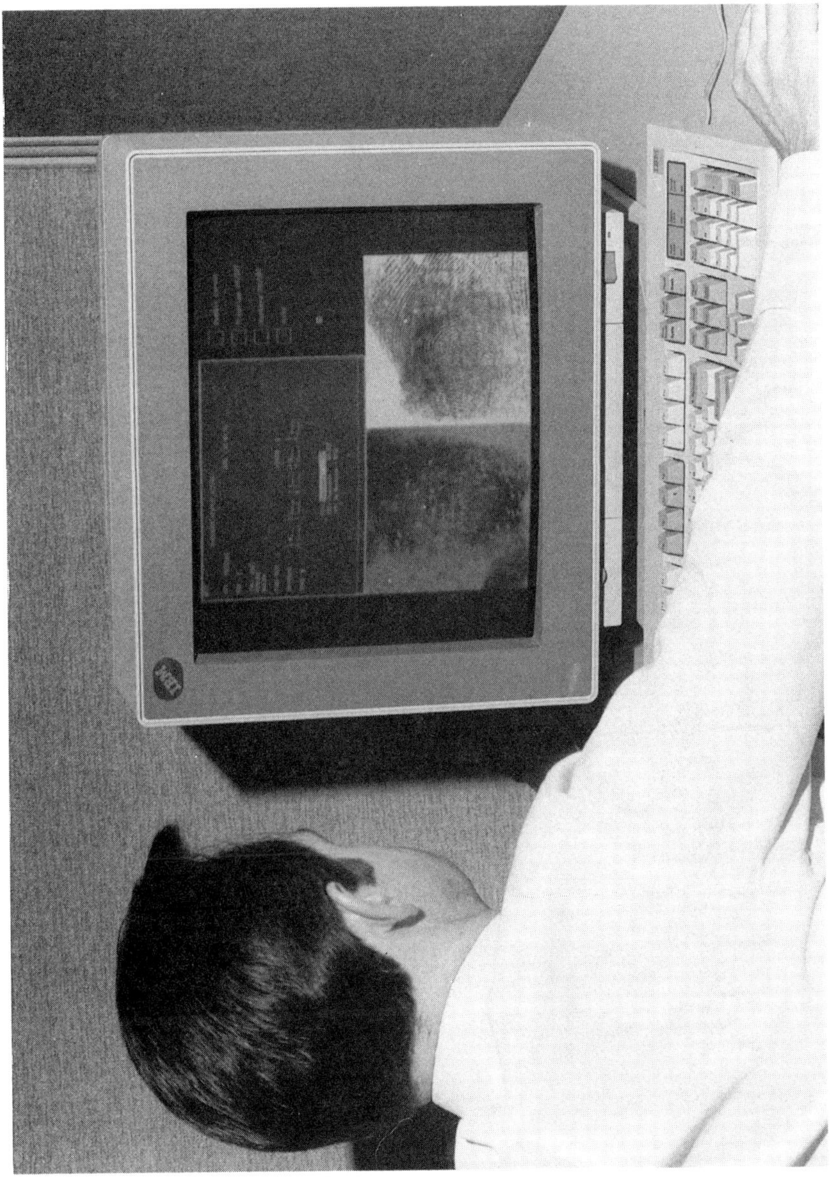

Forensic Analyst III Don Lock compares a latent fingerprint from a crime scene to a possible match from the data base of the Automated Fingerprint Identification System (AFIS) at the Missouri State Highway Patrol Crime Laboratory in Jefferson City.

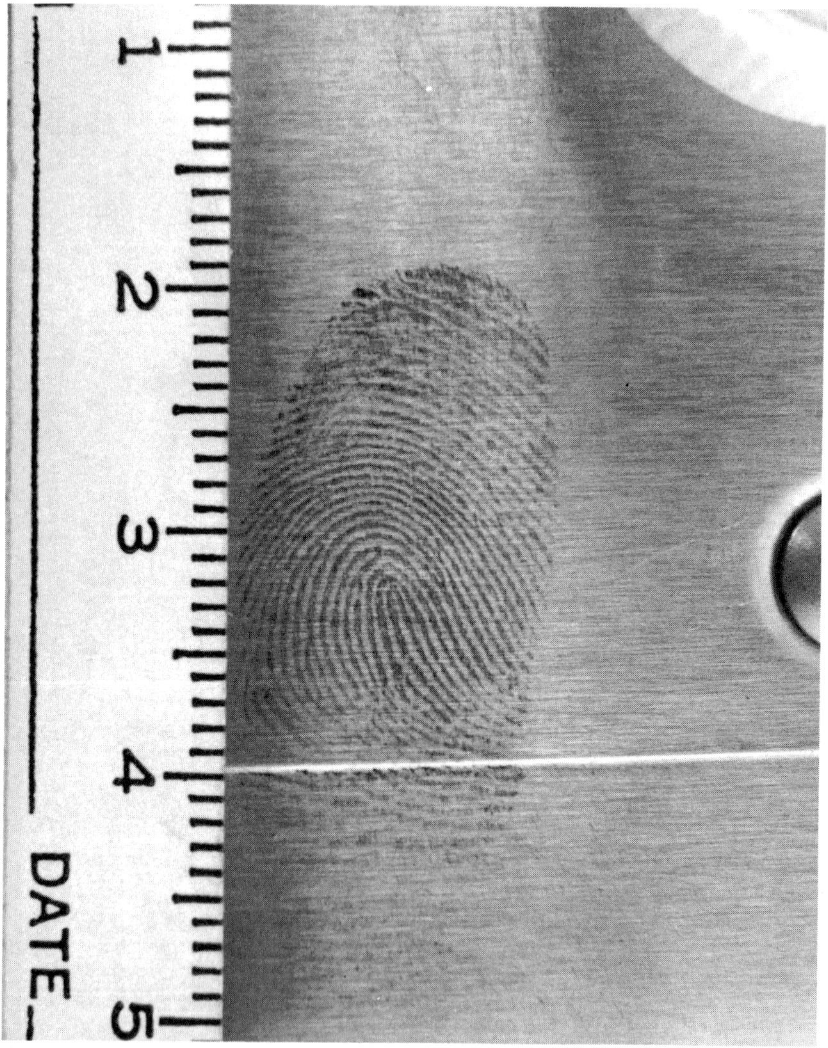

No need to dust and "lift" a print. A close-up photograph is sufficient for use in court. (Photo from Cape Cirardeau Police Department).

Photograph by Sheriff Theron Jenkins Taney Co. Missouri and Chip Mason, Major Crime Investigator was positively matched to boot of one suspect and tennis shoe of another resulting in guilty plea.

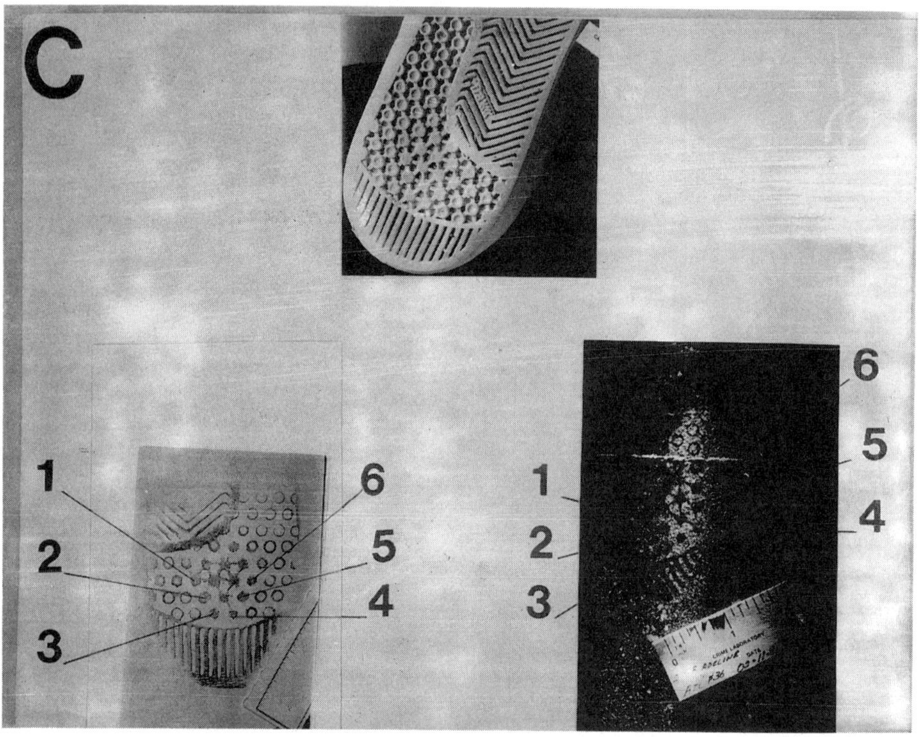

Two-dimensional footprint developed by photographic techniques by C.R. Longwell, SEMO Regional Crime Laboratory, Cape Girardeau, and David Warren, Evidence Technician, Cape Girardeau P.D. (SEMO Regional Crime Laboratory, Cape Girardeau).

Tom Buell, Missouri State Highway Patrol, makes a footprint comparison measurement by placing an inked roll bar on the known show and checking transfer pattern. He is looking for imperfections, wear characteristics and unusual dimension to compare footprints with those found at the scene of the crime.

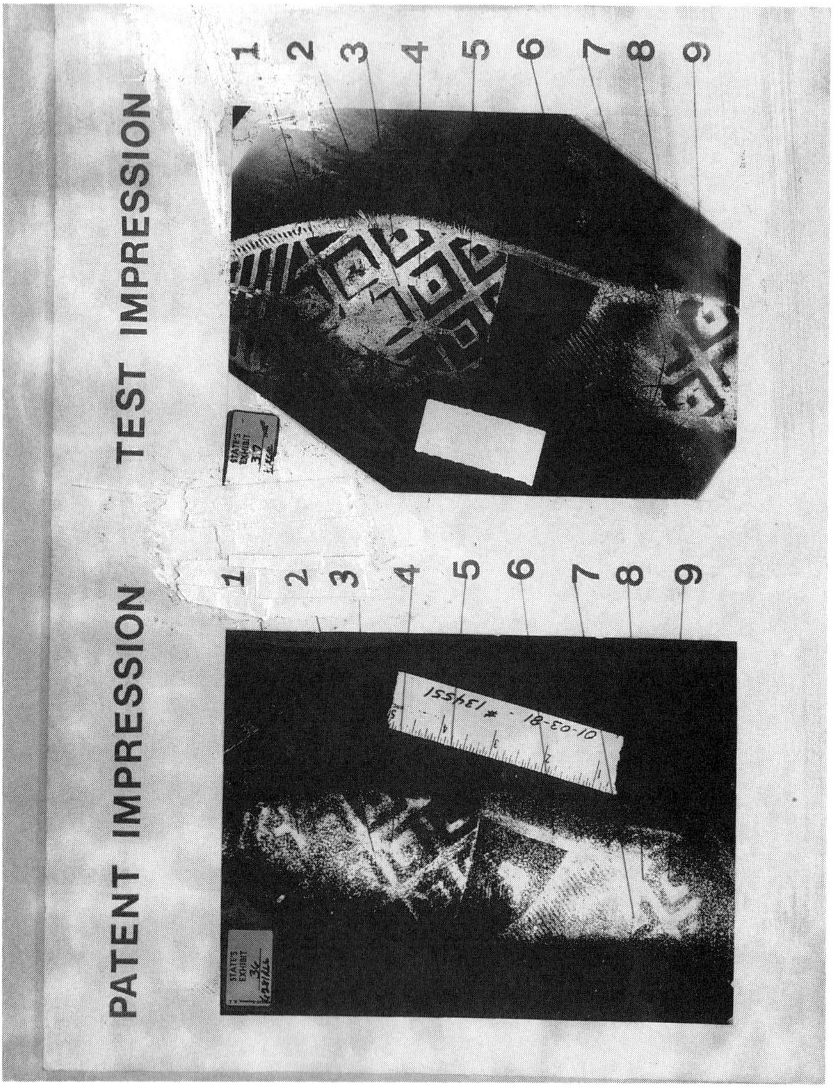

Two dimensional footprint developed by photographic techniques by C.R. Longwell, SEMO Regional Crime Laboratory, Cape Girardeau, Missouri, and David Warren, Evidence Technician, Cape Girardeau P.D. (SEMO Regional Crime Laboratory Cape Girardeau).

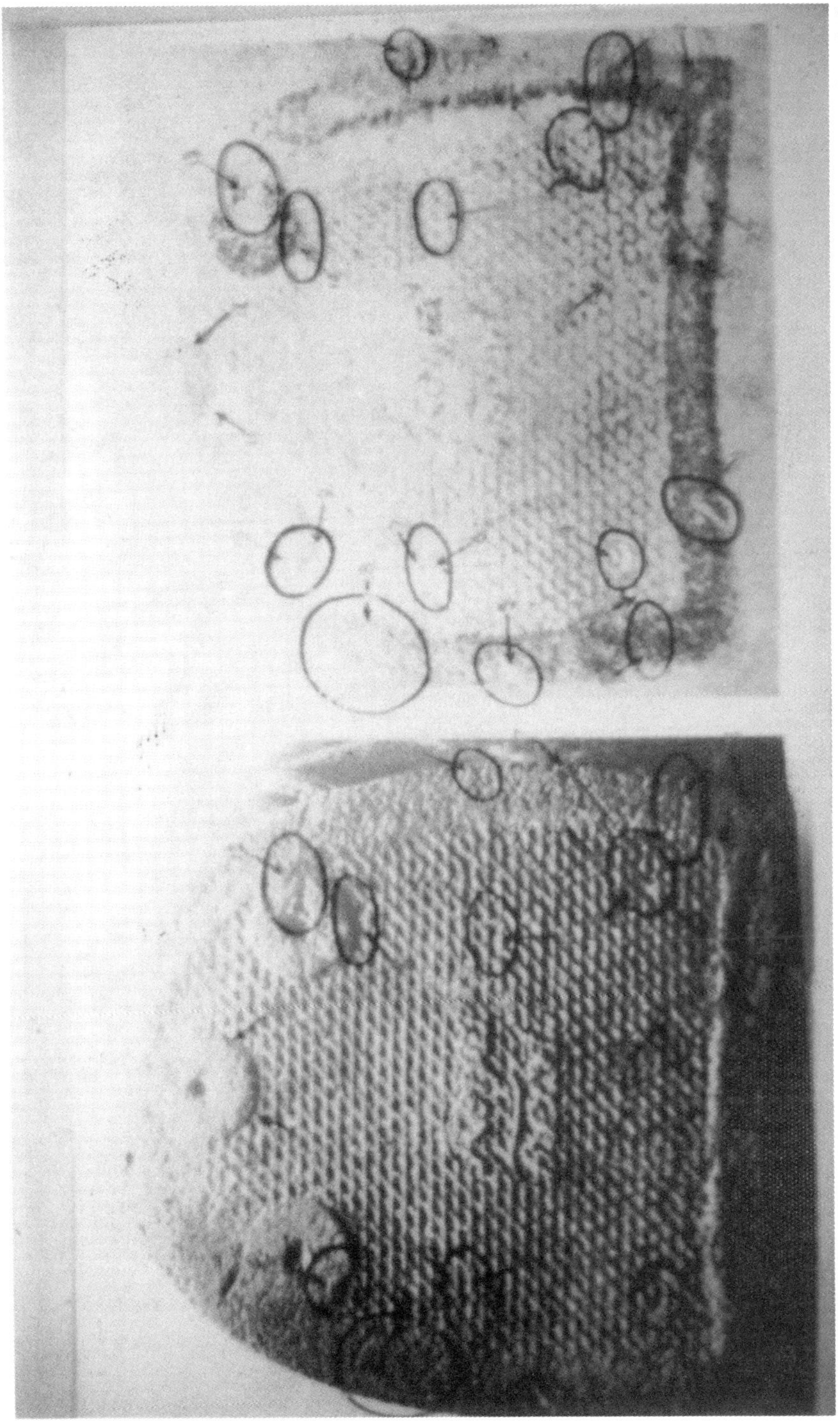

Heel Print analysis by comparison Photographs, is impressive to juries. Such evidence often makes the difference which results in a conviction.

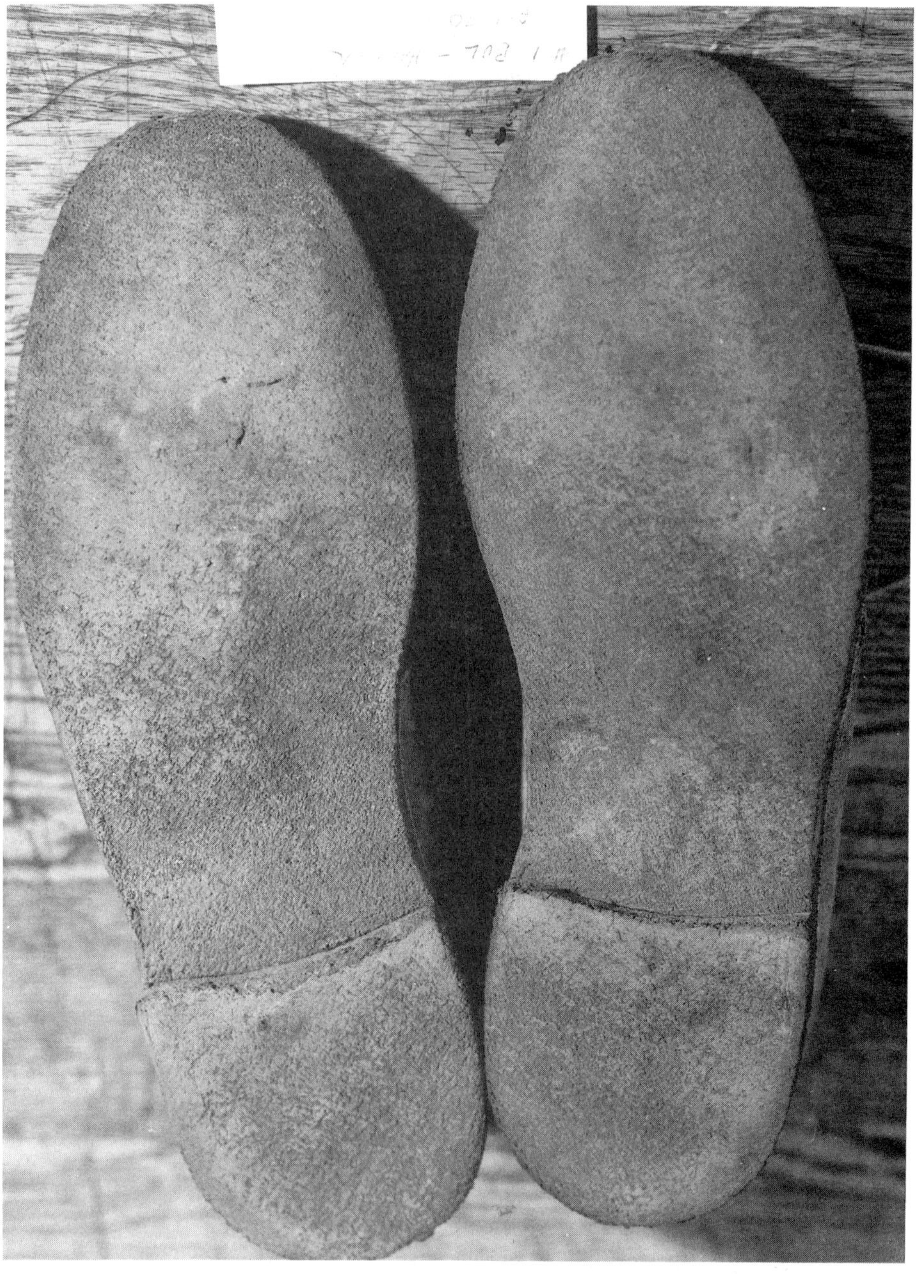

Close up photo of suspects' shoes can be matched with shoeprints found at crime scene (Jefferson City P.D.).

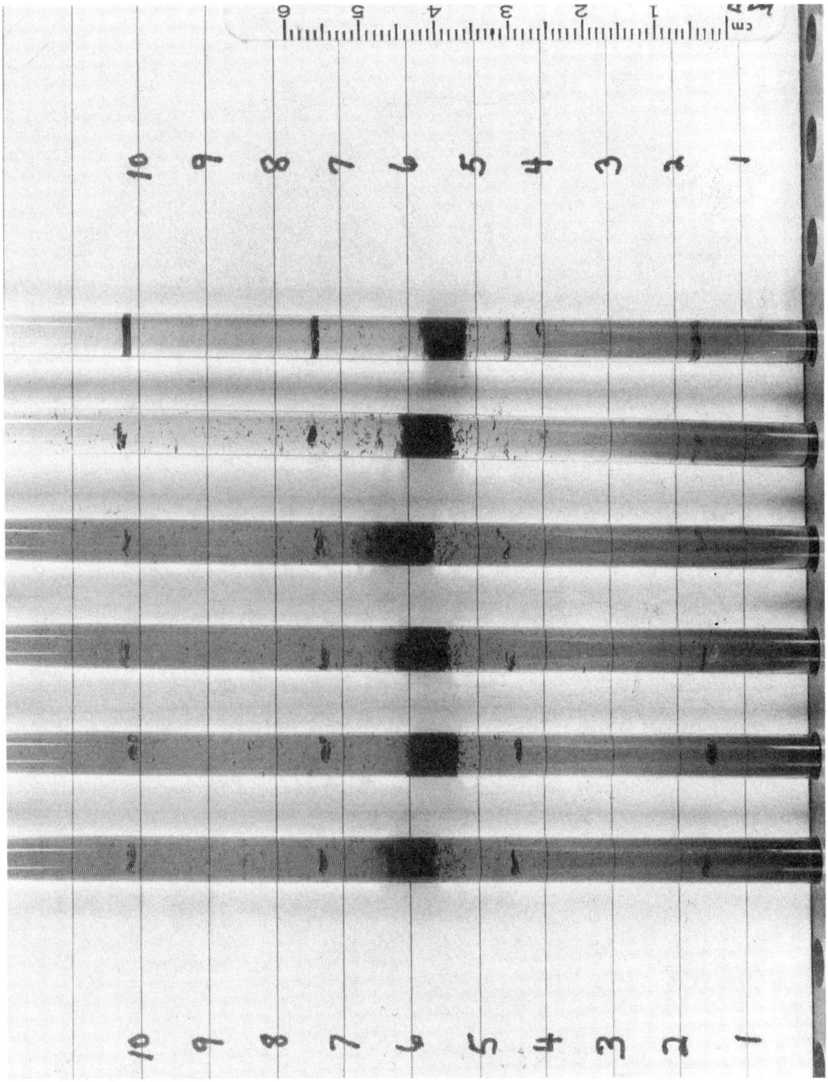

Missouri State Highway Patrol lab technician photographs density interfaces of soil found at the burglary scene.

Keen police work matched this footprint with a shoe taken from a suspect (Hannibal Police Department).

Marshall High School Principal Jim Tobin and Chief of Police James B. Simmerman examine tire track marks at high school burglary scene.

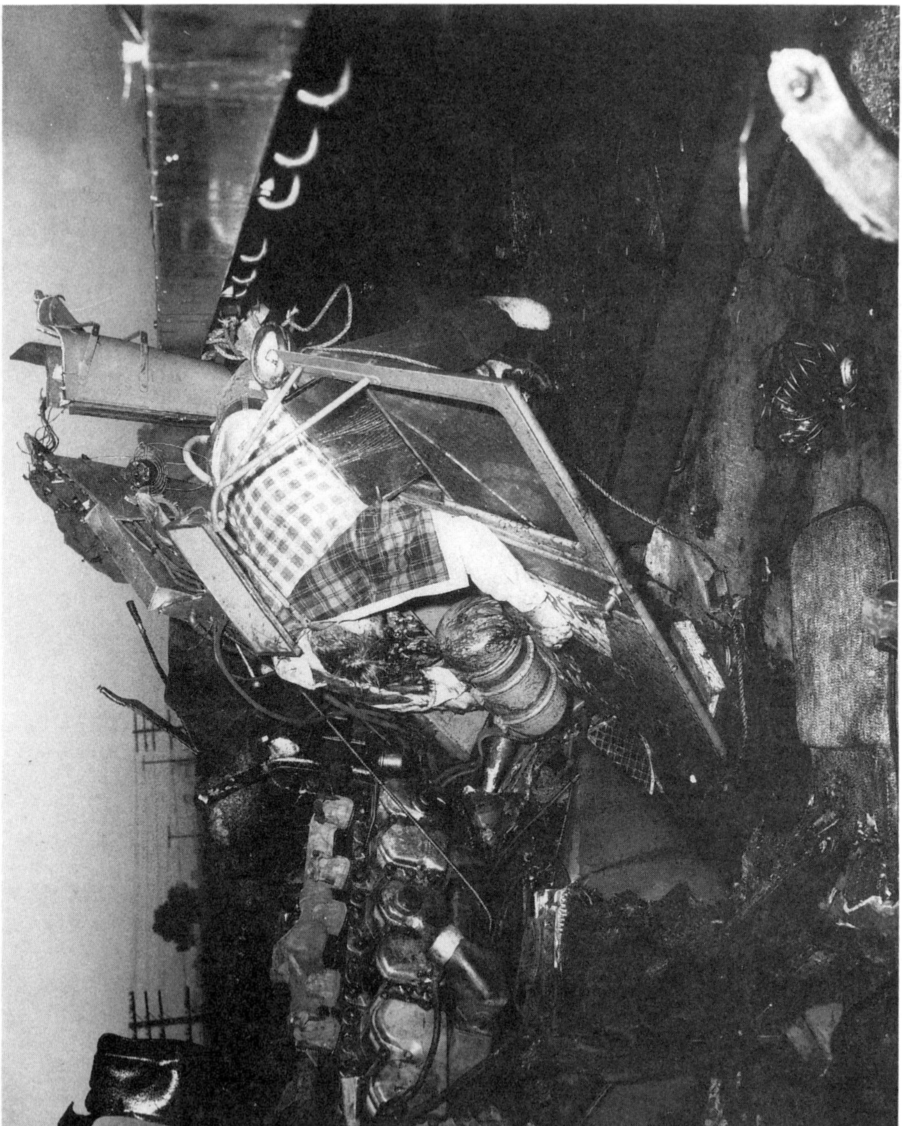

Missouri State Highway Patrol chemist does a blood alcohol extraction using the titration method, using the colori-metric blood ranges. Some individuals automatically test .03 of 1% due to alcohol and other substances in their body and the blood test is much more accurate.

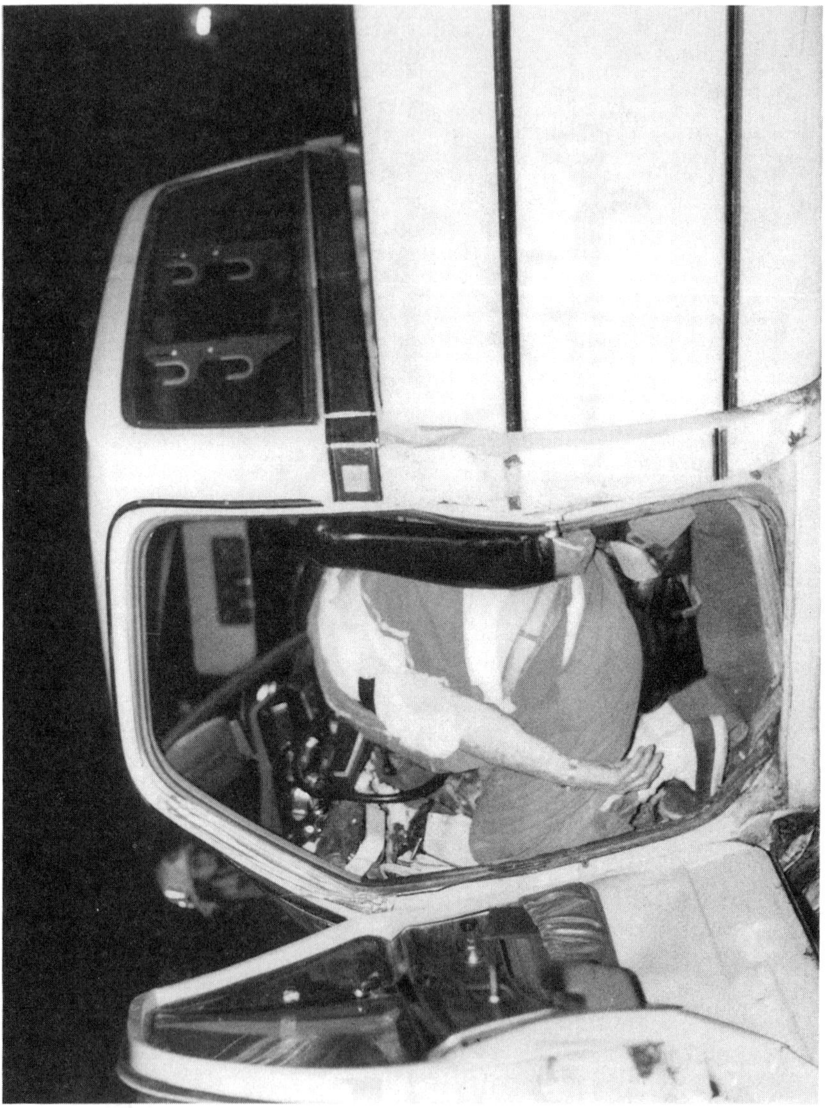

Fatal accident in Joplin (Photo courtesy Stephen D. Weston Jasper County Sheriff's Department).

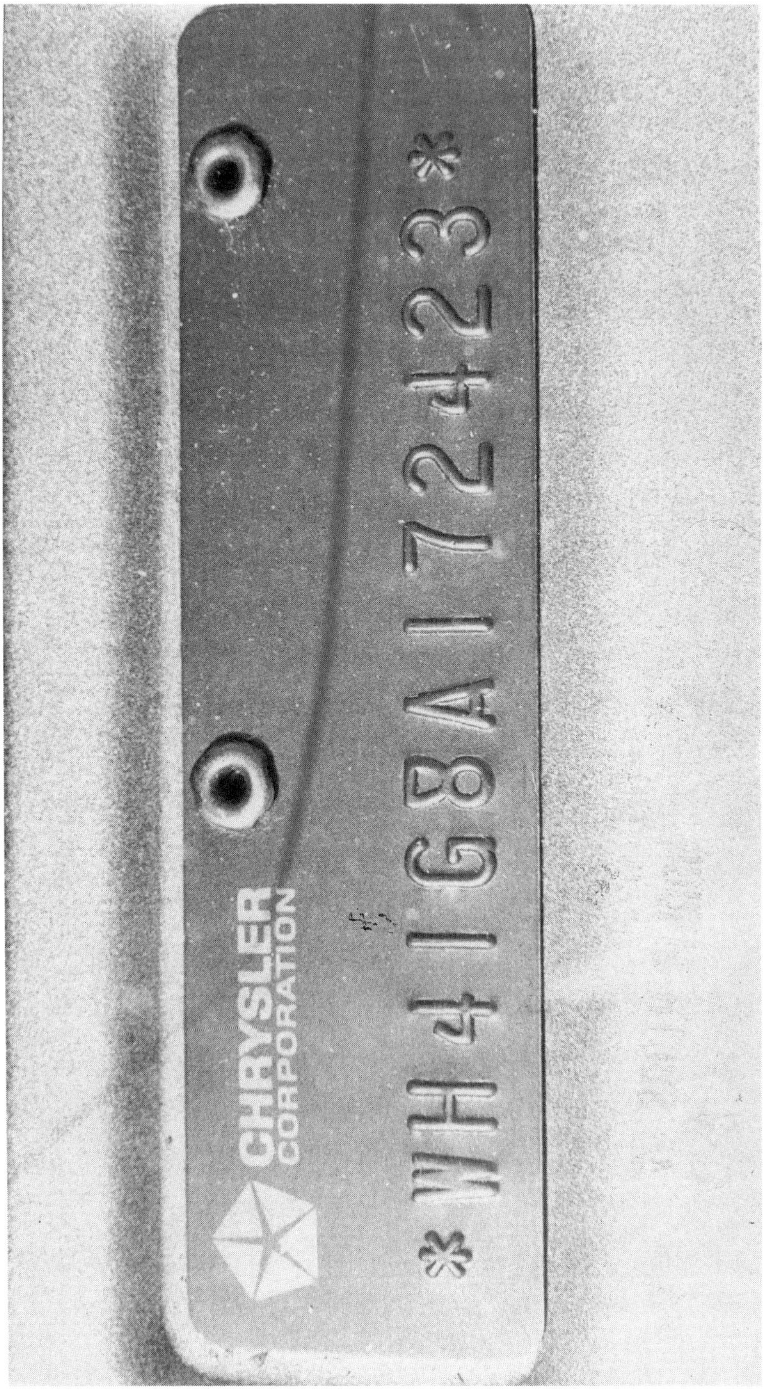

Close-up of photographs of even the simplest evidence can be impressive to a jury and turn an otherwise close case into a conviction of the guilty.

Pieces of broken headlights from the scene with a hit and run match those found on the accused's bumper grill.

Leaving scene accident - Photo of front of vehicle to be compared with close-up of missing/recovered chrome pieces.

Leaving scene accident - Captain Davis matches recovered hubcap to other hubcap of suspect vehicle.

Close-up photo of damaged area missing part of chrome on leaving scene accident case.

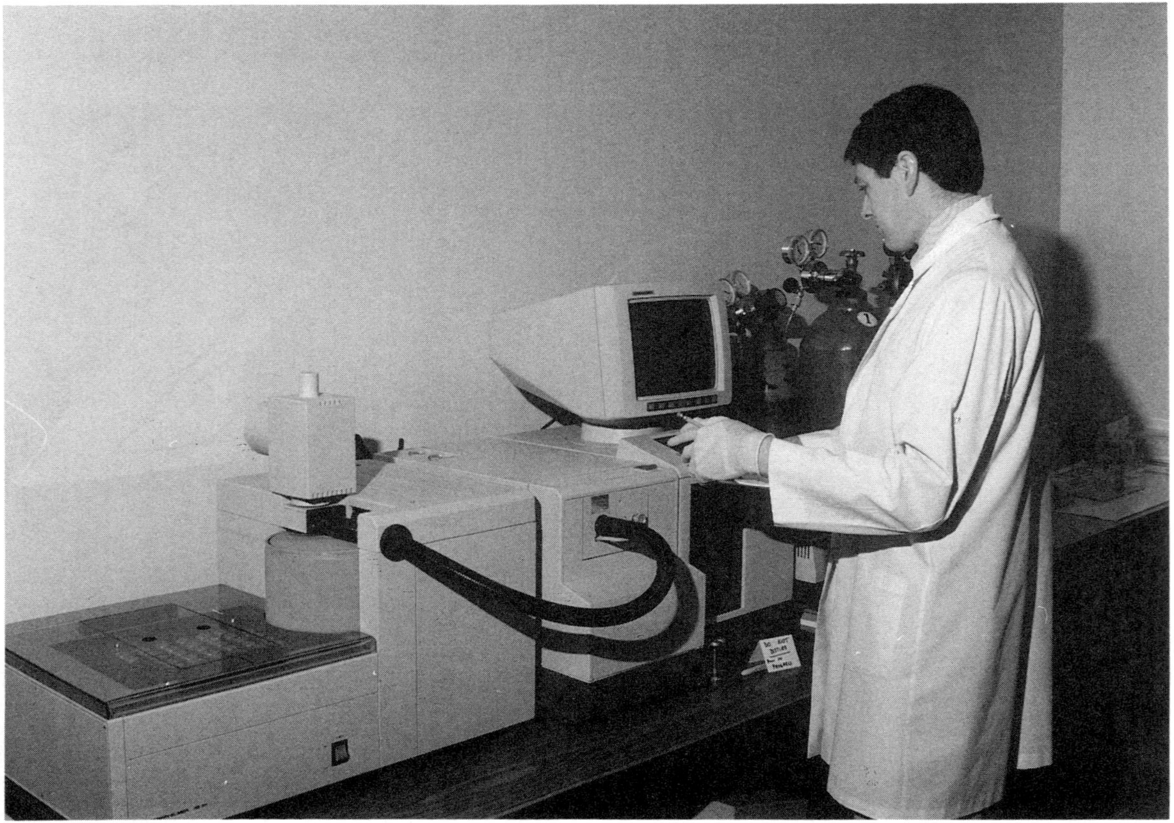

Forensic chemist Bill Barbaker performs a Headspace Gas Chromatograph analysis of blood alcohols at the Missouri State Highway Patrol Crime Laboratory in Jefferson City.

Have A
Happy
Day

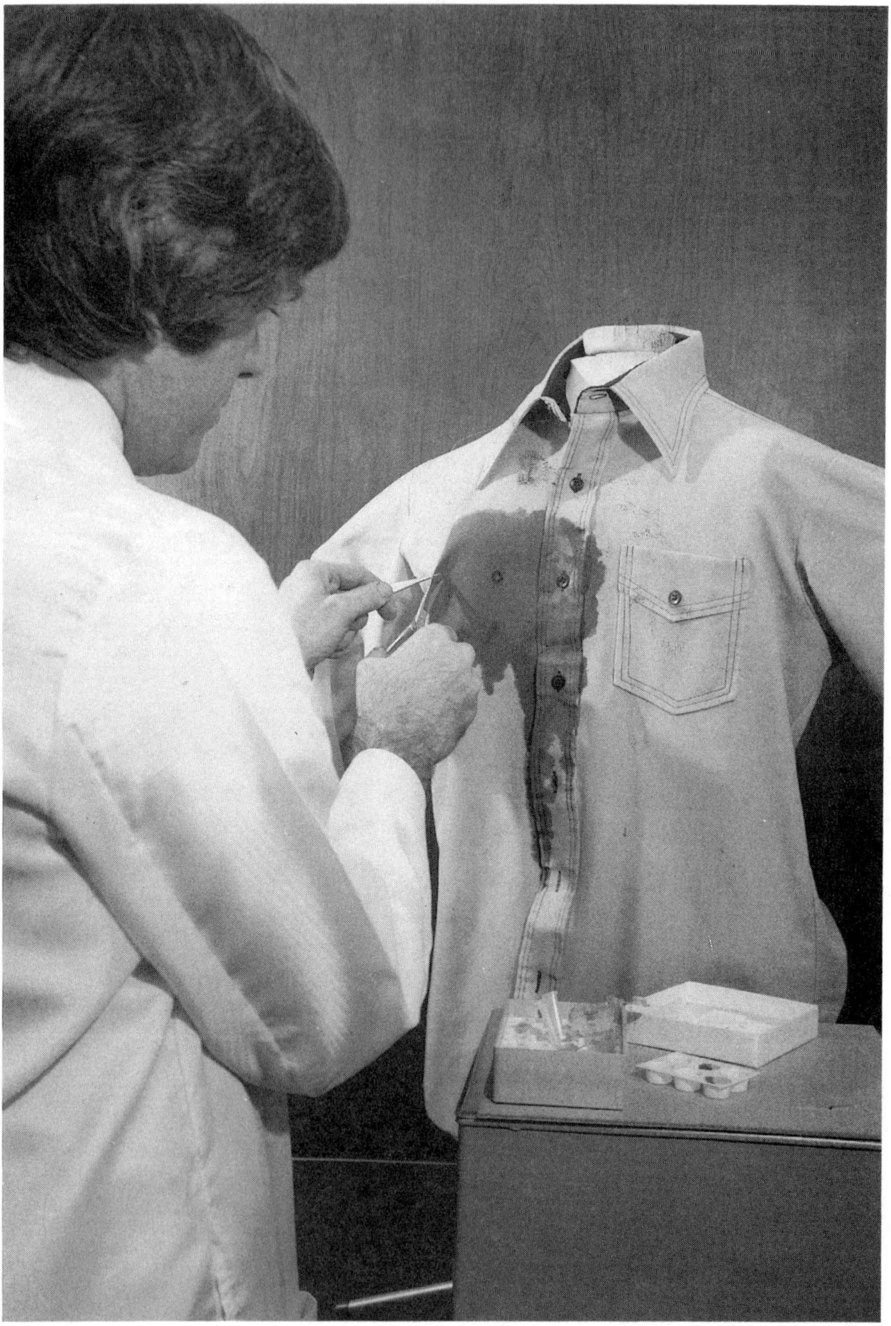

Tom Grant, Missouri State Highway Patrol, takes threads from a shirt preparatory to running an absorption clution test to check for A, B or O blood group, and for the iso-enzyme testing.

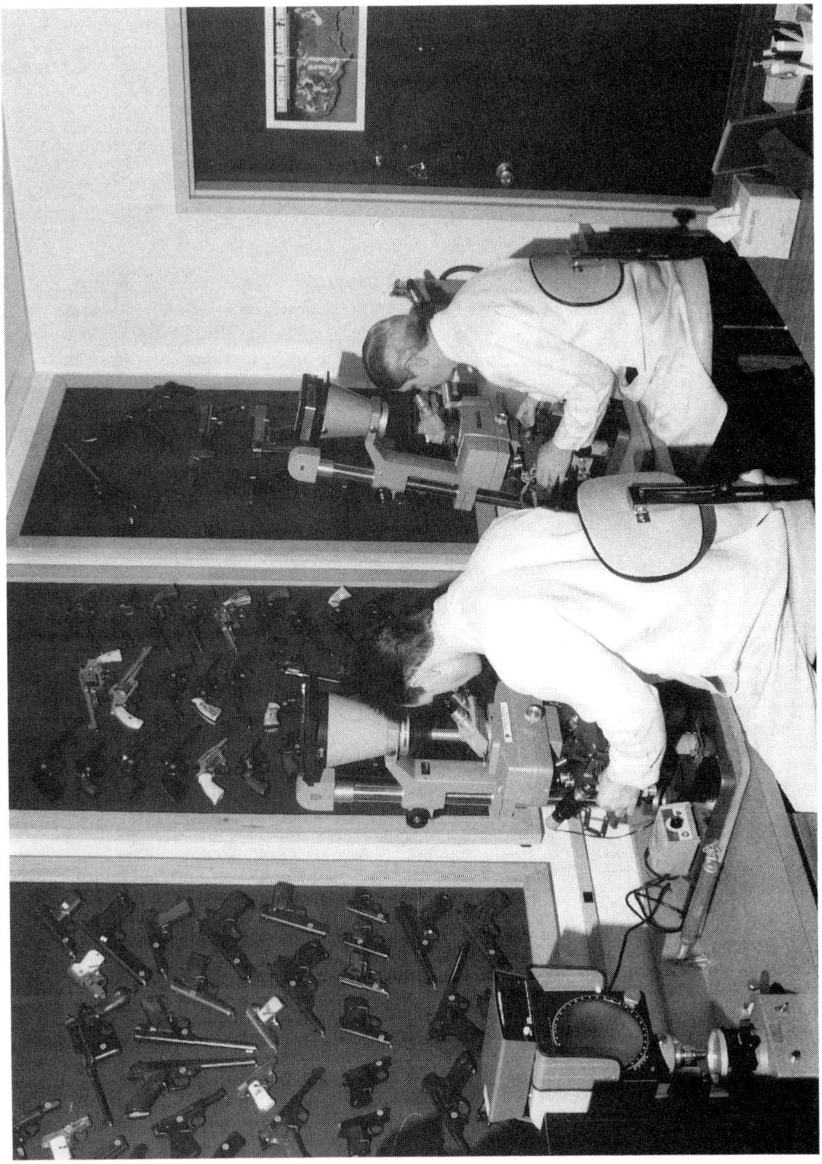

Forensic Analyst I Todd Garrison and Forensic Analyst Supervisor Thomas Buel Perform Forensic microscopic examination of bullets and cartridge casings at the Missouri State Highway Patrol Crime Laboratory in Jefferson City.

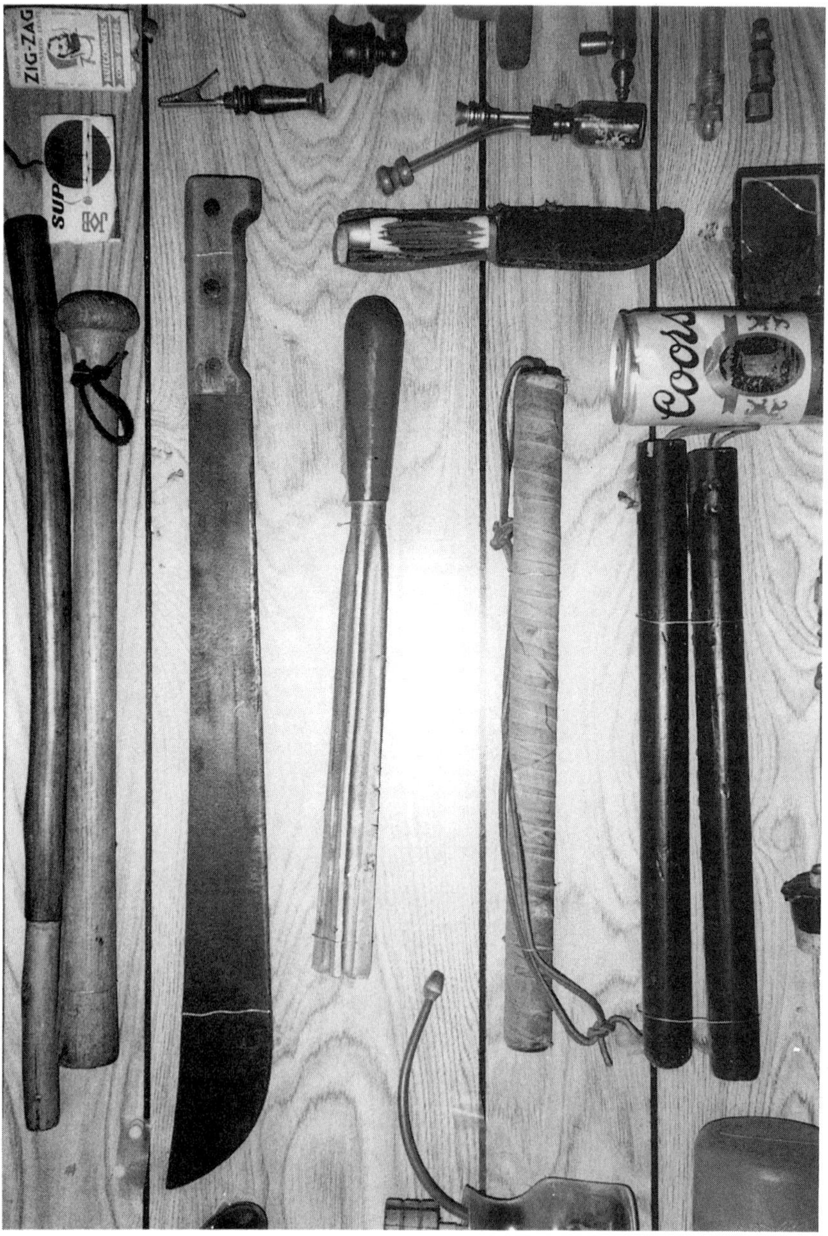

Homemade weapons, a class D felony, deadly and dangerous (Branson Police Department).

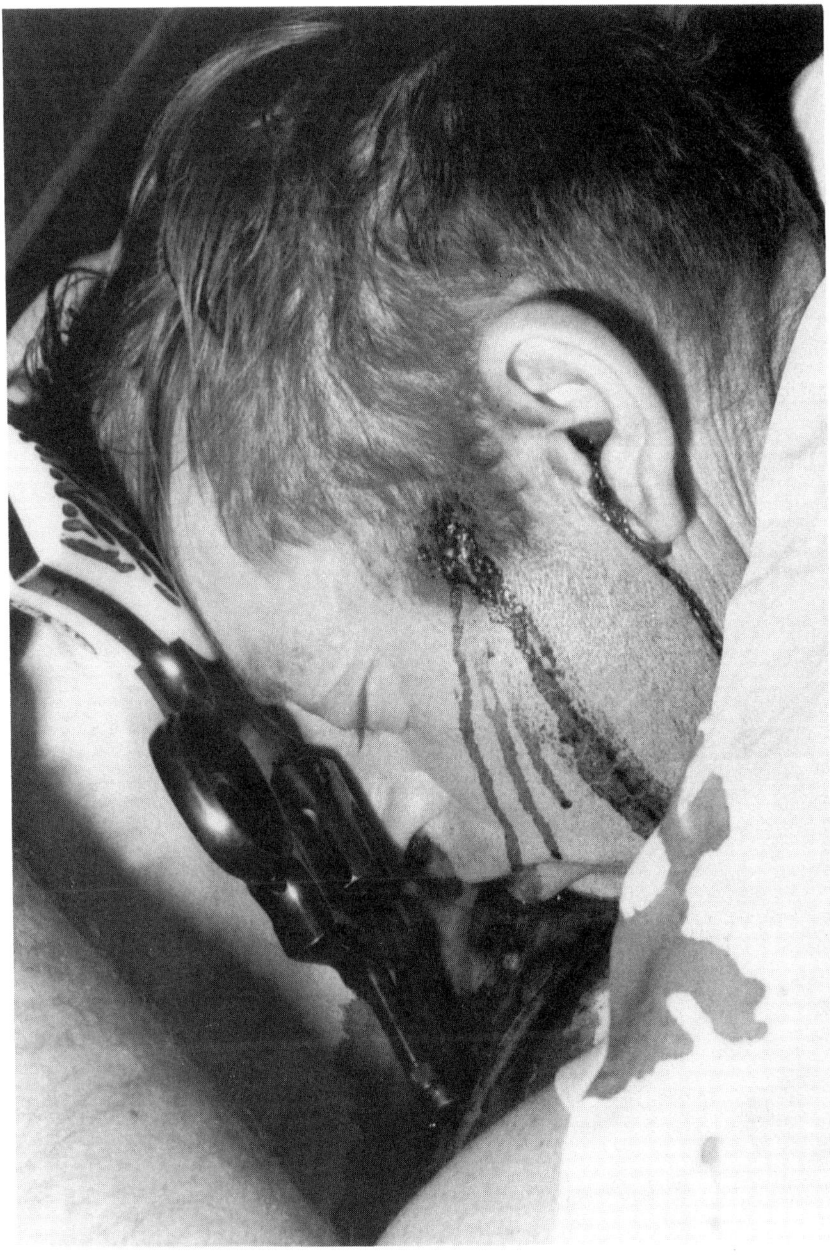

Entry Wound on deceased showing powder burns and tatooing from close range.

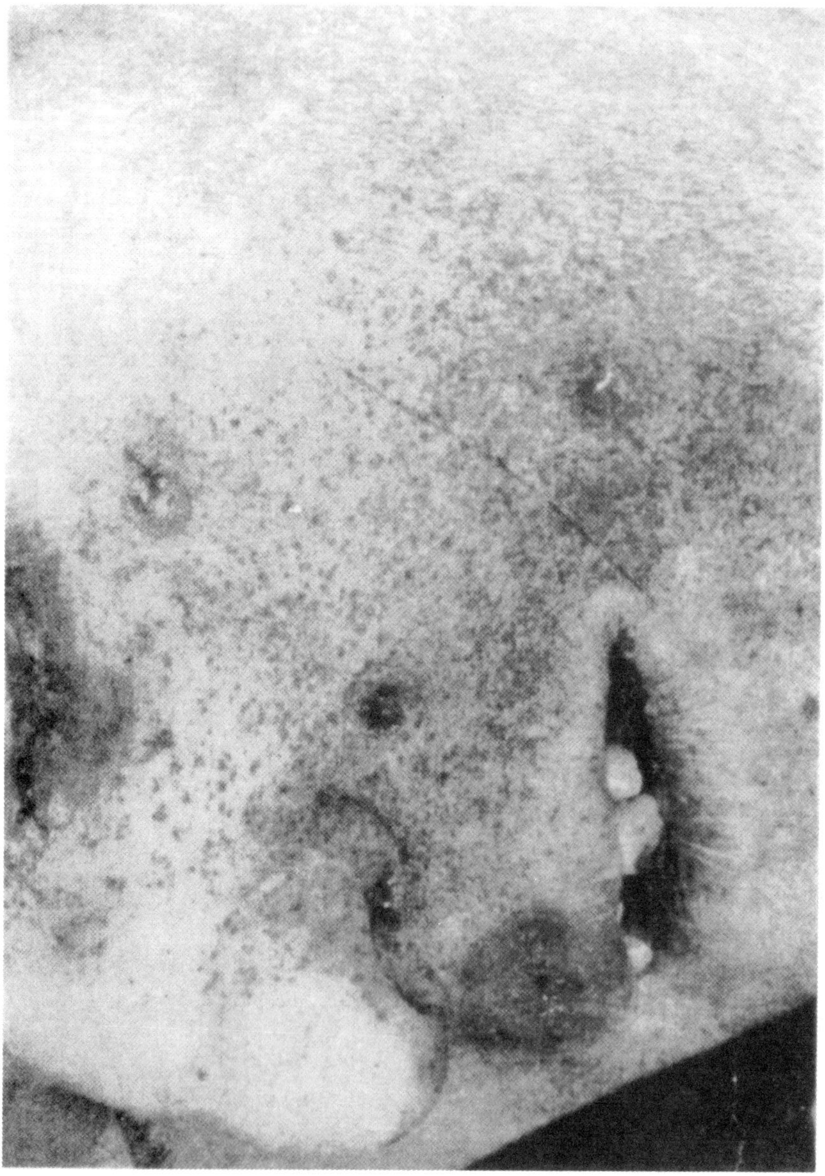

Chemists can determine the distance from which fire arms were discharged from the deceased by the "tatooing" of the powder burns.

Blood splatters are used to assist in determining where the victim was, and in what position at the time the shot was fired.

Blood splatters tell a forensic chemist much about the angle and force of blows.

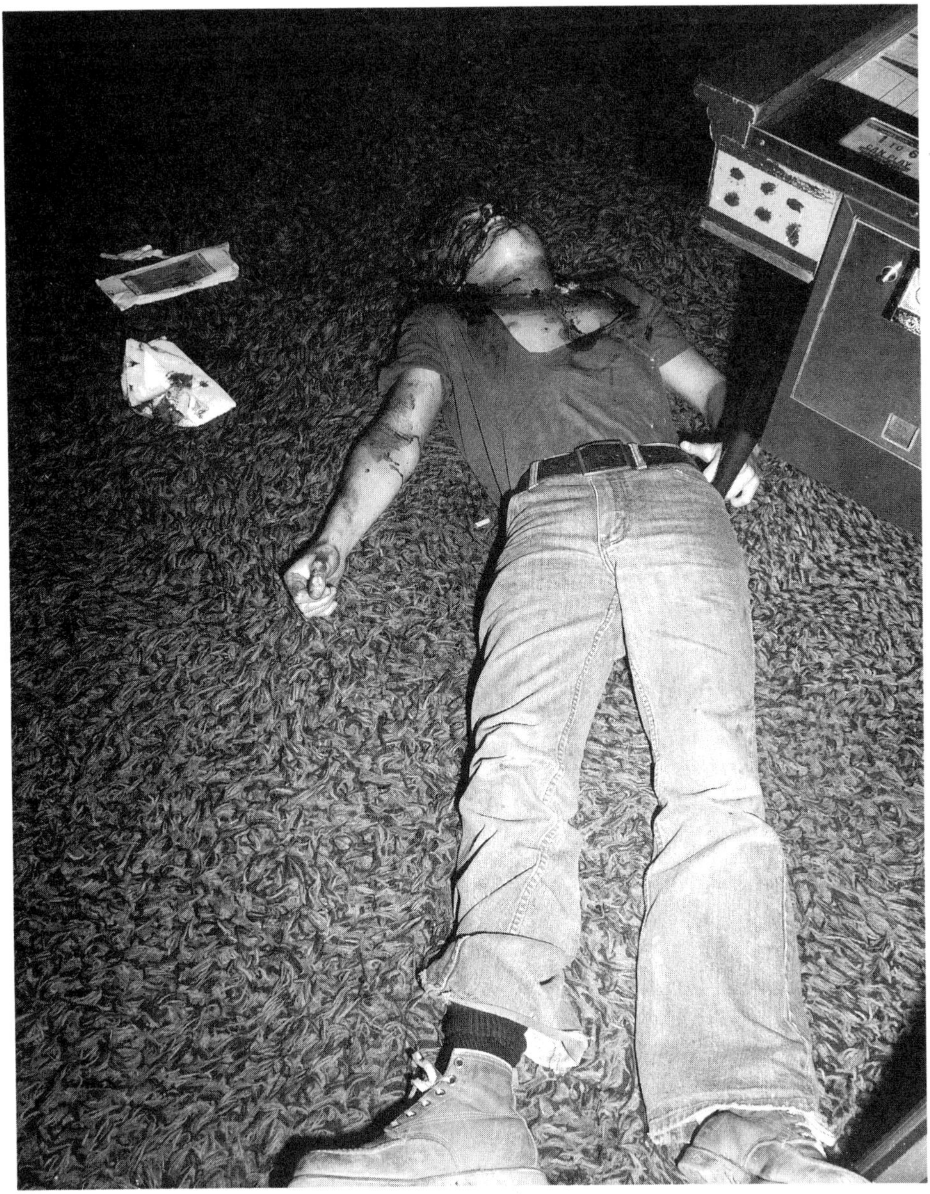

Chapter 12

The War on Drugs

"Find me a 40 to 50 year old person who didn't have a go-around with drugs, and I'll show you somebody who was a social invalid."

Don Johnson

"Consider somebody who wants to smoke a joint of marijuana. If he's caught, he goes to jail. Now is that moral? I think it's absolutely disgraceful for our government to be destroying their lives, putting them in jail. That's the issue to me."

Milton Friedman, 1991
Nobel Prize Winning Economist

Missouri Marijuana: A Bountiful Harvest

Police are losing the war on drugs. As long as demand remains high, enterprising persons will always invent new ways to manufacture and transport (mule) drugs.

We are winning the war on drugs in the classroom. With training and education, youngsters will learn that drugs are bad for your body, expensive and illegal.

Marijuana doesn't get as much publicity as cocaine, but it is still the most popular illegal drug. There are a large number of pot users willing to pay high prices, which keeps the cost high. The national war on drugs has helped reduce the number of marijuana smokers, but demand remains strong.

The *Kansas City Star* in 1991 estimated 100,000 people in the metropolitan Kansas City area are using marijuana at least once a month and 25,000 using it weekly or daily.

Eradication programs, tougher border patrols, fewer marijuana dealers (many having been already arrested), and diminished supply because of weather conditions and other factors, have increased the price. An increasing source is indoor cultivation.

The National Organization for Reform of Marijuana Laws (NORML) estimates 40 million people smoke pot nationwide.

Cocaine

Cocaine used to be a rich person's drug. No more. The powder is now being consumed by blue collar workers, college students, and high school teenagers.

Young female users look to achieve an intimacy in cocaine they cannot find naturally which comes from a dysfunctional family with a poor father role model or no father. Cocaine users are nearly always victims of grandiosity, seeing themselves as "unique" or "special" and the reversal of this sense of uniqueness is essential in the successful treatment of cocaine patients.

Ninety percent of cocaine patients have one or more parents with a drinking problem.

As in all drug patients, urine screen testing is needed and aftercare sessions once a week are a must. Cocaine treatment alumni need phone numbers to call and may need nightly recovery program meetings.

Physical rehabilitation is important, and many adult males having heart attacks under the age of 40 are regular cocaine users.

Peer support groups are a must for adolescents as patients need to listen to people their own age to lean on each other.

Who is in danger of being a potential user? Second and third shift workers, people who work in isolation, people with two jobs, nursing staffs working nights and surgical personnel, and other high risk occupations involving high stress, hyperactivity and image issues.

Stopping Cocaine

Given the power of the Columbian cartels, cocoa leaf production will increase. The epidemic will not somehow fade away. It will not deline sufficiently as long as supplies are abundant and prices are low.

Over 22 million Americans have admitted using cocaine at least once. Overdose complaints have soared more than 700 percent since 1983. The emergency room trend of overdose complaints is a clear sign that cocaine dependency is taking hold.

Taking the offensive against cocaine will take time, cost more money, and will include:

1. *Diplomacy*. Diplomatic priorities are needed in Columbia, Mexico, Peru, and Bolivia the most implicated in cocaine production and trafficking. Extraditing and prosecuting major traffickers is a primary objective. Destroying cocaine processing laboratories and warehouses is a major objective and economic pressure including trade sanctions should be used as a bargaining tool.
2. *Interdiction*. Bulk shipments of cocaine are concealed in air-freight and seaborne cargo. Customs must adopt pressure point tactics inspecting all shipments in a particular airport or harbor.
3. *Targeting traffickers* is a top priority. There is a decapitation strategy aimed at busting major American dealers and key players in the Columbian cartels.
4. *The Demand Side*. Prevention is one of the least expensive items. Every addict who stops using becomes a walking advertisement for abstinence. America has no choice–it must begin to fight back.

Crack

Crack is a highly potent, extremely addictive form of cocaine that can kill after just one use. Crack is more life threatening because it is a purer form of the drug and reaches the brain faster when smoked. The result is a more intense *high* for about 10 minutes, but the higher you go up, the farther you have to fall.

Crack seems cheap at first, but gets more expensive fast because you need more to keep from coming down. You get addicted before you know it, and some are addicted after just one use.

What Does Cocaine Actually Do?

Researchers believe the sense of stimulation that cocaine causes is from nerve cells in the brain being activated to release *dopamine*, a natural chemical in the brain that causes an increased sense of alertness and pleasure.

Cocaine tricks the brain into producing dopamine and blocks the nerve's ability to return to normal, the result being a continued feeling of pleasure for 10-20 minutes.

The more it is used, the more dopamine is depleted, which results in the user's inability to feel pleasure without the drug. After continued use of cocaine, the brain loses its ability to control the release of dopamine so that even small amounts of the drug can cause severe dopamine reactions in the form of seizures or sudden bursts of psychotic behavior.

> **RULE: COCAINE IS HIGHLY ADDICTIVE. IT TRICKS, DEPLETES, AND TRIGGERS. IT IS DANGEROUS, EXPENSIVE, AND ILLEGAL.**

Ice

Ice is not a new drug, but a smokeable version of an old one—crystallized methamphetamine—known as *crystal meth.*

Smoking ice provides a high for 8 hours or more compared with less than 30 minutes for crack.

The frustrating prospect is that if the effort to stop the cocaine flow from Latin America makes crack harder to get, users will simply shift to easily available speed.

Heroin and Opium

Opium crops in the world's three major production areas, Southeast Asia, Southwest Asia, and Mexico have doubled in the past 10 years.

Chasing the dragon calms the frantic high and person gets from smoking crack cocaine and softens the landing. Heroin shows signs of a dangerous resurrection known on the streets as a "parachute".

Cooked crack, crystallized with heroin, prolongs the high and reduces the after shock of depression and suicidal ideas that often occur when crack wears off.

Synthetic Heroin

China white is several hundred times more powerful than heroin, and even extremely small amounts can be fatal.

The presence of China white (also know as Persian heroin and gasoline dope) has killed several hundred people.

Victims are at the mercy of drug dealers who do not check the quality of drugs manufactured and sold. Three granules are enough for one dose, and is one of the most powerful drugs known.

Methamphetamine (Speed)

Made in a growing number of clandestine laboratories, methamphetamine (speed) is surging across the nation.

Speed is a powerful stimulant to the nervous system. It started with diet pills diverted for illegal use and popularity jumped in recent years with the increase of makeshift laboratories, turning out an off-white powder that can be snorted, injected or taken in a beverage.

Speed is simple to make and lucrative to market: $175 of chemicals yield a pound of pure meth which can then be weakened to make two pounds and sold for $32,000. Although raids on clandestine laboratories are increasing, huge quantities of speed are still being made.

There has been a sharp increase and pattern of agitated, violent behavior in addicts that resembles paranoid schizophrenia.

Users of crack can turn from the cocaine derivative to meth (known as *crystal* or *crank*) as well as speed. In addition to the cheaper "high", speed does not have the deadly reputation that cocaine has.

Growth in meth production poses new problems. Unlike cocaine which begins as a plant grown overseas, speed is synthesized in domestic laboratories, if Columbians do not traffic it up from South America. All that is needed are chemicals, most readily available in the United States.

Federal officials have tried to limit the manufacture of meth by outlawing chemicals like phenyl-2-propane, used in the production of perfume, and ephedrine, the active ingredient in several over-the-counter cold medications.

No special expertise is necessary, although the flammable materials involved pose a certain risk. One gallon of meth creates two gallons of toxic waste that is often dumped beside the road or left to contaminate rented houses that the drug cookers have abandoned. The waste from meth production includes carcinogens, mutagens, explosives, and hazardous metals like lead and mercury. Plastic gloves, boots, and coveralls are standard with breathing apparatus.

Vicks Inhalers

Meth is an illegal drug but the Food and Drug Administration (FDA) has approved a combination of ingredients for use in Vicks inhalers which is an isomer or diluted form of meth. There is a special law exempting Vicks inhalers, a nose spray sold over the counter.

Proving a Drug Case

It is unlawful to possess any quantity, however small, of a controlled drug. Certain drugs may not be possessed under any circumstance (marijuana, cocaine, LSD, crack, meth, stimulants) and others may be possessed pursuant to a valid prescriptions in limited quantities (codeine, desoxyn).

If you are charged with possession of a controlled drug that may be obtained by prescription, you have the burden to prove your possession is legal.

It is illegal to manufacture, possess, have under control, sell, give, distribute, compound, cultivate, grow, or by any other process, produce or prepare any illegal drugs.

You may not transport, carry, or convey in any vehicle, boat, or aircraft. A vehicle used to transport any of the drugs is subject to forfeiture by public or private auction with proceeds going to the state. The arresting officer takes possession and secures it in a safe place, then through the Prosecutor, files a forfeiture petition in Circuit Court declaring the vehicle a public nuisance.

All crimes, particularly drug offenses, must be committed *intentionally* and willfully which must be proved *beyond a reasonable doubt.* The state must prove you had the *intent to possess*, which can be shown by a large quantity of drugs easily visible on the premises. If only a few particles of marijuana are found near you, or in your car, it will be difficult to show you *knew* about and *intended* to possess the drug. *Knowledge may be shown by circumstantial evidence* or by incriminating statements. *Your mere presence* in an apartment or house, along with other people, is insufficient to establish possession of a drug but your proximity or location to the drugs may, in itself, support *constructive* possession. The possession of narcotics need not be exclusive where it is reasonable to infer intentional control and possession, but if there is joint control, there must be *some other evidence* to link you with the drugs. Control of premises in not automatically deemed possession of all things therein. A drug is possessed where the evidence shows that you had *knowledge* of the drug, access to it, and was involved in its use, which is the concept of *constructive possession.*

Drugs legally obtained must be kept in their original container. Pharmacists, physicians, veterinarians, and dentists, must keep strict records, which are open to the law officer. It is illegal to possess narcotic paraphernalia or devices, for the use of any prohibited drug.

You may not purchase or attempt to obtain any narcotic drug by fraud, deceit, misrepresentation, subterfuge, or by forgery, alteration of a prescription or written order, concealment of a material fact, or use of a false name or address.

Police must get a court order before any illegal drugs are destroyed. The order must specify all the details of the destruction and a return must be filed with the court within ten days.

Before drug charges are filed, the drug is analyzed by a qualified chemist. The exact type of drug is determined and botanical name (example: marijuana is botanically known as *cannabis sativa L*) in order to properly allege the crime. A field test is not legally sufficient.

The most common problems experienced in the prosecuting of drug offenses are those of arrest, search, and seizure. The arrest must be legal and there must be probable cause to search. Police try to make consent searches whenever possible to avoid these problems.

If the Prosecutor has demonstrated a valid arrest, search, and seizure at the suppression hearing, and has a valid chain of custody on the drugs, few defendants request jury trials.

In sale cases, the usual defense is entrapment unless you deny the sale. Entrapment means the criminal intent did not originate with your mind, but was planted or was the result of the officer's creative ability. If police or an informant solicit, encourage, or induce you to engage in conduct when you were not ready and willing to engage, it is entrapment.

Field Tests

Police use a quick, presumptive test that uses chemicals in a special kit to decide, at the crime scene, whether a "white powdery substance" is cocaine or baking soda. It determines the presence of specific drugs, blood, or gun powder.

The test does not tell with virtual certainty the presence of illegal drugs, but enables police to go forward with their investigation. Field tests are not admissible into evidence since they are not scientifically reliable.

Drug Courier Profile

In 1989, the U.S. Supreme Court in *U.S. vs. Sokolow,* allowed police to use a *profile analysis* to stop individuals on a hunch or suspicion they are transporting drugs based on:

1. Out-of-state license plates
2. Mexican or black males occupying a motor vehicle
3. Rental car checking to a third person
4. Out-of-state newspapers and maps in the car
5. Presence of air fresheners to hide the smell of drugs
6. Occupants carrying weapons or large sums of cash
7. Rear end of the vehicle riding low indicating heavy weight in the trunk
8. Nervousness of the occupants or inconsistencies in their stories
9. An older car but with new tires
10. Traveling from a source state
11. Presence of taped boxes
12. Other indications believed by police to commonly exist by drug transporters.

Courts disallow sole reliance on the Drug Courier Profile for the basis of an arrest. It may be used in conjunction with other suspicions the veteran trained police officer has observed. The law still requires police to prove they had probable cause to stop and arrest.

Marijuana sniffing dogs are often used in the *investigative detention* to sniff automobiles or luggage.

Drug Testing in the Work Place: (Urine and You're Out)

The U.S. Supreme Court has ruled that employer urine testing is legal investigation but regulates a perceived threat to the public and employee safety in the work place. The court considered whether such testing impermissibly infringes upon the Constitutional rights of citizens.

State and federal governments require certain industries to submit to searches and tests. Private employers can require, by *employment contract,* employees to submit to urine analysis testing.

Plastic Bags, Vials, and Rolling Papers

Certain containers and packages give police extra suspicion to search further and suspect the presence of drugs. If police look in your car and observe drug paraphernalia (bongs, pipes, roach clips, syringes, zig zag papers) or containers that are often used (vials, plastic bags) they search further to look for drugs.

Some containers, although *opaque* do not support a reasonable expectation of privacy because their contents can be inferred from the outward appearance.

Drug Package Profile

The U.S. Postal Service and DEA developed a Drug Package Profile to stop drug trafficking through use of the mails. The government decided your Fourth Amendment notion of being *secure* in your *personal effects* must give way to society's interests in law enforcement to win the war on drugs.

The Profile is developed to detect mailed parcels likely to contain illegal drugs noticing:

1. Size and shape of the package
2. Package heavily taped to close and seal all openings
3. Handwritten labels
4. Unusual return names and addresses
5. Unusual odors coming from the package
6. Fictitious return addressee
7. Destination of parcel
8. Multiple packages sent to same address, but to different persons
9. Packages mailed to arrive for delivery on a repeated basis.

Suspicious packages are removed from conveyor belts of mainstream mail and placed in a special area for a trained narcotic sniffing dog. If the dog alerts to the package, a search warrant is obtained, the package opened, and contents analyzed, and a controlled delivery made and an arrest.

Mail sent by Federal Express, United Parcel Service, or other *private agencies* can be opened by those companies legally, but if it is the U.S. Postal Service (the *U.S. Government*) it can only legally be opened with a search warrant based on probable cause.

The Postal Service has rules regulating itself to prevent arbitrary openings, but these agency regulations can be ignored and courts will still uphold the profile.

You do not have a Constitutional right of privacy in the outward appearance of your mailed package. The fact that many innocent packages are held up and delayed in the mail, and subject to random seizures, has been given little attention by the courts.

Packages are delayed and as long as the delay is reasonably brief, it is legal. Delays of up to a week are allowed.

Taking a Bite Out of Crime: Dogged Pursuit (The K-9 on Trial)

Since 1900, our canine friends have not had the best job assignments. At the turn of the century, New York City police first used police dogs as a "first responder". Later, visions of well trained and ferocious German Shepherd war dogs appeared during World War II. In the early 1960's the use of the German Shepherds by "Bull" Connor, in Birmingham, left an unfavorable impression. In Vietnam, many were used to sniff mines, alert soldiers to trip wires or enemy ambushes.

The growth of K-9 units soon became a fad used by many police departments. The "bite and fight" image was replaced by "crowd control" duties, later for search and rescue missions, and the images of police dogs improved. Citizens began to view police dogs in a more favorable light as success rates soared. K-9 unit perception has come a long way, the "old dogs are gone" and a transition has occurred.

The FAA has 100 dogs in major airports. Major police departments now use dogs in a variety of functions, including explosion detection, screening and clearing areas, looking for escaped convicts and missing persons.

Their keen sense of smell, by different estimates, has been held to be at least 100 times more sensitive than human's. The ability of dogs to detect the scent of humans, explosives, or drugs, is unquestioned *if* properly trained. An *alert* or *reaction* caused the dog to bark, whine, snarl, or paw in the area of the scent. Some dogs are passive indicators and sit quietly at the smell of drugs.

The dog reacts to the scent, and not the *presence* of drugs.

It is not documented whether dogs react in different degrees depending upon the strength of the scent, or quality of drugs found.

Those who contend evidence of *dog sniffs* is legal evidence claim the use of the dog's olfactory process is not a physical search. Especially in public places, the Fourth Amendment has been held not applicable because the accused *does not have any justifiable expectation of privacy* in the molecules of the sniffed air, as no physical intrusion or trespass has occurred. Even if held to be a search, it is regarded as "reasonable" under the Fourth Amendment.

Search warrants have been upheld if there is strong foundation of canine reliability and handler expertise. Courts determine: (1) Did a search and seizure occur? (2) Was the use of the dog reasonable?

Passengers of commercial airlines, trains and buses have little reasonable expectation of privacy and use of dogs will increase.

Police dogs will increase because:

1. Domestic terrorism will increase the need for explosive detection;
2. Narcotics trafficking and the burgeoning war on drugs will demand dogs trained, as no equipment has yet been invented to replace a dog's nose;
3. Budget restraints, decreasing funds, and the need for increased police forces will add to the demand.

Male German Shepherds have especially demonstrated size, temperament, loyalty, quick adaptability and intelligence.

The I-44 Pipeline

Daily across the bustling interstate highways cutting across Missouri from Joplin to St. Louis, police take in pounds of illegal dope as the interstate drug pipeline continues to flow.

Day after day, hundreds of pounds of drugs are transported along Interstate 44 stretching nearly 700 miles from Texas to Illinois and connecting to highways to both coasts.

Each year thousands of pounds of marijuana and hundreds of pounds of cocaine are seized, accounting for millions of dollars "street value".

The imaginative ways of stashing drugs has increased: hidden in furniture; false compartments; inside food; spare tire compartments and spare tires; wrapped in layers of paper; smeared with mustard and pepper to throw off drug sniffing dogs.

Use of air fresheners, coffee grounds, inside extra layers of sealed trash bags fools some patrolman but not their dogs.

For every 10 lbs of seized, 100 more lbs. get through to anxious users.

Forfeiture Laws ("Seize and Freeze")

Federal and state laws provide that any vehicle, boat, or plane which transports *any quantity* of drugs (the zero tolerance rule), plus any money, guns, or anything else of value in connection with drugs be declared a *public nuisance* and forfeited to the government.

The *res* (thing) is seized by police. The owner or other interested person must then come forward to explain why he was unaware of the presence of drugs.

The owner may take the Fifth Amendment and refuse to answer, but if so, has little chance of getting his property returned.

It is a civil lawsuit and no *stay* of the criminal trial is granted. Interrogatories, depositions, and other discovery may occur so that each side may better prepare for trial.

The civil forfeiture proceeding occurs whether or not the defendant is ever convicted and is separate from the criminal charge.

Defenses used to have property returned include:

1. "The defense of *$8,850*"
2. "The defense of *Pearson Yacht*"
3. Duress, necessity and impossibility
4. Equitable estoppel
5. Entrapment
6. Stolen property defense
7. DeMinimis defense
8. Defendant acquitted in criminal case.

The defense of *$8,850,* (undue government delay) is the one most frequently used. In bringing lawsuits, the government sometimes delays and may have violated deadlines. Courts use the *Barker-Wingo Balancing Test* which balances:

1. The length of the delay
2. The reason for the delay
3. The defendant's assertion of his Constitutional rights
4. The prejudice to the defendant.

RULE: ALWAYS DEMAND A SPEEDY HEARING IN A FORFEITURE CASE AND CLAIM CONSTITUTIONAL RIGHTS.

In the Pearson Yacht defense, if you have property stolen or taken from you without permission, it would serve no purpose to forfeit your property. If your vehicle is seized and drugs are found, you will have to prove what you have reasonably done to prevent the criminal use of such property.

In the *equitable estoppel* defense, you argue the government agent caused you to take a wrong action or fail to take action in time to avoid the forfeiture.

In the *deMinimis* defense, you argue that the drugs found were so small or that your car was so expensive or important to you that a forfeiture would be against public policy and be extremely harsh. It seems unfair to forfeit a $30,000 car if only a small residue of drugs were found.

In the *acquittal* defense, if you are subsequently cleared of the criminal charge, you can claim that forfeiture would be unjust.

Forfeiture laws enacted to combat drug scourges need to be drastically rewritten.

The laws were aimed at big time dealers. The idea is not to send them to jail, but to deprive them lavish possessions—fancy cars, yachts, and mansions—that their illegal drug trade has allowed them to acquire.

Instead, automobiles are being taken from casual drug users stopped for minor traffic violations.

A conviction is not necessary before police can confiscate your car. Administrative seizures can be undertaken by the state and later *adopted* by the federal government, and whether you are ever convicted of any crime, the *burden of proof is on you.*

In state court, police must report to the seizure within three days, and within five days thereafter must file a petition with the court. In federal court, authorities take plenty of time, advertise your name in *U.S.A. Today,* and presume you are guilty.

Unless forfeiture laws are reformed, the nation's drug war increasingly becomes a pretext for exploiting citizens.

Lawyer's Fees

The money might come from drug trafficking, insider trading, loan sharking, embezzlement, or burglary. Until recently, two things were always true. No matter how ill-gotten it may be, the wrong doer was always free to spend it on a lawyer. The lawyer was always free to accept it.

In the past years to curb the narcotics trade, prosecutors now challenge this time honored tradition where legal fees are not held sacrosanct if traced to illegal sources.

The *Federal Comprehensive Forfeiture Act of 1983* forces racketeers and narcotics dealers disgorge illegal profits become the exclusive property of the United States.

This powerful law gives federal Prosecutors the right to *seize and freeze* your funds before trial (but not take back the fees after trial). In addition, anything purchased with such funds such as boats, planes, land or jewelry can be traced and seized.

The Sixth Amendment guarantees a lawyer but not a lawyer of one's choice. Thus, such illegal monies can be seized by the government and the accused required to obtain a public defender.

As U.S. District Judge David Edelstein put it:

> "In a same manner that a defendant cannot obtain a Rolls Royce with the fruits of a crime, he cannot be permitted to obtain the services of the Rolls Royce of attorneys with these same tainted funds."

In our system of law all defendants are presumed innocent. Isn't a defendant entitled to employ a lawyer and pay by whatever funds a defendant has?

One well-known attorney states:

> "This practice enables the government, literally at whim, to prevent certain defendants from retaining private council and prevent certain lawyers with demonstrated expertise from participating in the process."

Lawyer's fees are expensive. The more experienced the lawyer, the higher the fee, since he charges for his *time* and *service*.

Forfeiting Freedom

We can suffer a greater injury from our war on drugs by surrendering our sacred freedoms in order to win the war.

Drug abuse is a serious matter. But the sacrifice of basic human rights and the fundamentals of democratic principles are too great a price to pay. We can meet the challenges of these times without selling off our American birthrights and our liberties.

When Missouri forfeits the property, 90% goes to the school fund. Most large forfeitures are now being *adopted* by federal agents in which 100% goes to the federal government.

If you're caught driving with enough marijuana for one joint in your glove compartment that your cousin Betty stashed, they can forfeit your entire car.

The U.S. Supreme Court has upheld the right of police officers to search your car, briefcases, and trunks; to sift through your trash, fly over your house and scan your backyard; secretly tape your phone of face to face conversations; to stop, detain, and question travelers who resemble drug couriers, all without a search warrant. Your car and property can be kept without a trial or conviction. Your bank accounts can be frozen, prohibiting you from hiring an attorney.

Police no longer need *reliable sources* to gain a search warrant since an anonymous tip is now plenty. A nameless phone call has now become the drug war equivalent of *probable cause.*

Whom can you trust? Not your own attorney–sometimes. The government calls upon attorneys to testify against their own clients. Attorneys have to warn their own clients that sometimes what they say to their attorney can be used against the client.

Laundered Money (Dirty Dollars)

Automobiles, antique dealers, jewelers, pawn brokers, lawyers, real estate and insurance agents, all may know something the government needs to know. The government needs to know who big cash spenders are.

Each may be the recipient of requests to purchase services, products, or property with large amounts of cash. Large cash purchases are a way for drug dealers to hide the sources and amounts of their money.

The *1970 Bank Secrecy Act* and the *1984 Tax Reform Act* are intended to reduce the use of banks to launder money. Any business or person receiving more than $10,000 in cash from one customer must report all such transactions (IRS form 8300), which must be filed within 15 days of the payment (Cash Transaction Report "CTR").

Prescribing Controlled Drugs Within the Law

State and federal pharmacy laws regulate doctors and pharmacists, which result in revocation of licenses or future loss of privileges to prescribe medicine.

When a doctor prescribes drugs, he must list the patient's full name and address, actual date the prescription is written, drug name, strength, and quantity, instructions for use of the drug, the physician's signature, doctor's complete address and DEA number, and number of refills. The prescription pads must be numbered and kept secure.

Detailed regulations prohibit the use of facsimile signature stamps, Roman numerals, office nurses to sign for a doctor, or handing out signed prescription blanks. Refills for certain drugs are forbidden, and limited refills for less addictive drugs are limited.

Occasionally, telephone prescriptions are permissible, but the doctor should follow up the telephone call with a written prescription within 72 hours. Certain drugs may only be prescribed once a month, and others may be prescribed every 90 days.

The Missouri State Board for the Healing Arts, the State board of Narcotics and Dangerous Drugs, and the DEA place restrictions on prescription and emphetamine-like drugs for hyperactivity, attention deficit disorder, obesity, and narcolepsy. Doctors must keep history and physical examination records on blood pressure, pulse, weight, height, and completion of appropriate tests.

Defending Yourself Against a Drug Arrest

Places where drug arrests most likely occur are:

1. In a car along the shoulder of a highway after being stopped for a minor traffic violation.
2. Arrested after disembarking from a plane at an airport.
3. Arrested in your home while police are serving an arrest or search warrant.
4. Arrest while selling or buying drugs.
5. Persons transporting drugs (known as "mules") are often stopped on interstate highways traveling from the West to the East Coast. Police use their *sixth sense and intuition* and look for common characteristics to decide if you fit the *Drug Courier Profile*.

If your vehicle has out-of-state plates from a *source* state (Arizona, California, or another western state), headed eastbound towards St. Louis, Chicago, Detroit, in a rental car, which has air freshener (to mask the smell of drugs), then police will separate you and the passenger and ask *routine questions*. They will inquire as to your destination, purpose and length of your trip, and the contents of your vehicle. They will then compare notes, keeping you and your passenger separated, and decide if you have give inconsistent statements.

They ask for permission to *look* in your car or sometimes for permission to *search* your car and its contents.

They sometimes use *written consent* forms, but more than likely only ask for *oral consent.* This sets up a factual situation where it is your word against theirs as to whether you consented *and they will always win.*

If you stand on your Constitutional rights and refuse permission to search, they take this to mean that you are hiding something.

If you give them consent to look or search, they will go ahead and search and find any drugs you have hidden.

Their initial stop of your car will be on some minor traffic offense, such as failing to signal a lane change, weaving, following too closely, or on interstate highways in St. Louis, Springfield, and Kansas City (designated as "urban areas" by the state and federal government), the *65* mph speed limit is *lowered to 55* and they can stop you for going one mile over the speed limit. It makes no difference as to why you're stopped, once stopped they will begin incessant questioning.

If you refuse the search, they use a drug sniffing dog. If the dog *hits* or makes an *affirmative response* on your vehicle, police consider this probable cause to search your vehicle whether or not you consent.

If police have probable cause to search your car, they will search your trunk, glove compartment, locked suitcase or other closed areas.

Police have no absolute right to detain you on the shoulder of a highway and question you beyond the non-culpable traffic offense for which you have been stopped. There is no absolute duty of a citizen to *jaw* with police and answer every question asked.

> **RULE: DRIVE STRICTLY WITHIN THE LAW AND AVOID BEING STOPPED. IF STOPPED, ANSWER THE OFFICER POLITELY, PRODUCE YOUR OPERATOR'S LICENSE, AND SAY NOTHING MORE. THE MISTAKE MOST CITIZENS MAKE IS THEY TALK TOO MUCH. THE "MOUTH" IS YOUR WORST ENEMY. IF ASKED YOUR DESTINATION, ORIGINATION, PURPOSE AND LENGTH OF YOUR TRIP, POLITELY TELL THE OFFICER YOU DECLINE TO BE INTERROGATED. IF HE HAS A TRAFFIC TICKET TO GIVE YOU, THEN GIVE IT, AS YOU DO NOT WISH TO BE DETAINED FURTHER.**

Do not aid in supplying probable cause to search your vehicle. If he asks you to get out of the vehicle—comply. Do not respond to any other demands. If he demands the key to the trunk, suitcases, glove box, or that you identify your luggage, you are not obligated to say or do anything except to respond, "Officer, I wish to resume my journey." The less you say the better.

If the officer searches and finds drugs, he may misquote or misunderstand anything you have previously said. Once it is written in his report, it is etched in stone and will be used against you at trial. Rather than say anything which may be misunderstood by him to mean consent, inconsistent statement, or confession, it is better to say nothing.

Most citizens believe that if they are polite, kind, and cooperative, the officer will go away and they can somehow fool him or trick him into not finding contraband. Don't count on this!

Should you be stopped at an airport, bus, or train station, you will be questioned if you look suspicious. If you are carrying too much luggage (or not enough), are first off the plane (or last), had a short trip (or long), paid for your ticket in cash, or if you look nervous or excited, you may be stopped and questioned by airport police, D.E.A., F.B.I., or U.S. Customs agents.

If you are innocent and have no contraband on you, you should fully cooperate and be released. If you are carrying contraband, they will not leave you alone unless you fully cooperate or satisfy their desire to conduct a complete search. They are going to search you—legally or illegally.

If you say nothing, do not respond to their questions or pay any attention and walk a straight line for the door, they have the burden of proof to show probable cause to stop you and conduct a search. If you do not add fuel to the fire by giving inconsistent statements or stopping to give them an opportunity to observe other unusual things (such as suspicious bulges in your wearing apparel or luggage) they will have less legal justification to use in court.

If you are in your home or business and police knock on the door announcing their identity and purpose, you are not required to do or say anything. If you do not answer the door allowing them entrance, they have the right to knock the door down to gain entry.

You are not required to identify yourself, take police on a tour of your house, answer questions, or explain the contents in your house. Your best course of action is to sit down in the living room and relax, saying and doing nothing. The more you say, the deeper you will be mired in your own problems.

If you are in a parking lot, public street, or some other place where a drug purchase or sale has just transpired, or have committed a crime in the presence of an undercover law enforcement officer or wired informant, they have the right to arrest you immediately. You do not have the right to a speedy arrest and if the officer or informant is undercover they have other cases in the work and do not wish to reveal their identity as they are currently protecting their secrecy. They may go ahead and make a drug purchase from you, make their report to the Prosecutor, but no formal charges are filed for a year until they have made a number of other cases and then "resurface" as a uniformed, clean shaven, police officer. Drugs will have to be chemically tested and there may be a delay of several months, as the crime laboratory is testing drugs. Once formal charges are filed, a warrant is issued for your arrest and police then come to your door to arrest you. In the process, attempting to get you to walk from room to room to get dressed and get your personal belongings, they may search rooms, closets, dresser drawers and areas that you are near (in order to look for weapons that you might grab).

Don't keep contraband, guns, or large sums of cash because, if they serve an arrest warrant, they will make a limited *protective sweep* search and if items are observed in plain view, you will be charged with another crime.

Conclusion

RULE: WHEN POLICE SERVE AN ARREST OR SEARCH WARRANT, YIELD TO THEIR DEMANDS AND SUBMIT YOUR PERSON OR PROPERTY TO A SEARCH. DO NOT ARGUE WITH POLICE OR THEIR AUTHORITY. CLAIM YOUR CONSTITUTIONAL RIGHTS IN TAKING THE FIFTH AMENDMENT. DO NOT DISCUSS THE CASE UNLESS YOU HAVE HAD AN OPPORTUNITY TO TALK WITH A LAWYER AND GET EXPERT LEGAL ADVISE. YOUR LAWYER CAN FILE A MOTION TO SUPPRESS AND QUESTION THE VALIDITY OF THE SEARCH AND JUDGE WILL DECIDE WHETHER THE SEARCH WAS LEGAL AND THE EVIDENCE SHOULD BE USED AGAINST YOU. YOU ARE NOT REQUIRED TO COOPERATE WITH THE LAW ENFORCEMENT OFFICERS ANSWERING THEIR QUESTIONS AND CONDUCTING THEM ON A TOUR OF YOUR PROPERTY IS THE COMMON MISTAKE MADE BY MOST CITIZENS

TRYING TO BE POLITE AND HELPFUL TO POLICE, WHOSE MAIN PURPOSE IN BEING AT YOUR PROPERTY IS TO ARREST YOU AND SEE THAT YOU ARE FOUND GUILTY AND PUNISHED. WHY FEED THE HAND THAT HURTS YOU? YOU ARE NOT REQUIRED TO SPEAK, GIVE ORAL OR WRITTEN CONSENT, OR DO ANYTHING TO HELP POLICE. THEY ARE GOING TO ARREST YOU AND/OR SEARCH YOUR PROPERTY ANYWAY, SO LET THEM CONDUCT THEIR INVESTIGATION AND ANSWER THEIR OWN QUESTIONS.

You presented your case and despite your best efforts—you lost. The jury rejected your testimony. The presentence report is concluded, allocution granted, and you've been sentenced to prison. All is not lost.

Stings and Reverse Stings

Sometimes police work undercover and recruit confidential informants (CI's) to infiltrate loose knit gangs and groups. Police pose as gang members or businessmen buying stolen property or drugs and engage in an ongoing business with criminals until a case has been made. When an arrest is made undercover cops reveal their identity. These are *sting operations* where police buy contraband or drugs.

A *reverse sting* is where police intercept drugs or stolen property in transit and get an informant to *roll* with the contraband and sell it to a criminal, reverse sting simply meaning that the contraband are being sold rather than being purchased.

Courts approve these police practices unless police become involved in the criminal activity or they engage in criminal misconduct. Police usually video and audio tape the buys.

Gang Violence

Gang related violence, drive-by shootings, and drug turf battles continue to be a big problem for local police of which there are about 500,000 nationwide. There are over 100 different gangs in most major American cities.

Street violence is growing. State prosecutors charge individuals, federal laws prosecute drug and firearm offenses and conspiracies and large groups.

Street gangs such as the Crypts and Bloods are rapidly multiplying. FBI, ATF, and DEA federal agents are assisting local police.

The main reason for gangs is the breakdown of the family unit, complete absence of one parent (usually the father), total disrespect for the law and authority, lack of respect for personal and property rights of another and no motivation to succeed in school.

Missouri State Highway Patrol dog handlers with their specially trained drug dogs.

Marlene Ash and Dannette Dunson are subjects of a drug sniffing dog "Wiko" of Trooper David A. Henson, Missouri State Highway Patrol at the Springfield Muncipal Airport. (Picture is posed.)

Sgt. Steve Ijames, Springfield Police Department Crisis Action Team (CAT), finds cocaine while serving a residential search warrant.

Marijuana and guns confiscated by Wayne County Sheriff Bud Snyder, Greenville.

Illicit clandestine laboratory in Northeast Missouri produced methamphetamine.

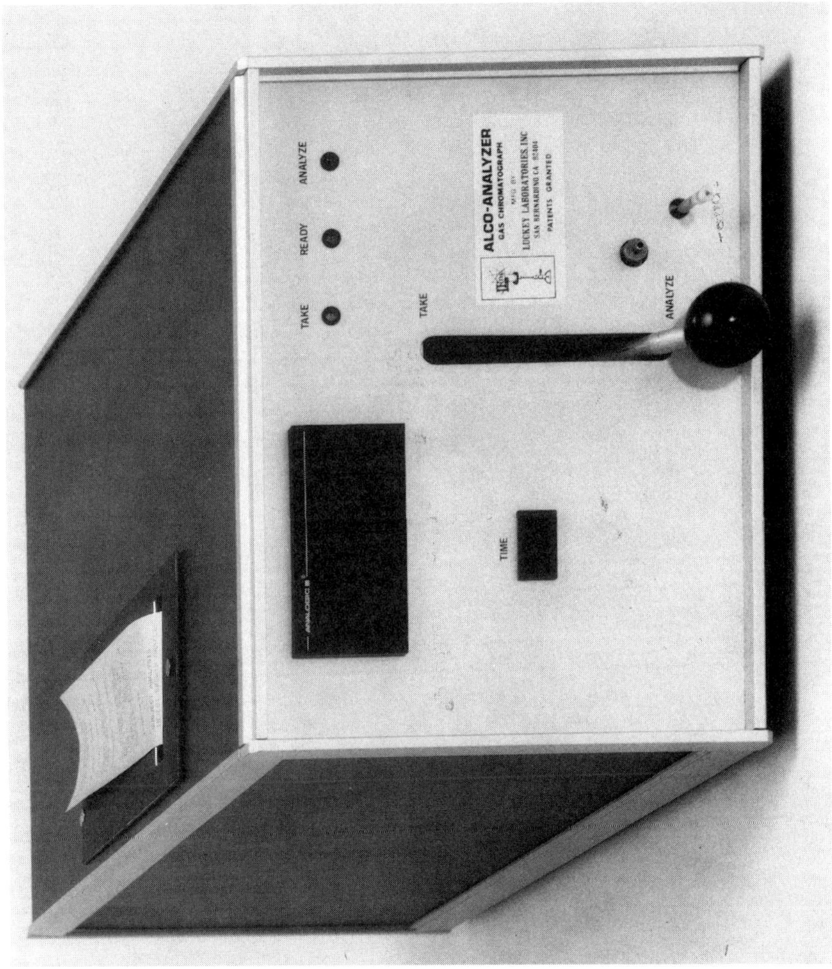

Replacing the Breathalyzer 900 is the Alco-Analyzer commonly used in DWI cases to determine the percentage of alcohol in your lungs.

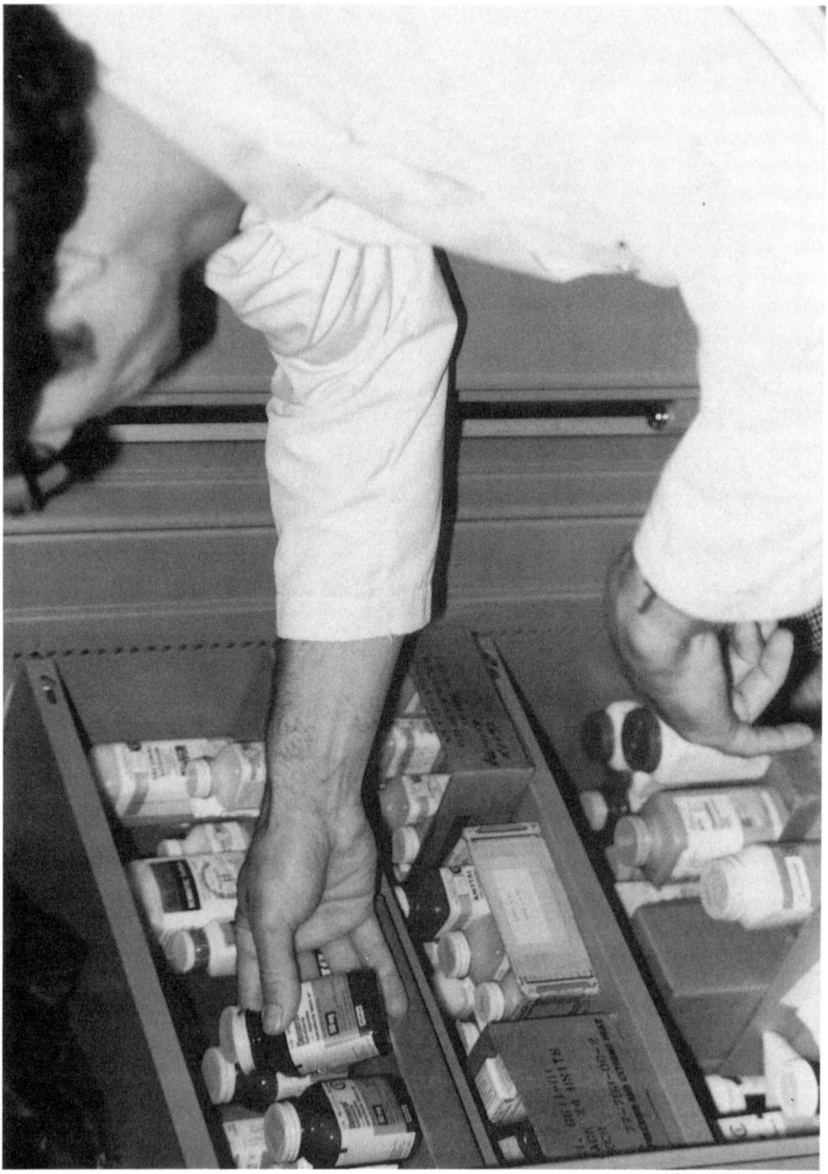

All narcotics and controlled substances must be kept locked and secured by pharmacists and are not allowed outside their marked containers.

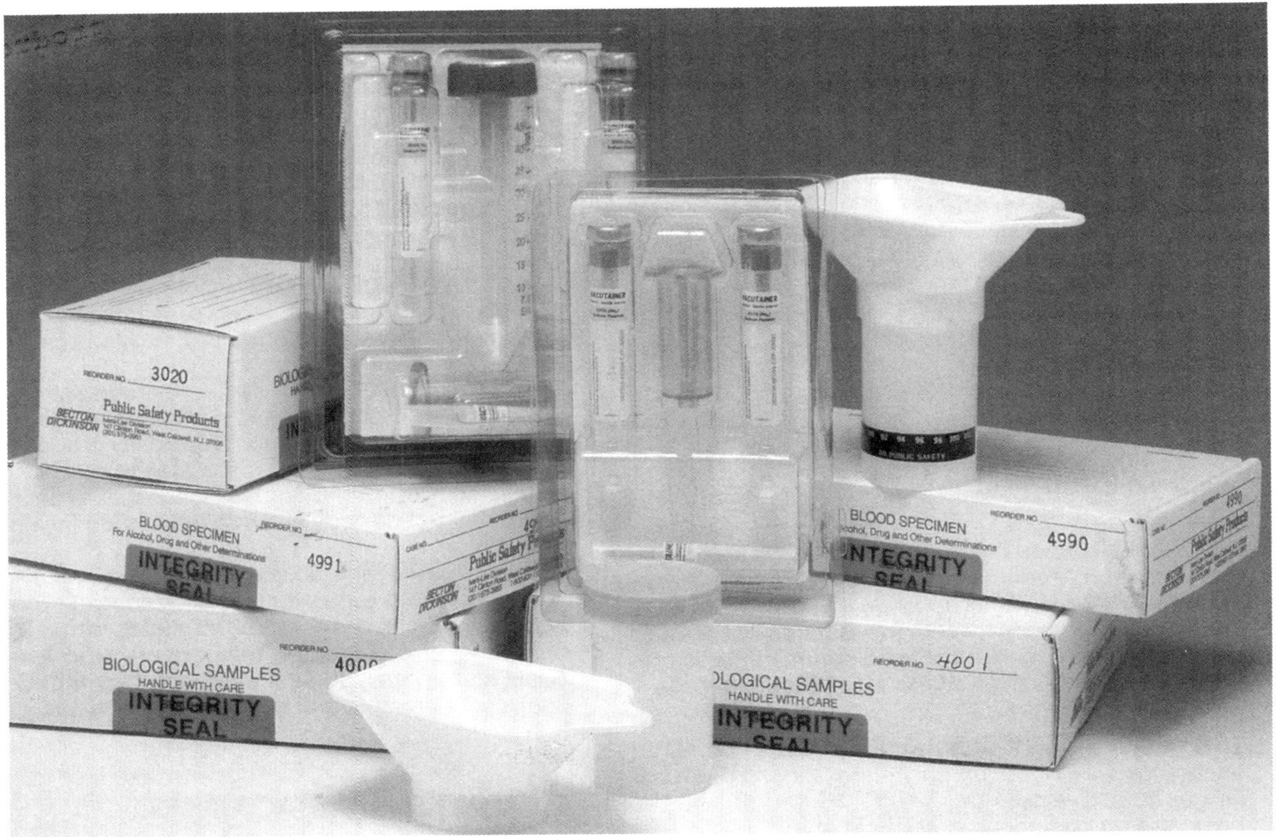

Specimen collection kits are specially designed to provide chain simplicity in collecting blood and urine specimens.

Trimming down the drug supply. Ernest Sjoblom (left), chief of the DOH bureau of Narcotics and Dangerous drugs and Garland Land view more than 250,000 confiscated diet pills. The drugs represent the largest quantity of drugs since 1976 to be brought into the Jefferson City office for destruction. The capsules were surrendered by a southeast Missouri physician who was illegally prescribing and dispensing the medication. The BNDD monitors and investigates activities with controlled drugs, takes adminstrative action to suspend or revoke controlled substances registrations issued by DOH, and destroys outdated, deteriorated and unusable controlled drugs.

ALCOHOL LEVELS BY WEIGHT

	CONSUMED PER HOUR	BODY WEIGHT			
		100	140	180	220
BEER	GLASSES				
	1	.05	.04	.03	.02
	2	.08	.06	.05	.05
	3	.11	.09	.08	.07
WINE	GLASSES				
	1	.03	.03	.02	.02
	2	.06	.05	.04	.03
	3	.08	.06	.04	.04
DISTILLED SPIRITS	OUNCES				
	1	.04	.03	.02	.02
	2	.07	.05	.04	.03
	3	.09	.07	.06	.05

The active ingredient in marijuana (THC) acts as a depressant on the brain. (Sgt. James Baker (L) and Sgt. Randy Evans (R), Carthage Police Department.

Calloway County Sheriff Harry Lee happily harvests a marijuana crop near Fulton.

Missouri State Highway Patrol Troopers harvest a local crop of marijuana in Central Missouri.

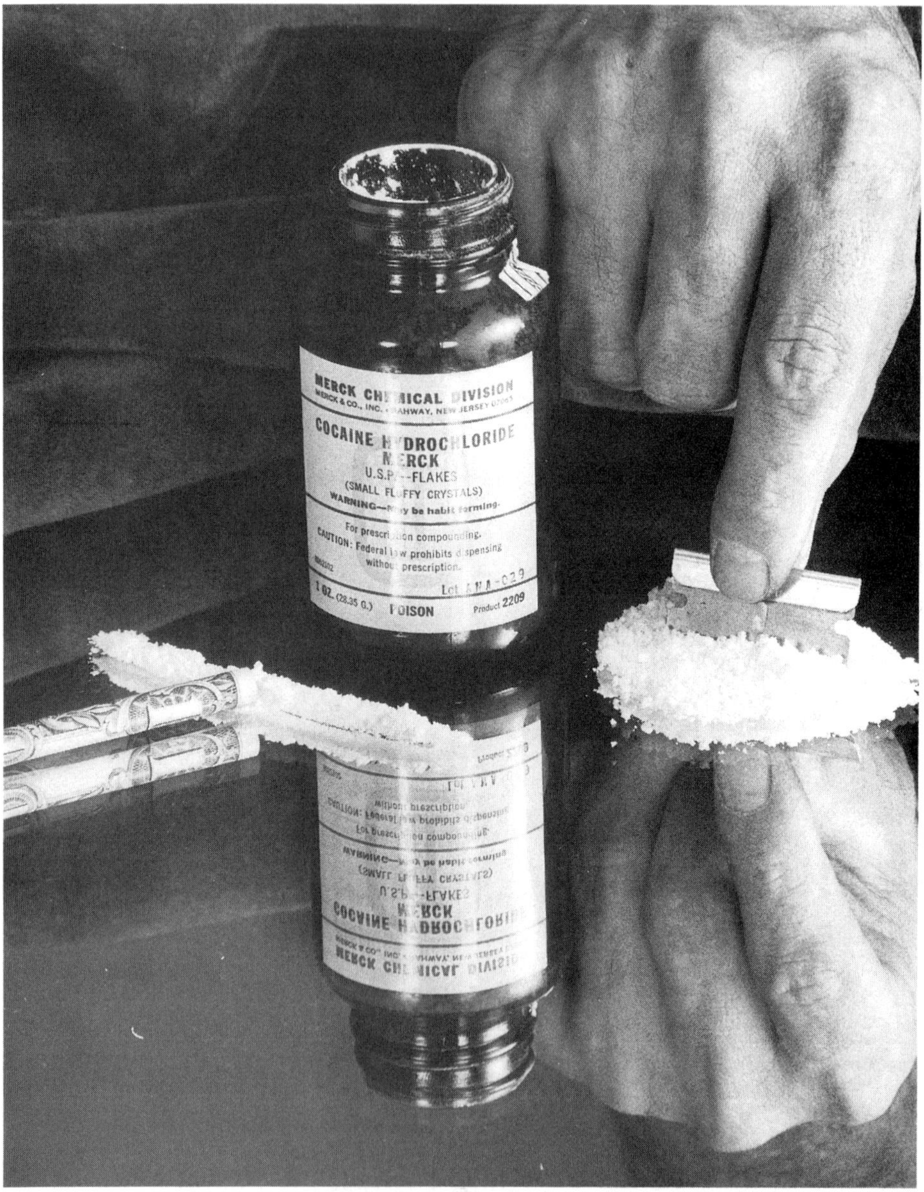
COCAINE
(SMALL
For prescri
CAUTION: Federal
1 OZ. (28.35 G.)
Product 2209

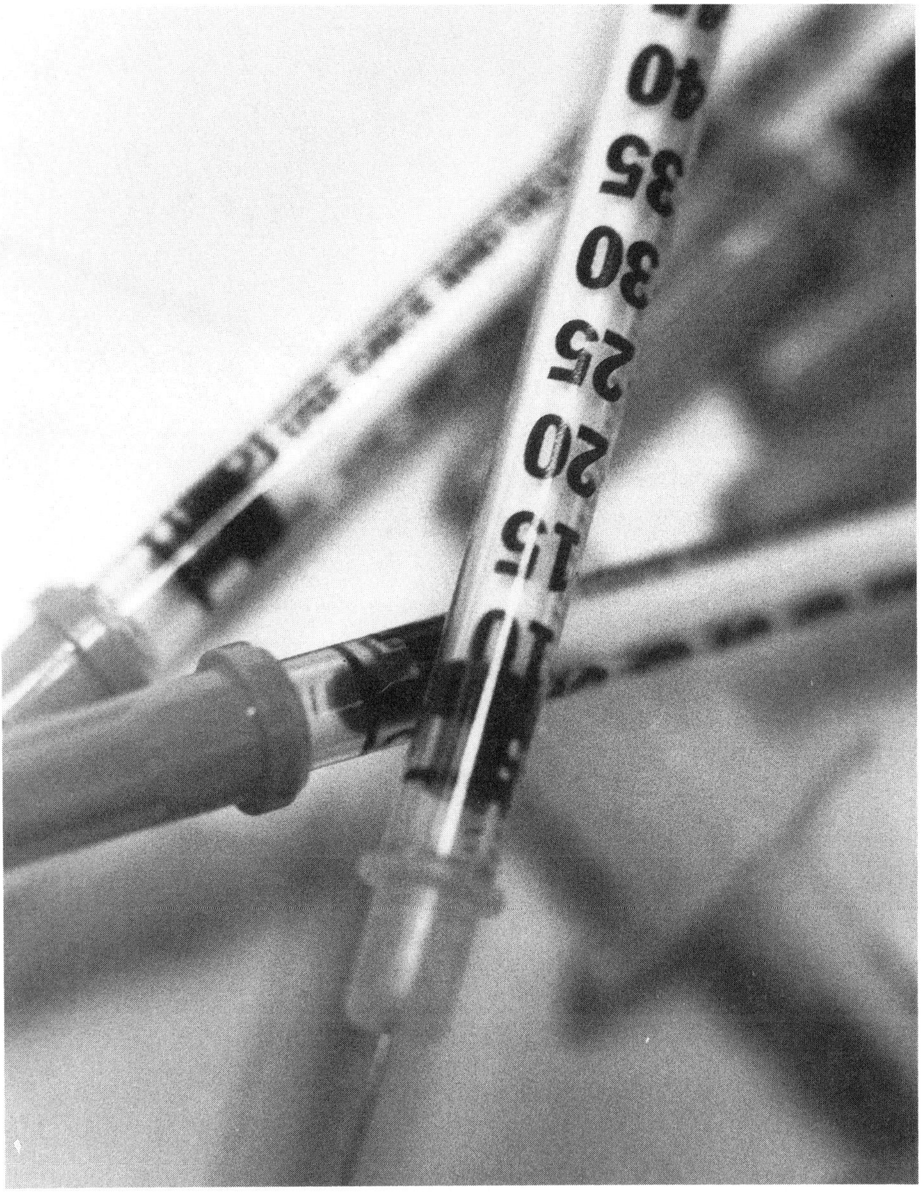

Crack: A Non-Traditional Form of Freebasing

COCAINE BASE

CRACK

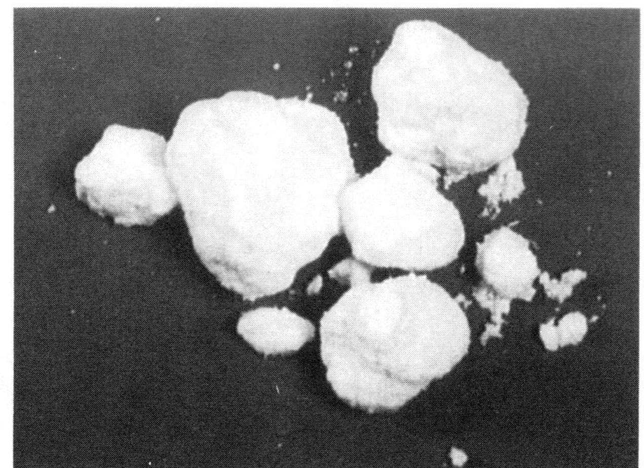

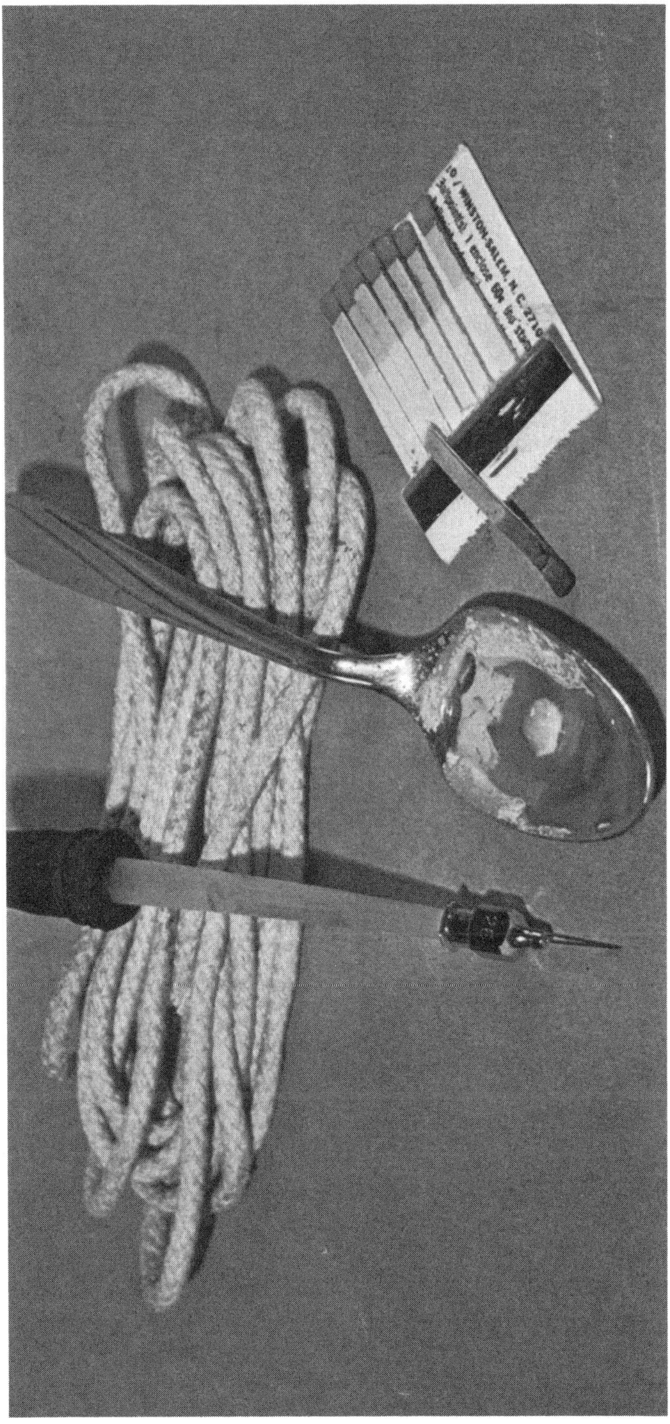

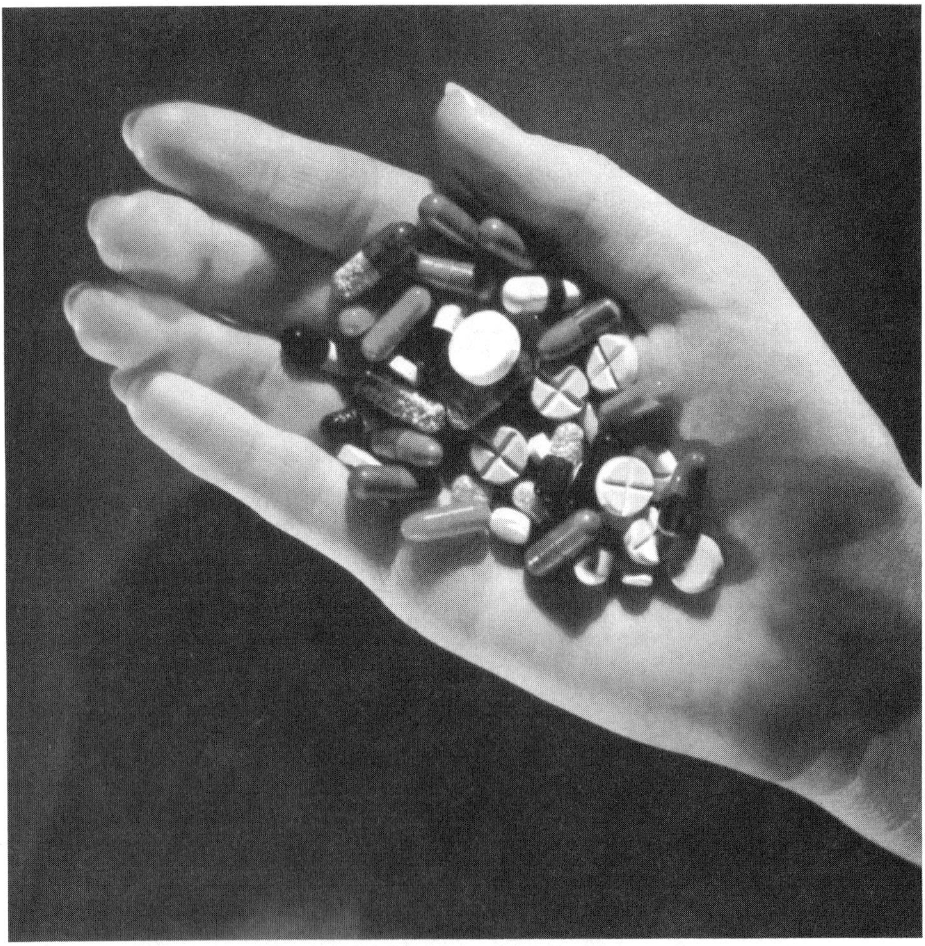

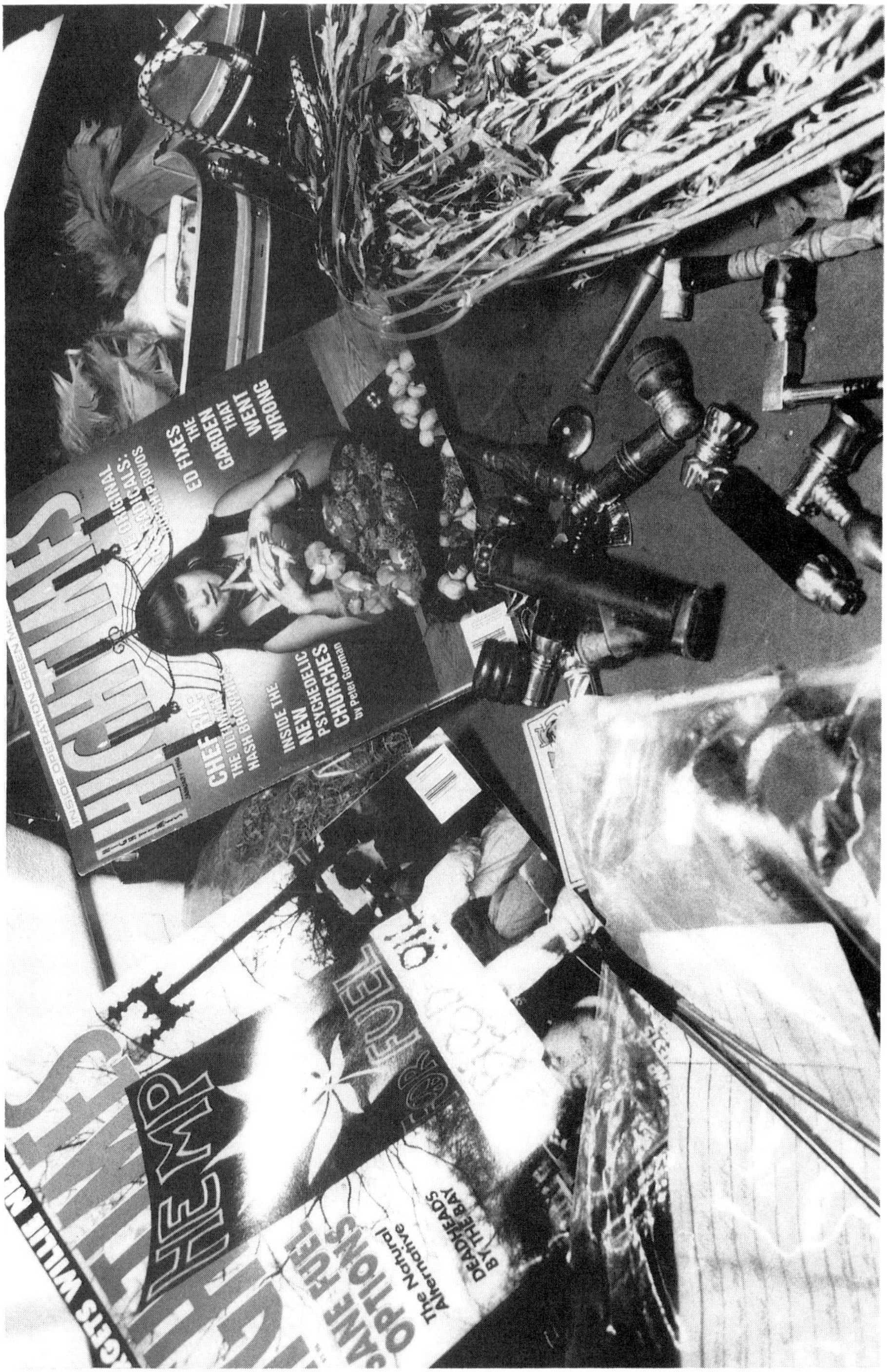
HIGH TIMES
CHEF RA: THE ULTIMATE HASH BROWNIES
INSIDE THE NEW PSYCHEDELIC CHURCHES
by Peter Gorman
ED FIXES THE GARDEN THAT WENT WRONG
HEMP
OPTIONS
The Natural Alternative
DEADHEADS BY THE BAY

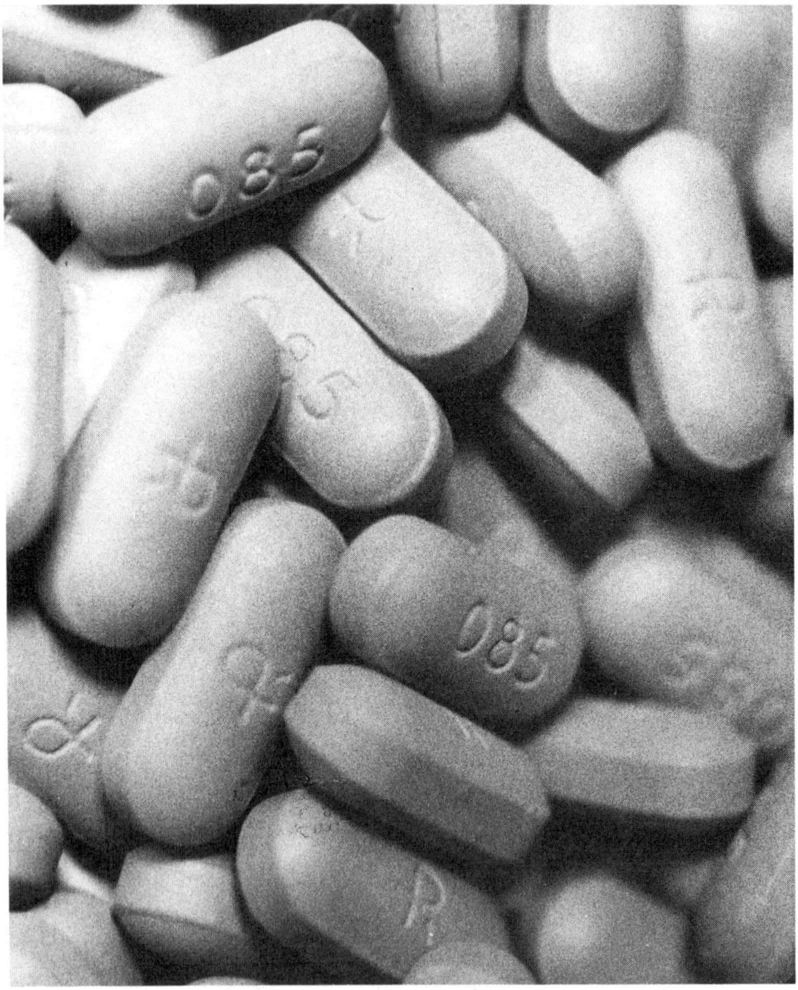

Opium poppy and Derivatives - crude opium, codeine, Heroin & Morphine

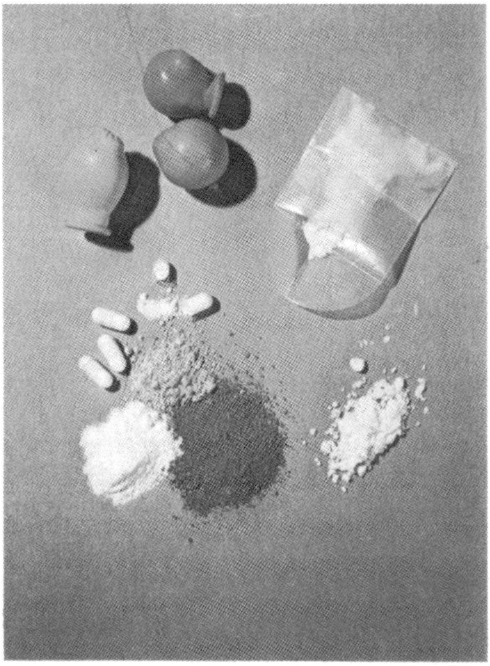

Forms of Heroin

Coca leaves & Illicit forms of Cocaine

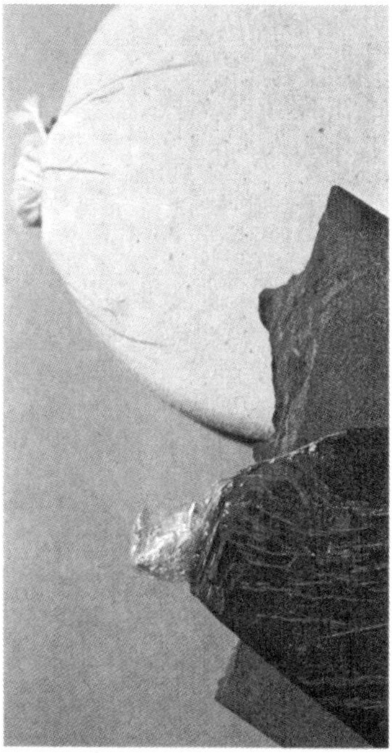

Hashish

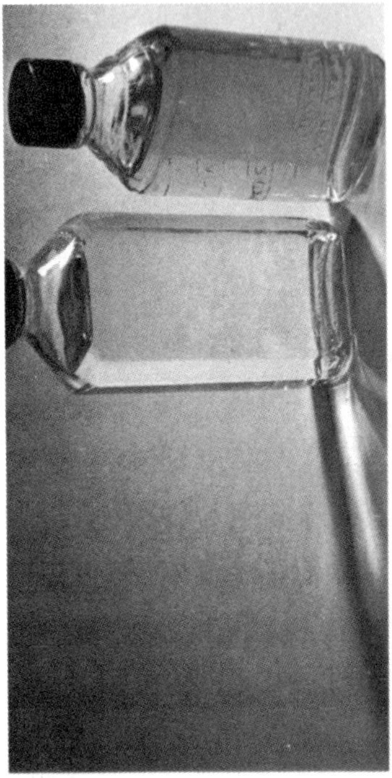

Exempt Narcotics - cough syrup with codeine

Manicured Marihuana, cigarettes and seeds

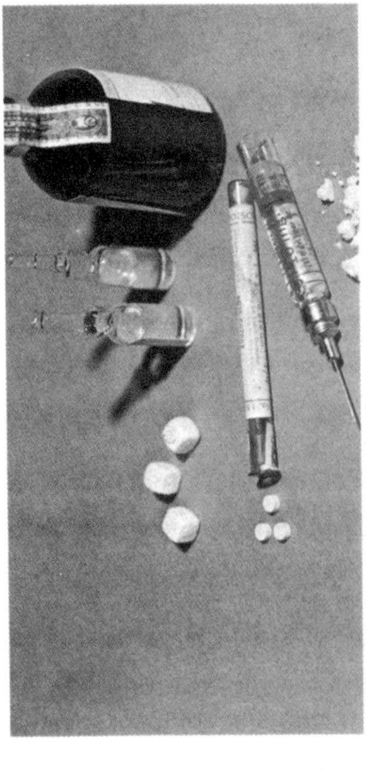

Forms of Morphine

Kilo bricks of Marihuana

Illegitimate forms of Lysergic Acid Diethylamide (LSD)

Dimethyltryptamine (DMT) on Tobacco and Parsley leaves

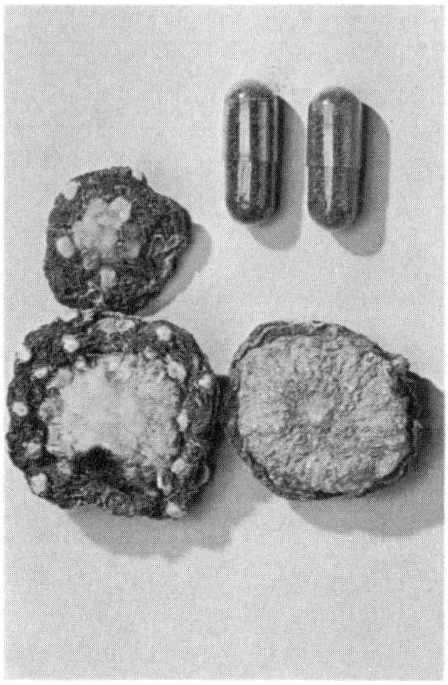

Peyote Buttons and ground Peyote

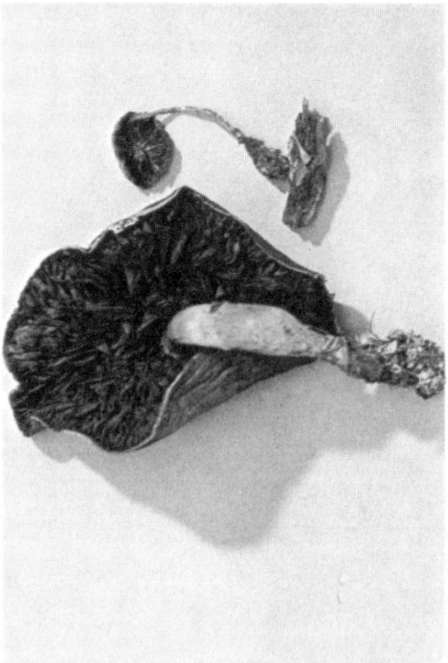

Psilocybe Mushrooms

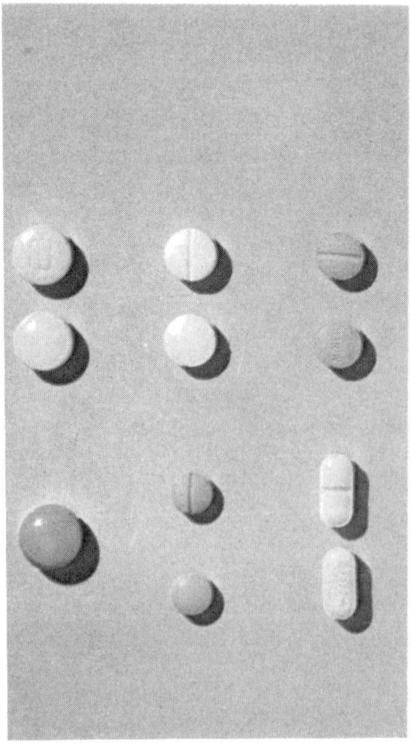

Miscellaneous Barbiturate Tablets

Amphetamines

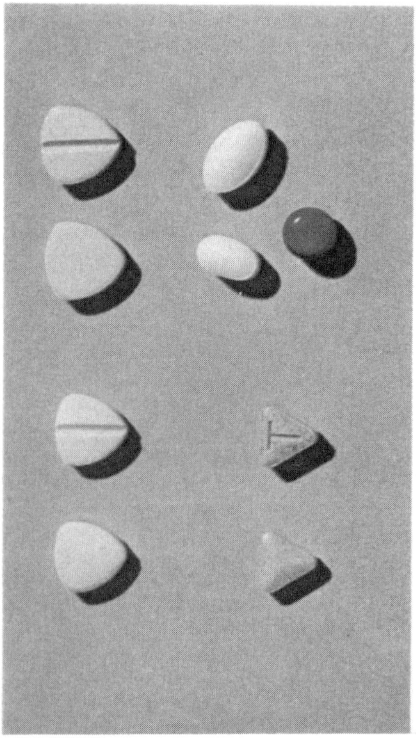

Stimulants

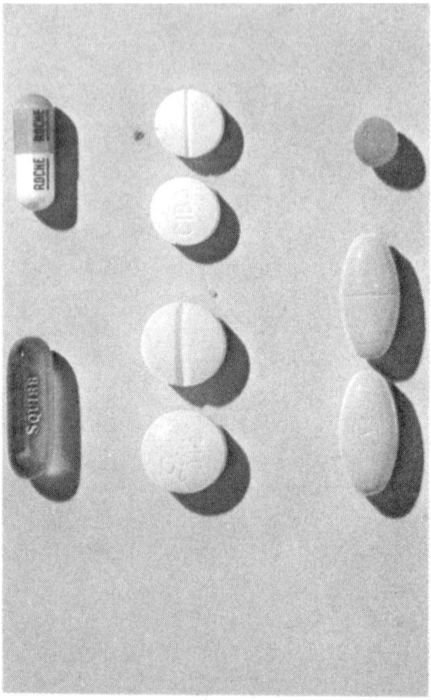

Depressants

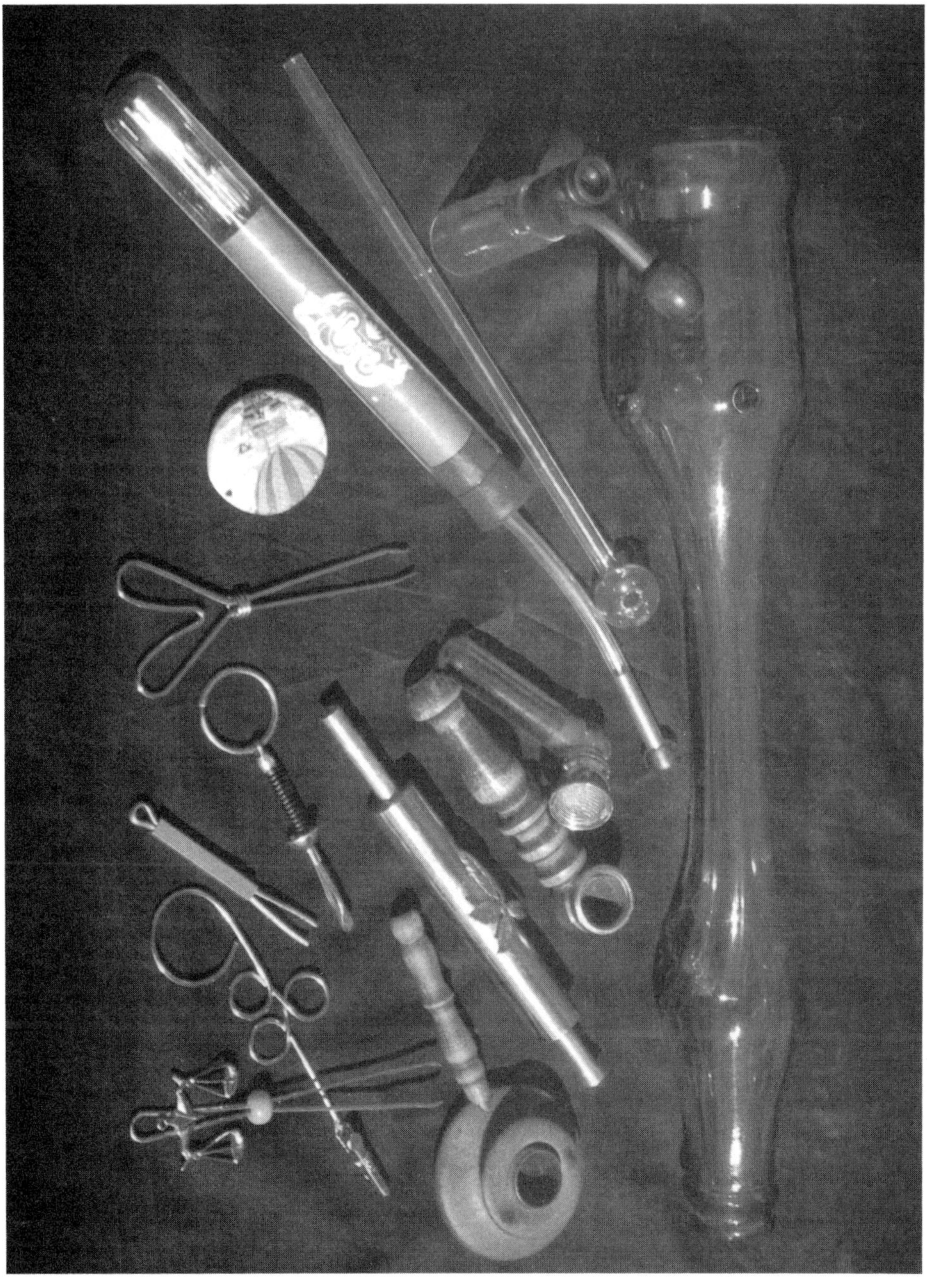

DEPARTMENT OF JUSTICE
DRUG ENFORCEMENT ADMINISTRATION
US
SPECIAL
AGENT
DEA

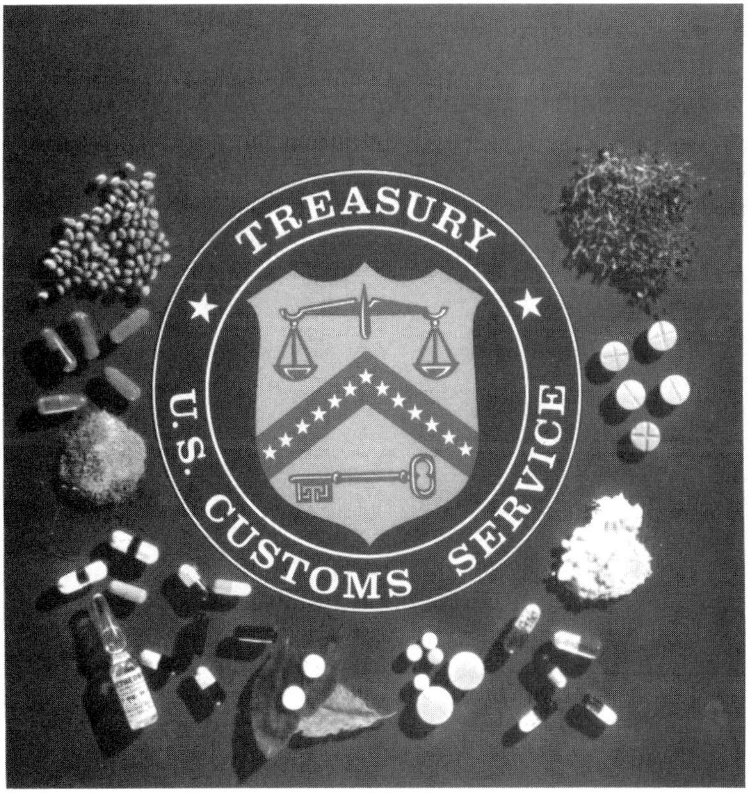
TREASURY
U.S. CUSTOMS SERVICE

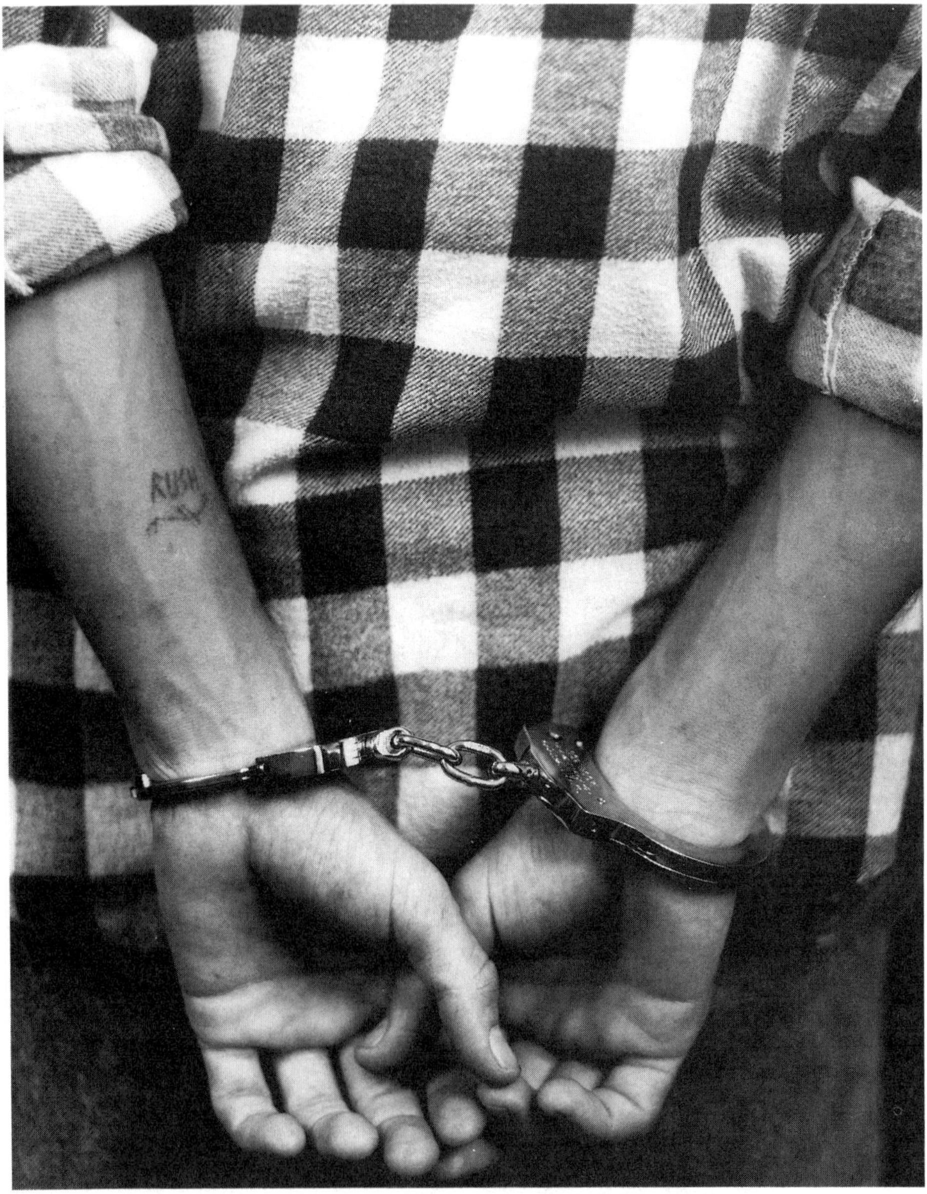
RUSH

Chapter 13

Off to Prison

"Every criminal represents a failure of society to control a criminal, as well as a failure on the part of the criminal to respond to social control."

J.B.S. Haldane

"I may hate sin, but never the sinner."

Clarence Darrow

"In imprisonment, the public is seeking its own salvation, not that of the lawbreaker."

G.B. Shaw

Despite best efforts, sometimes it is impossible to avoid being convicted and going to prison.

Discretion may be the better part of valor and a *negotiated plea of guilty* may be your best course of action.

In *state prisons,* only a small percentage of most prison terms must actually be served behind bars. A higher percentage of time must be served in federal prisons but the conditions are much nicer.

If you are going to prison, you get credit for *good time* (no write-ups or disciplinary problems in prison); *back time* (any time you originally served at the original time of arrest); and may also be eligible for early release to a *halfway house,* or for *house arrest.* These are possibilities that are more meaningful towards the end of your prison term.

While in prison, do the following:

1. Keep yourself meaningfully busy, physically and mentally occupied.
2. Volunteer for every job imaginable.
3. Enroll and successfully complete high school and college courses, earning GED and college credits.
4. Attend and participate in every self-improvement program offered, whether you think you need to or not (including NA and AA).
5. Become a trustee.
6. Stay out of gangs, cliques, groups, and fights.

Your *out date* (release date) may be placed far off, but may be moved up sooner, as the time gets closer.

In state court, upon formal sentencing you go to the county jail and await the sheriff to transport you to Fulton, Missouri, to be tested, classified, and eventually assigned to the Department of Corrections (DOC) to one of the 10 state prisons.

In federal courts, the prison location is not designated by the Bureau of Prisons (BOP) until actual sentencing. Your lawyer should ask for special permission to personally report to the institution. You are placed in a lower security risk category.

Sentencing

Possible sentences include:

1. Imprisonment
2. A fine
3. Probation
4. Suspending the imposition of sentence
5. "Shock" probation.

If a fine is assessed, the money goes to the school fund or if sentenced in city or municipal court, then to the city revenue.

You must enter a plea knowingly and intelligently and a full and complete record made as to the facts of the case, the reason for entering the plea, and whether you are in fact guilty. You should be advised of the range of punishment and a number of other important Constitutional rights.

If a *Pre-Sentence Report* has been requested, you have the right to contradict any part that you believe is false. If a plea bargain has been entered into, the Court is not obligated to accept the bargain. If the Judge does not accept the plea bargain, he gives you an opportunity to withdraw your plea. The Prosecutor only agrees to recommend a certain sentence to the Judge, *which is not a guarantee* that you will actually receive that sentence. As long as the state does what it promises, then it has kept its part of the plea bargain.

You may be given a *Suspended Imposition of Sentence*, which means no sentence is actually imposed after the plea of guilty and the court actually takes the matter under advisement for a period of time.

Plea bargaining is a proper procedure in which the court does not usually participate. The court will disclose whether or not it will follow the agreement.

Post-Trial Matters

A prisoner may petition the trial court to set aside the conviction if the conviction or plea was caused by a denial of some Constitutional right.

Grounds for successful motions include:

1. Ineffective assistance of counsel
2. Denial of lawyer at trial
3. Denial of lawyer at motion for new trial
4. Denial of lawyer at prior conviction
5. Involuntary waiver of jury trial
6. Denial of right to confront witnesses
7. Incompetence to stand trial
8. Forced confession
9. Conviction based on perjured testimony
10. Double jeopardy
11. Insufficiency of criminal charge
12. Unconstitutional identification
13. Use of improper prior conviction
14. Involuntary abandonment of right of appeal.

Unsuccessful grounds

1. Matters which were raised on prior motion
2. Matters already decided on appeal
3. Matters waived on appeal
4. Failure to allege facts
5. Illegal arrest
6. Unlawful search or seizure
7. Newly discovered evidence
8. Lack of speedy trial

9. Failure to give Miranda warnings
10. Dissatisfaction with penal conditions
11. Irregularities at preliminary hearing
12. Illegal evidence, confession, insanity, entrapment
13. Imperfect criminal charge
14. Important trial errors
15. Errors in admission of evidence
16. Cruel or unusual punishment.

You may file a Motion for New Trial alleging specific trial errors. Subsequent appeals can include only those matters contained in the motion, or those which constitute *plain error* and result in a *manifest injustice*. You may file a *Writ of Habeas Corpus* alleging an unconstitutional deprivation of freedom.

Post Conviction Motions

The two procedures by which you can return to court to contest your imprisonment:

RULE 24.035

After a *plea of guilty*, if you are sentenced to imprisonment and claim the plea was involuntarily entered, the sentence was unconstitutional, your attorney was incompetent or *ineffective*, you were not properly advised of your rights, or the sentence was illegal, you can file one post-conviction motion where you must state all grounds known to you and raise every claim you desire to challenge your sentence.

RULE 29.15

After a *trial*, if you believe your lawyer was incompetent, that illegal evidence was used against you, that the trial Judge made errors in ruling on evidence, you may return to court and file one post trial motion to attack your conviction.

You must be in custody, under a sentence, conviction of a felony, and actually serving time in prison.

After sentencing the trial Judge asks questions to determine whether there is probable cause to believe you did or did not receive effective assistance from your lawyer. A probable cause finding is made immediately.

Post conviction motions must be filed within 90 days after commencement of the sentence and may be amended thereafter, one time after a lawyer makes an entry of appearance or a public defender is appointed.

The court will make a preliminary finding as to whether an evidentiary hearing is required on the motion and if not, may summarily refuse to hear prisoner's arguments. The Judge may order a hearing, in which testimony is heard.

RULE: THE OBJECT OF POSE CONVICTION REMEDIES IS TO DISCOVER THOSE RELATIVELY FEW CASES IN WHICH AN INMATE HAS SUFFERED A GENUINE DEPRIVATION OF HIS CONSTITUTIONAL RIGHTS.

Pardons and Paroles

A *pardon* can only be granted by the governor, and is an act of grace.

A *judicial parole* is a conditional release, with the objective being the rehabilitation of the prisoner. A Judge can grant only two paroles for any one crime. A parole comes only after judgment and sentencing. A court can revoke a parole, if within the time of the original parole. Any conviction felony can be paroled, given a suspended imposition of sentence, or the Judge may actually pronounce sentence and suspend it, under any conditions including "shock probation."

The State Board of Probation and Parole has authority to hear parole applications for prisoners confined in state correctional institutions and conducts all pardon investigations.

The board gives physical and mental exams, considers employment, social history, attitude criminal record, conduct, and considers the best interest of society.

Court parole violation warrants are bondable. At the hearing, reliable hearsay evidence may be received. You should be represented by counsel. If the violations are admitted, no hearing is necessary.

Punishments

Missouri has the following punishments:

Class A Felony - death, life imprisonment or imprisonment for a term of 10 years or more
Class B Felony - 5 to 15 years
Class C Felony - maximum 7 years prison
Class D Felony - maximum 5 years prison

Class A Misdemeanor - 6 months to one year in jail, or fine of up to $1,000
Class B Misdemeanor - 30 days in jail, or less fine of up to $300
Infraction - no jail, fine of up to $200, except where a person has been convicted of a misdemeanor or infraction in which he derived economic gain.

Persistent or Dangerous Offender

A Judge may sentence you to an *extended term of imprisonment* if you are persistent or dangerous offender and have a prior felony record.

Going to Prison

There are differences between state and federal prison which make a large difference in the *amount of time* and the *quality of time* served.

Your lawyer must send medical and mental reports to the prison, favorable police reports, letters of good character, and copies of certificates, awards, or degrees that you have earned so the prison has proof of your *good characteristics* in assigning you to an institution. To impress officials who will be designating you to certain prisons, they need all possible favorable information.

Once sentenced to prison by a state court judge, you immediately go to a county jail where you are held for several days until transferred to Fulton to be *classified* and assigned to one of the ten state prisons. Your criminal history is graded as a *salient factor score.*

120 Day Call-Back Law

The Judge retains jurisdiction of your case for up to *120 days from the date that you enter the prison.* He can order a report from the prison to see if you are a suitable candidate for a 120 day *call-back.* If so, he can order you to be released from prison. This authority rests *solely* within the trial judge. You may not move for 120 day probation. It is granted as an act of mercy by him, although an enterprising attorney can present helpful information to the Judge as to why his client deserves parole. If paroled, you under supervised probation of the State Board of Parole and Probation and the Circuit Judge.

If you do not obtain 120 day probation call-back, you serve as much of the sentence as the State Department of Corrections desires.

If you commit a violation, the probation officer can place you in jail without bond and the Department of Corrections will decide if you are to be returned to prison. If you are paroled under the 120 day law, the trial judge decides whether your parole is to be revoked.

Remember, when you are on parole or probation you are a *second class citizen*. You're not allowed to violate any law. You cannot possess firearms, associate with convicted felons, and report all changes of address, employment, and marital status within hours. Any parolee who refuses to do these things is a fool and is asking for a one-way ticket back to prison.

You are eligible for *house arrest* in which you wear a monitoring device on your leg which requires you to keep stringent curfews.

It is important you attend all useful and constructive classes and programs offered—obtain your high school equivalency degree, attending college courses, Alcoholics Anonymous, Narcotics Anonymous, sexual offenders programs, counselling and therapy sessions, and volunteer for work details.

Depending upon your prior felony record, you will be eligible for parole after serving approximately one-third of your time. A parole board hearing will be held, giving you a few minutes to state why you believe you are ready to return to society. You're entitled to have a friend, relative, or attorney present with you at the hearing which is tape recorded.

Whenever possible you will want to make trusty status by indicating your hard work, good faith, and sincere desire and efforts to improve yourself. If you have any pending criminal charges or detainers, demand speedy disposition of those detainers.

Parole Hearings

You will be given a parole hearing when the *Missouri Board of Probation and Parole* visits your institution. You are present with one person (a relative or lawyer) to speak for you. The hearings are recorded, informal, and are very brief.

RULE: THE MISTAKE MOST PRISONERS MAKE IS TO TRY TO MINIMIZE OR EXPLAIN AWAY THEIR ORIGINAL CRIME, A SURE SIGN YOU ARE NOT REMORSEFUL OR HAVE ACCEPTED RESPONSIBILITY. YOUR BEST BET IS TO ADMIT THE PAST, ACCEPT

RESPONSIBILITY AND BE POSITIVE ABOUT THE FUTURE. WHAT ARE YOUR DISCIPLINED PLANS FOR THE FUTURE, YOUR HOME, EMPLOYMENT, AND CHURCH, UPON YOUR RELEASE? THE PAROLE BOARD DOES NOT WANT TO BE EMBARRASSED BY A NEW PAROLEE IMMEDIATELY COMMITTING ANOTHER CRIME.

RULE: AT PAROLE HEARINGS, LIKE SENTENCING HEARINGS, ALWAYS PRESENT A BROCHURE OR SCRAPBOOK WITH PHOTOGRAPHS OF YOUR FAMILY, HOME, FUTURE EMPLOYER, CHURCH, CERTIFICATES, AWARDS AND DEGREES THAT YOU MIGHT HAVE EARNED, TOGETHER WITH NUMEROUS GOOD CHARACTER LETTERS. THIS BROCHURE WILL GET THE ATTENTION OF THE JUDGE OR PAROLE BOARD, AND MIGHT MAKE THE SLIGHT DIFFERENCE IN THEIR ATTITUDE OF GIVING YOU PROBATION.

Habeas Corpus

A *writ of habeas corpus* ("you have the body") is a command by a judge to have a person held in custody, brought before the court for the purpose of determining the legality of confinement. Without this guarantee, police could take people into custody and keep them there indefinitely. When the Bastille was stormed during the French Revolution men were set free who had been imprisoned without trial for years. The Writ protects against such actions and can be suspended in the event of rebellion or invasion, or when "public safety may require it". Only twice in our nation's history, once during the Civil War and once in Hawaii during the Second World War, was the Writ suspended.

Jailhouse Lawyers

The law recognized the absolute right of a prisoner to file lawsuits on his own behalf. The U.S. Supreme Court in *Johnson vs. Avery* (1969) ruled it was the Constitutional right of a prisoner to receive free access from someone with training in the law. Prisoners may file *pro se* or *inpropria persona* (for himself) lawsuits. Most of these are frivolous, poorly written, and rarely succeed. They work for cigarettes and other favors.

Prisons: The Punishing Cost

Every week like clockwork the total number of prison inmates grows by 1,000 people. Their cost is between $15,000 and $30,000 a year to feed, house, and guard. With over 1,000,000 men and women behind bars in the state and federal prisons, the U.S. already has the highest incarceration rate in the Western World, and four times the per capita rate as England or France.

Legislators are afraid to complain about the spiraling costs, lest they be labelled soft on crime. Nobody wants to be accused of being a wimp. Everyone wants to get tough, and toughness is translated into longer sentences.

Sooner or later you have to ask whether you are willing to let your kid have a mediocre education in order to send a few more people to prison.

The opposite view is though while it may cost thousands to keep a man behind bars, it may cost as much as $430,000 yearly to let that man run free, committing crimes with calculations based on the idea that criminals in prison would each commit 187 crimes a year if they were running free.

Calculations show that the average crime costs society about $2,300.

Less than 1% of all crime result in a prison sentence, so even doubling or tripling the incarceration rate has a little real impact.

What about rehabilitation? Overstretched budgets and terrible crowding in most prisons preclude all but the most minimal rehabilitative efforts. Worse, prisons often unwittingly function as graduate schools for crime.

Halfway houses, work release, and community service, provide regular counselling and supervision without the expense of constant guarding and concrete walls may be the answer of the 21st Century. At sentencings, Judges must be convinced to use them, saving the state money and giving offenders a chance to re-enter society in a controlled way.

Prisoners Pay for Jail Upkeep

Prisoners who have sufficient assets and money have to pay some of the costs of their incarceration under Missouri Incarceration Reimbursement Act.

The law empowers the Missouri Attorney General to collect thousands of dollars per prisoner toward the cost of the inmate's incarceration.

Prisoners often conceal or transfer assets once they learn of the state's interest in recovering money.

In the Pre-Sentence Report, information is gathered about financial assets, and this information is given to the Attorney General and assets seized, collected, and assigned to the state Department of Corrections. This includes Workers' Compensation, pension benefits, previously earned salaries or wages, bonuses, annuities, retirement benefits, settlement or claims against the state, or judgments received by the prisoners against a state officer. Exempt assets include homes less than $50,000, and inmate's wages up to $2,500.

The prisoner is given 30 days notice before his case is heard by the court, and the state may not recover more than 90% of the value of the prisoner's assets.

The sentencing judge can assess as *court costs* reasonable costs of the county jail, which the inmate must pay.

Overcrowding at Federal Prisons

Federal prisons are now at 150% capacity, by 1995, 100,000 prisoners will be confined, and by the year 2000, 137,000. Nearly 60% of all prisoners are confined on drug related crimes.

An impact can be made on crime through *rehabilitation* since eventually the prisoner will be released into society which includes the following steps:

1. *Literacy*. Every federal prisoner is required to have a high school diploma before he can take part in any preferred federal prison program.
2. *Drug treatment* programs are now required.
3. *Work*. Every federal prisoner must work. Prison industries employ over 15,000 prisoners every day.

Recidivism

About 50% of all prisoners are back in prison within three years. People can change, but often they don't change, don't want to change, or are not getting the help to make the change. We want to keep people permanently out of prison and provide successful and corrective environment the first time.

Prisoners need *real world contacts*—help from people on the outside, to show an interest or to make a call on a prisoner's behalf.

World's Top Jailer

Our total prison system overflows with 1.1 million inmates in 3320 jails. While inmate population has increased, so has violent crimes with a record number of murders.

Costs of inmates costs over $20 billion each year, $20,000 per inmate—about the same as tuition at a top college.

Innovation and alternative sentencing should be used:

1. One useful approach is jailing low risk prisoners at home (house arrest), electronically monitored at less than 1/4 the cost of prison. They can work and support themselves, but their activity is restricted.
2. Other approaches are *half-way houses*, drug and alcohol treatment programs.
3. Community service performing several hundred hours.

That's smarter than being the world's top jailer.

Women Behind Bars

There are 17 men doing time for every female prisoner. The reason for this explosive increase can be put in a single word: "drugs".

About 50% of all women in federal prisons have been convicted of drug-related offenses, but that's only part of the story. Other crimes, such as theft, armed robbery, bad checks, prostitution, are also drug related.

About 80% of women entering prisons are mothers; most have custody of their children. By contrast, only 60% of male prisoners are fathers, and less than half have any custodial responsibility.

The number of women inmates has tripled in the past 10 years. They face a system designed and run by men for men.

Prisoners' Rights

Prisoners often file lawsuits against prison wardens. Writs of habeas corpus are used to challenge conditions of confinements, especially overcrowding. Lawsuits under the Civil Rights Act of 1987 are common, known as a "1983 action" (42 U.S.C. §1983).

A due process hearing is necessary before an inmate can be punished for violating prison rules. In addition to disciplinary rules, the

U.S. Supreme Court in *Johnson vs. Avery*, held that unless a state can provide a reasonable alternative, it cannot prohibit one inmate from assisting another in the preparation of writs, (jailhouse lawyers). Prison law libraries are required. Inmates cannot be denied access.

Medical care for inmates has become the subject of judicial concern. Some prisoners use the medical claims as ancillary claims against overall prison practices both other cases have reviewed the entire scope of prison medical programs, using the regular standard of negligence rather than the previous one of international action.

Cases involving religion, access to the news media, censorship of mail and many other areas have given prisoners limited rights. Prisoners' mail is censored.

Court decisions, though controversial, are aiding prison officials in stepping up needed reforms in a complex area that is suffering from growing pains.

What You Need to Know About a Criminal Conviction

Being a convicted felon is serious business and has many collateral consequences.

If you're convicted of a felony you can lose certain federal and state benefits. A person convicted of distribution of drugs can be ineligible for federal benefits for up to five years for the first offense, and forever on a third and subsequent offense. Federal benefits means any "grant, contract, loan, professional license, or commercial license provided by any agency of the United States."

A tenant or any person in the household or guest under the tenant's control are not allowed to engage in any criminal activity on the premises and loss of benefits can result.

The Immigration and Naturalization Services (INS) considers drug enforcement a high priority and there is substantial likelihood that any state drug conviction of a non-citizen will come to the attention of the INS, and can be deported for being a drug addict, whether or not the person is convicted. Passport revocation may occur.

If you become a "cooperating witness" however, a denial of federal benefits may not apply.

Currency reporting requirements requires that cash payments in excess of $10,000 be reported to the IRS. Failure to do so in violation of federal law, especially under the "Undercover Sting Operation in Money Laundering Cases."

In state court, you lost your right to vote (disfranchisement) as the County Clerk removes your name from voter roles. You are forbidden to own or legally possess a firearm. Convicted felons lose their operator's license if a motor vehicle was used in their crime. You are forbidden to enter bars and tap rooms, and are severely limited in obtaining any licenses from the state (nurses, doctors, lawyers, accountants, barbers).

Sentencing in Federal Court

"No, no," said the Queen. "Sentence first–verdict afterwards."

Lewis Carroll from
Alice in Wonderland (1865)

The *Federal Sentencing Guidelines* divide all federal crimes into 43 levels of seriousness and set *base sentences.* Many Judges have rebelled against the Sentencing Guidelines as bureaucratization of the sentencing process. The Sentencing Commission used a pool of 10,000 past convictions and averaged out the actual time served for each category of crime. The base sentence can be ratcheted up and down by an array of *offense characteristics* such as the amount of money stolen or drugs possessed.

The tough sentencing laws in federal court require almost any convicted felon to actually do time in a federal penitentiary. Only if the felony is extremely unimportant, and you have a spotless record, *and cooperate* with the federal government by *agreeing to testify* against others, you do have a chance for probation, house arrest, home detention, or confinement at a halfway house.

The Commission sets up *guidelines ranges* from which the Judge may select a sentence, although under certain circumstances the Judge may *depart up* or *down* from the guidelines. The purpose of the law is to have an effective and fair sentencing system with honesty, uniformity, and proportionality, depending upon the criminal history of the defendant, whether a weapon was used, the amount of property stolen, or damage done, and hundreds of other factors and categories, in order to determine the appropriate punishment. The punishment is scaled to offenders culpability and the resulting harms.

The law requires the Judge to consider seven factors:

1. The nature of the offense
2. The history and characteristics of the offender
3. The kinds of sentences available
4. The guidelines and policy statements of the Commission
5. The need to avoid the unwarranted disparity
6. The need for the sentence to serve the purposes of deterrent, incapacitation, rehabilitation and retribution
7. The sentence must reasonably comply with these four purposes of sentencing.

There are a large number of *relevant* factors that determine the guideline range, including *acts* and *omissions* that the defendant *aided* and *abetted* in doing the *risk of harm* that resulted in whether his acts were *intentional, reckless*, or merely *negligent*, and his *state of mind*, bearing on intent, motive and purpose in committing the crime.

Federal sentencing is extremely complicated. A creative defense attorney has a number of grounds he can argue for a *downward departure* from the guidelines having to do with his client's youthfulness, unique family upbringing, exceptional military service, diminished mental capacity, motive for committing the offense, and a number of other factors.

Getting Into Club Fed

Throughout the United States there are *Regional Designators* who coordinate placement of newly sentenced defendants and assign them to federal prisons.

A prisoner will be allowed to *voluntarily report* to the designated prison unless the prisoner is already in jail or is denied permission from the Judge. If allowed to voluntarily report, you are placed in a lower security category in prison which gives you more freedom and benefits.

The Regional Designator will consider:

1. Your past criminal record.
2. Whether you've ever been confined in a prison.
3. The seriousness of your crime.
4. Whether you are considered violent.
5. The location of your family and friends who would be visiting you.
6. Whether you have a skill or trade that might be used within the prison system.
7. The availability of bed space.

8. If the sentencing Judge recommends you be confined in a particular prison, some weight will be given the Judge's wishes.

The defense lawyer can serve his client well by providing information to the Regional Designator to make it more likely you will be confined in a low security prison near your home and make your stay in prison more convenient and enjoyable than you might expect.

There are some federal prisons designated as *camps* where considerable more freedom is given a prisoner and makes confinement more akin to being in the military service. The higher security prisons are guarded carefully with regular daily countdowns, little or no freedom outside your cell, and you are confined in small spaces with other dangerous, violent prisoners. These prisons should be avoided at all costs, and can make your confinement a "living hell".

Snitching

"Nobody talks, everybody walks."

In federal court, it is especially important to *accept responsibility* for criminal conduct. If you assist or *cooperate* with the government in some way, it will lower you sentence on the complicated guideline scale, which means less time in prison. If you provide *substantial assistance* to the government, the judge can be requested to assess a lower sentence.

Some people make a career out of breaking the law and when pinched, snitch out (roll over) and cooperate with the police.

Insiders of organized crime (La Cosa Nostra) referred to the Sicilian tradition of loyalty and silence that has long held insiders together as *omerta*. Government handlers recruit criminals for the snitch business and try to put a favorable *spin* on their credibility. They later become star witnesses and testify against one or more former friends so that the snitch does not have to spend the rest of his life in jail or pleads to lesser charges.

By breaking the code of silence, the Feds push a noble view of their man and the snitch brokers himself a chance at a rebirth as a law abiding citizen.

Being a snitch is dirty business. Tattling on your best friends, talking behind their back, causing them to be arrested and charged with a crime, will not leave a good taste in your mouth.

It can be dangerous if the target finds out "you're the one" who caused him grief. Your friends and family may disown you, you may fear for your life, and your immediate family. The sinking feeling in your stomach will linger into sleepless nights.

On the other hand, you may be doing your target a favor by turning him in and causing him to get help from a drug or alcohol addiction. After all, you didn't cause him to deal in drugs, he did it on his own. You're not getting him in trouble, he chose his own path; and besides, isn't reporting crime your civic duty? Like your mother always told you —always tell the truth and you'll never get into trouble.

You've been arrested, your house searched and the pressure is on. You are soon to be charged with a crime—you good name plastered in the media. You are facing massive attorney fees, lose of job, and disrespect and ridicule from everywhere. The cops tell you "there is a way out", by helping them and becoming a "cooperative individual". What are the rules?

1. *Get advice.* Consult a knowledgeable lawyer, one who has been down the road with other informants. Make sure he can cooperate with police and doesn't object to representing you. Listen to his advice as he weighs the pros and cons about your life as a snitch. See what he recommends. There are different ways to skin a cat!
2. *Tell the truth.* If you do cooperate and meet with the police—tell the truth. Don't start out by lying and trying to mislead the cops about your involvement and that of your friends. They know better. They'll discover your lies. "Don't bullshit bullshitters." Tell the truth.
3. *Hit and run.* See if you can give them just enough accurate information, enough to make them happy, so they'll leave you alone. If their case against you is average, the cops may be happy with a few tidbits and left-over information and will let you go.
4. *Act Secretly.* See if you can act as a *confidential* (CI) informant, without your name being broadcast to the world. Give confidential but reliable information. Police check it out to confirm your truthfulness. Then they obtain search warrants, using you only a "Reliable Confidential Informant". Maybe no one will ever know you "were the one".
5. *Introduce.* The next best thing is to "introduce". The cops will assign an unassuming narc to you, (who fits right in) and will be your companion, "Joe, from out of town". Your job is to introduce him around as a trusted high roller who has connections.
6. *Let Your Fingers Do the Walking.* Try to make telephone deals. The cops will wire your phone while you call friends, engage them in

incriminating conversations. This is an "extra cherry" that cops use to prove "intent". They love to make tape recordings.

7. *Wearing a Wire.* The most dangerous thing you can do is to *wear a wire.* It could be an invitation to the morgue. If you are deeply involved enough that the only way out is to be the front man, wear a Nagra or high quality recorder which records and transmits to waiting cops. They monitor and move in when the deal "goes down". Imagine being searched by a drug seller when he finds you are a police informant. Good luck!
8. *How long is this hell?* Repeated buys. How long must you work? Cops will want you to make buy after buy. They'll bleed you dry if you let them. They let you work for months, making dozens of cases, still dangling carrots in your grasp, suggesting they will "inform the prosecutor of your cooperation" (that plus 50 cents will get you a cup of coffee) and intermittently other good things. Ask for their promises in writing and watch them run in the opposite direction. (Cops will *never* put anything in writing since they don't make the decisions–the prosecutor and judge are the bosses.)

Most cops want you to turn several tricks, with equal or high quantity of drugs for which you were originally arrested.

RULE NO. 1 - TALK TO YOUR LAWYER BEFORE YOU MEET WITH POLICE. DON'T LET POLICE SCARE YOU FROM GETTING ADVICE.

RULE NO. 2 - STRIKE THE BEST DEAL YOU CAN, MINIMIZING YOUR INVOLVEMENT.

RULE NO. 3 - TRY TO SATISFY THE COPS WITH CONFIDENTIAL "BACKGROUND INFORMATION" SO YOUR NAME IS NOT MADE PUBLIC.

RULE NO. 4 - GET IN AND GET OUT QUICKLY. HOPEFULLY, WITHIN SEVERAL WEEKS, AFTER ONE OR TWO DEALS, YOU ARE OUT WITH A FREE RIDE AND GET WHAT YOU WANT.

Rule 35 Motion

Once sentenced, the U.S. Attorney, within one year, can file a *Rule 35 Motion* asking your sentence be reduced on the grounds of cooperation and assistance to the government.

You can enter a *nolo contendere plea.* Plea bargain agreements are where the government and defendant enter into an agreement as to what is going to be said to the Judge, what the recommendations are on sentencing, and many other matters.

You may be allowed to enter an *Alford Plea* which means you plead guilty but state to the Judge that you really did not do the particular act in question, but the facts are of such that it would be likely a jury would convict you and, therefore, you plead guilty.

Son of Sam Laws

Efforts to make the proceeds of crime stories benefit victims of crime rather than the perpetrators reflects a compelling state interest in taking away the fruits of crime from criminals. Named after serial killer David Berkowitz, known as Son of Sam, who terrorized New York City in 1977.

Laws impose obligations on any person who contracts with a criminal to take the proceeds from a book or movie and pay the money over to a state agency to be held in escrow in case the victim wishes to file suit.

Notoriety for profit laws are meant to ensure that criminals do not profit from story telling about their crimes before the victims have a meaningful opportunity to be compensated for their injuries.

Laws usually apply even before the criminal is officially convicted. The law also applies to the author, his thoughts and the recollections and work product in filming the movie or writing the book.

The question whether the government may drive certain viewpoints from the marketplace presumes discrimination. The Constitutional right of free expression is intended to remove the government from the arena of public discussion and put that decision as to what views shall be voiced into the hands of each of us in the belief that no other approach would allow for individual choice. That free speech may be offensive is not a good reason for suppressing it, but all the more reason to give it Constitutional protection.

On the other hand, the state has the right to ensure that criminals do not profit from their crimes, to take advantage of their own wrongs, or to found any claim upon their own inequity, or to acquire property by his own crime.

Greene County Sheriff's Deputies Ken Clayton and Larry Alexander secure a prisoner at the Greene County jail (Photograph courtesy of Warden Les Ridenhour and Sheriff John T. Pierpont).

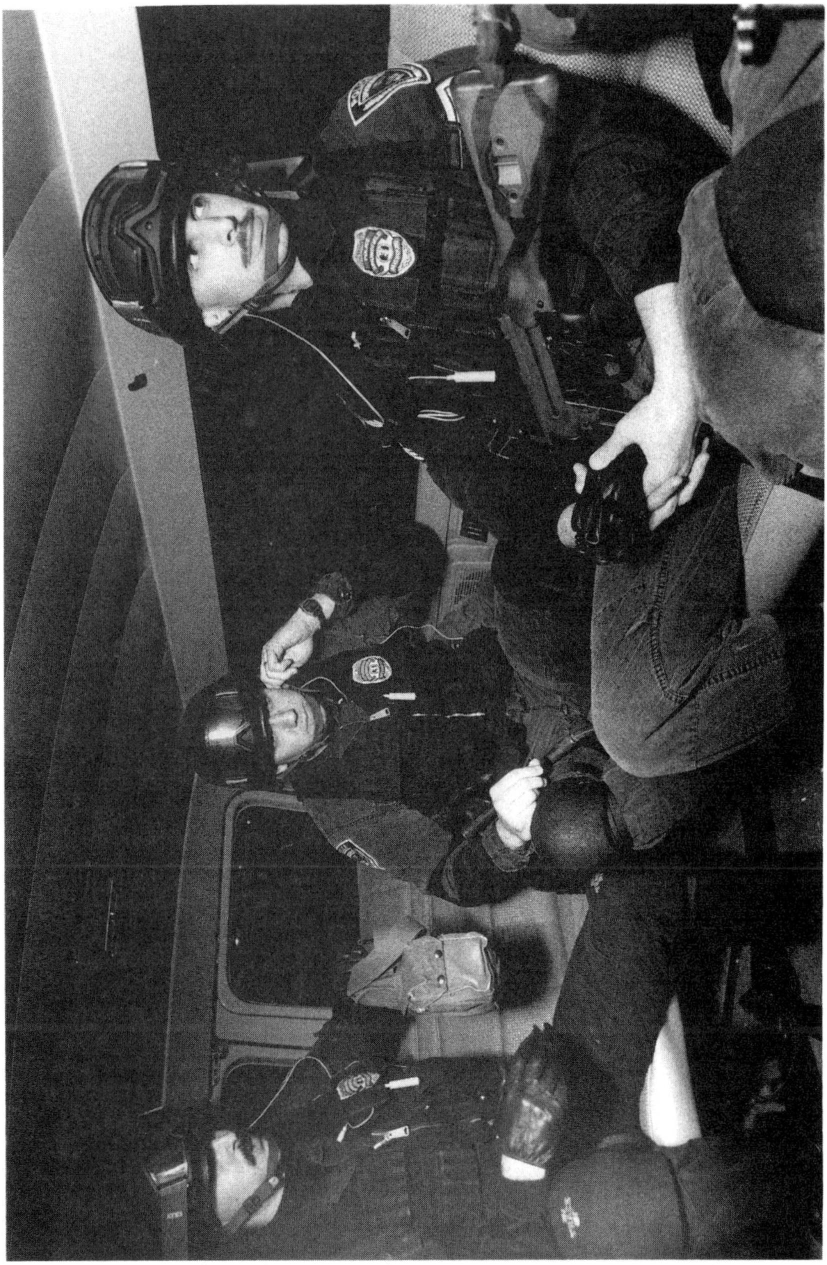

CAT Team (Bryan Atkins, Mike Owen, and Sgt. Steve Ijames) on route to complete a mission.

View of a cellblock at the Missouri State Penitentiary (Jefferson City).

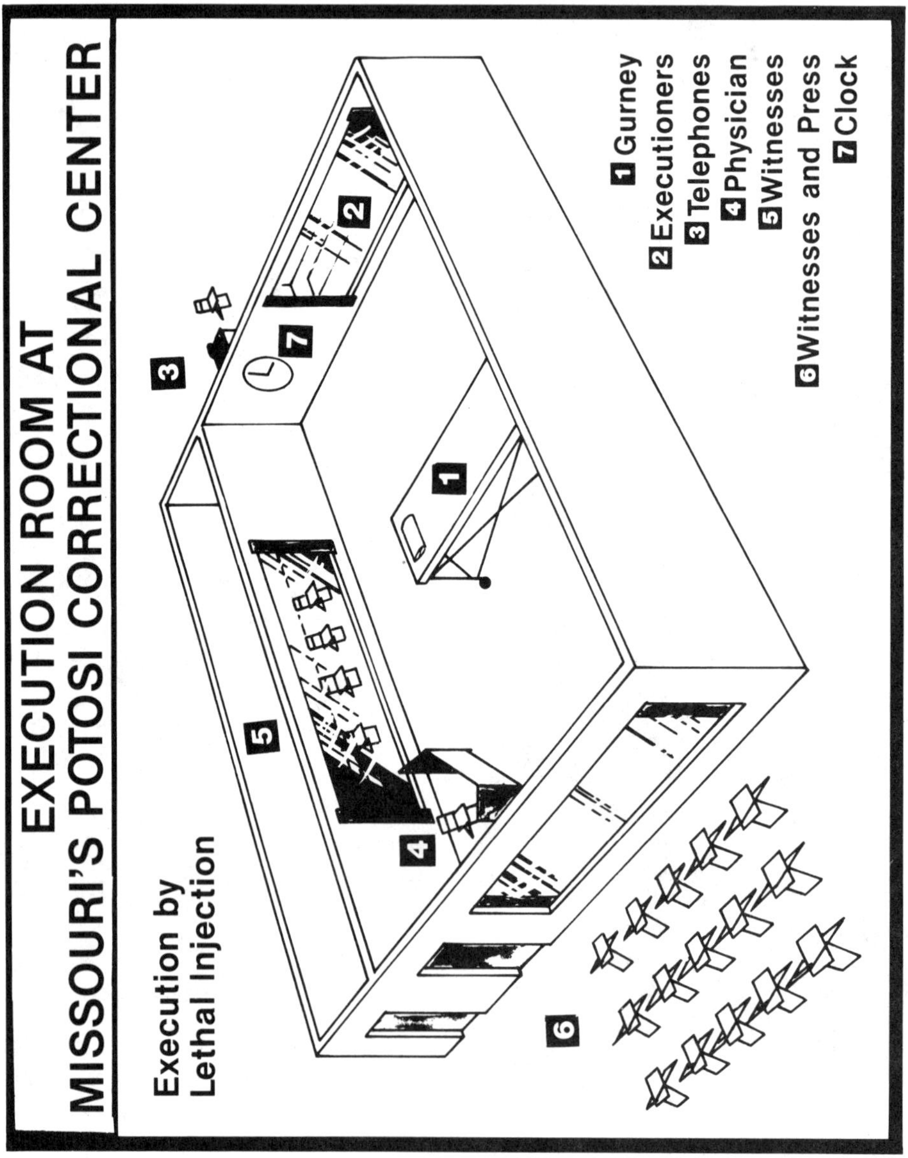
EXECUTION ROOM AT
MISSOURI'S POTOSI CORRECTIONAL CENTER
Execution by
Lethal Injection
1 Gurney
2 Executioners
3 Telephones
4 Physician
5 Witnesses
6 Witnesses and Press
7 Clock
1
2
3
4
5
6
7

Chapter 14

Questions of the Day (and Some of the Answers)

"Test everything. Hold fast to that which is good. Abstain from every form of evil."

I Thessalonians 5:22

"You must purge the evil from among you. The rest of the people will hear this and be afraid, and never again will such an evil thing be done among you. Show no pity, life for life, eye for eye, tooth for tooth. Hand for hand, foot for foot."

Deuteronomy 19:18-21

"What greater or better gift can we offer the republic than to teach and instruct our youth?"

Cicero

Defending yourself against Cops is really quite simple.

In the first instance, there is no substitute for staying out of trouble. Your own sense of right and wrong, letting your *conscience be your guide*, should give you enough good sense to know when you are committing a crime. If there is any question about whether your actions are illegal, contact a competent attorney for advice. An office conference will only cost a few dollars and may save you thousands of dollars later.

If you are arrested, keep your mouth shut! Don't give into intimidation. Don't try to be cute and outfox the police, who are veteran interrogators. You probably can't talk your way out of it—and you'll just make matters worse. Insist on your right to have a lawyer present.

If you are formally charged with a crime hire the best attorney as quickly as possible. Get started on your defense.

Finally, after your "trial by fire", once you have survived the investigation publicity and trial, whether you are convicted or eventually plead guilty, listen carefully to your lawyer's advice on "survival in prison". Doing time in prison is much easier if you are fully remorseful, accept responsibility and guilt for your acts. Resist the temptation to place blame on other people.

The Answer to Crime

> **"For there is no principle annunciated by the philosophers—at least none that is just and honorable—that has not been discovered and established by those who have drawn up codes of laws for states. For whence comes our sense of duty? From whom do we obtain the principles of religion? Whence comes the law of nations? Nothing more overt is so completely in accordance with the principles of justice and the demands of Nature as is government, without which existence is impossible...the universe obeys God; seas and lands obey the universe; and human life is subject to the decrees of the supreme law."**
>
> Cicero, The Republic and the Law

> **"Let us admit it fairly, as a business people should. We have no end of lesson: it will do us no end of good.**
> **Not on a single issue, or in one direction or twain, But conclusively, comprehensively, and several times and again,**
> **Were all our most holy illusions knocked high than Gileroy's kite?**
> **We have had a jolly good lesson and it serves us jolly well right!"**
>
> Rudyard Kipling

People ask why crime rates continue to soar, what can be done about the drug war, the reasons for increased teenage pregnancy, and juvenile delinquency? The answer: *The breakdown of the family unit* by moral decay.

Two-thirds of all black babies are illegitimate, born to unwed teenage mothers. Children everywhere are neglected without encouragement and praise. Less than 50% of Americans live in family units without a mother or father. Teenagers watch thousands of hours of television trash condoning violent and pornographic perverted lifestyles.

The problem will get much worse before it gets better. Until we reclaim the streets, return to church, and revamp the liberal lifestyle (If it feels good, do it!), crime as a social problem and multi-billion dollar expense will mount.

> **"Beneath the surface of everyone's life, especially the more mature, is an ache that will not go away. It can be ignored, disguised, mislabelled, or submerged by a torrent of activity, but it will not disappear. And for good reason. We were designed to enjoy a better world than this."**
>
> Dr. Larry Crabb, *Inside Out*

> **"We have lost our moral compass. There are lots of ways to control crime. The first way is the home and the neighborhood. The second way is to warehouse criminals. This carries an enormous cost and when the person gets out of prison they are worthless. We are losing a generation of people."**
>
> Chief Justice Gerald T. Joflat,
> United States Court of Appeals,

It's tragic that in our collective horror of the crime problem we have lost faith in our ability to take care of ourselves and each other. We have relegated the problem to the police, the courts, and social welfare agencies. Although the public should support these areas, the crime problem is too important to be left just to them.

RULE: COMBATING CRIME IS THE BUSINESS OF EVERY AMERICAN. NONE OF US CAN AFFORD TO ABDICATE OUR PERSONAL RESPONSIBILITY. THE CRIMINAL JUSTICE SYSTEM CANNOT GUARANTEE OUR WELL BEING ANYMORE THAN PHYSICIANS CAN GUARANTEE OUR HEALTH. EACH OF US MUST TAKE PRIMARY RESPONSIBILITY FOR OUR HEALTH WITH DOCTORS AS BACK UP CONSULTANTS. EACH OF US

MUST TAKE PRIMARY RESPONSIBILITY FOR OUR OWN SAFETY WITH THE POLICE CALLED UPON AS LITTLE AS POSSIBLE.

What really prevents crime? Most people shake their heads and say, "Nothing works."

Crime and crime prevention costs our citizens billions of dollars a year. Homicide is now the leading cause of death for black men 15 to 25 years of age, and is ninth for men of all ages. Crime takes a terrible toll on all of our citizens.

Zero Parents

The impossible goal of creating closer families and greater links between the school and home is tragic.

We are producing a new generation of orphans. Teenagers are growing up with drugs, drive-by shootings, AIDS, and illiteracy, and many are being abandoned by one or both parents.

The typical family home (consisting of four family members) is now being replaced by the single parent family, and soon the *zero parent family*.

Children are being shuffled to an aunt's home, foster home, and in 1991, five percent of America's 64 million children were zero parent children, soon to be nearly 1 in 10, living in a house headed by someone other than a parent.

Missing parents are from drug addiction, imprisonment, teenage mothers, and absent fathers. Children are often shuffled from one home to another and that creates defiant attitudes and behavioral problems. The next century may prove to be even uglier than pessimists predict.

Where Justice Is Denied

> **"There are more African-American men locked up in prisons than are in college and professional school. The criminal justice system has become the new slave-catcher for African-American men."**
>
> Randolph N. Stone,
> Professor of Law,
> University of Chicago School of Law

The real dimension about crime by blacks, though they comprise 15% of the population, account for 44% of all crime arrests, and nearly 50% of all violent crime arrests nationwide.

There is the *broken mobility escalator*. At various times Irish, Jewish, German and Italian immigrants all flooded to our country and sent crime rates soaring, but it disappeared as the economy worked its magical effect and moved them up the ladder of social mobility into the middle and upper classes.

Unfortunately, the unemployment rate of blacks remains alarmingly high, sometimes 50% for black teenagers. The great escalator of the American system has stalled.

A black experience in America seems to have been radically different than that of other immigrant groups. No other Americans were taken from their homeland and forced to come to this country and no others lived for generations under the degrading circumstances of slavery. As Alex D. Tocqueville wrote long before emancipation:

> "Slavery recedes, but the prejudice to which it has given birth is immovable."

There are myths we have developed about crime that need to be stripped away:

1. Most crime is committed by the poor.
2. Regulatory agencies prevent white collar crime.
3. Rich and poor and equal before the law.

Why are 48% of American prisoners black? Why is it so rare to see rich, prominent people sent to prison? What makes the detection of the crimes of the wealthy harder to detect is that their victims are usually unaware they have been victimized. The poor are odds on favorites to have their violations of the law detected.

When the rich are caught they are more likely to be treated as having suffered enough without resorting to incarceration, (exemplified by the trial of former Vice President Spiro Agnew).

It has been suggested that those who can afford to pay high fees obtain better legal counsel than those who have to rely on public defenders. They may be unfair to public defenders who are highly experienced, skilled trial lawyers, but unfortunately public defenders have large case loads and demands on their time. Private attorneys can delay proceedings while a client remains free on bail, take expensive depositions, find weaknesses in the prosecution's case, retain experts and character witnesses of high community standing. These opportunities give a considerable edge to the defendant who can afford experienced private counsel. A first class defense, even of a misdemeanor, can sometimes cost thousands of dollars.

Keeping Children and Friends Away from Drugs

RULE: TEACH STANDARDS OF RIGHT AND WRONG AND DEMONSTRATE THESE STANDARDS THROUGH PERSONAL EXAMPLE.

Children brought up to value individual responsibility, self-discipline, and a sense of right and wrong, are less likely to try drugs.

1. Set a good example and not using drugs themselves. Take a moral stand in your home.
2. Explain to children at an early age that drug use is wrong, harmful, and unlawful.
3. Encourage self-discipline through giving children everyday duties and holding them accountable.
4. Establish standards of behavior concerning drugs, drinking, dating, curfews, and unsupervised activities. Assure adequate supervision.
5. Encourage children to stand by their convictions when pressured to use drugs.

RULE: HELP CHILDREN TO RESIST PEER PRESSURE TO USE DRUGS BY SUPERVISING ACTIVITIES, KNOWING THEIR FRIENDS AND TALKING WITH THEM ABOUT THEIR PROBLEMS.

When parents take an active interest in their children's behavior, they provide the guidance and support needed to resist drugs.

1. Know children's whereabouts, activities and friends.
2. Work to maintain and improve family communications and listening.
3. Communicate regularly with the parents of their children's friends and sharing knowledge about drugs with other parents.
4. Be selective about children's viewing of television and movies that portray drug use as glamorous and exciting.

5. Encourage the development of a school policy with a clear no-drug message.
6. If guests are under the influence, don't allow them to drive.

Conclusion

"Our great legacy of freedom, belief in individual liberty, private ownership of property and opportunity through the free enterprise still serves us well for the future. The United States is still No. 1."

Lt. Col. Oliver North, USMC (Ret.)

"Hate evil, love good; maintain justice in the courts. Perhaps the Lord God Almighty will have mercy on the remnant of Joseph."

Amos 5:15

You want to go about business free from fear that you will be assaulted or robbed. You want your family safe on the streets, at home, and to retire at night secure they are not in danger.

The criminal law, whose primary function is to protect us from the criminal, must get on with its tasks. Some say we will never remedy the problem of crime unless we defeat poverty, ignorance and racial prejudices as the ultimate causes. Those who earnestly advance this argument never explain why much crime is committed by people who are neither poor, unintelligent, nor who have ever suffered a day of racial discrimination.

Moreover, we cannot wait until we have rebuilt society according to some utopian reformists' prescription before dealing with the all too common place everyday savagery of crime.

Willie "The Actor" Sutton, the dapper and ingenious bank robber whose exploits in the '40's and '50's put him on front pages, was examined by sociologists, criminologists, and psychiatrists. After they pinched, poked, and prodded every aspect of his life from toilet training on, with the assumption that Willie was somehow abnormal or had some particular genetic defect or environmental experience which compelled him to pursue a criminal career was asked, "Why do you rob banks?" Without a moment's hesitation Willie shot back: "Because that's where the money is."

That simple and honest explanation is worth a world of learned treatises on the causes of crime. Many commit crime because they chose to do so; they choose to do so because of the potential rewards, relative to the risks of being captured, tried and punished. The choice is a reasonable one. Crime is often the product of rational thought by a person whose physical and chemical processes are well within normal limits.

We must avoid the tendency to regard crime as a form of "mental illness" as a humanitarian disguise for the belief that we should not be held accountable for our acts.

The criminal will go on planning and committing crimes so long as he thinks the law is weak and yielding enough to give him a chance to evade it.

If you're considering committing a crime–don't! It's wrong and besides; it isn't worth it. The costs of lawyers, bail bonds, and expenses is great. The embarrassment among friends and family will last a lifetime. The inhumanity of jail and prison is a nightmare.

RULE: IN MORE WAYS THAN ONE, CRIME DOESN'T PAY.

We live in a Godless philosophy or *moral relativism*, dominant in America because parents have allowed it to exist, teachers and professors teach it, and churches have passively accepted it.

The only politically correct way to think is that immorality may be moral, traditional concepts of right and wrong are passé, and everything comes in shades of gray.

Why strip life of its only source of meaning? Since there are no absolute moral laws to contend with, and no God who promises to punish sin and hold us accountable, the obvious solution is to minimize risks as much as possible and continue doing what brings us momentary satisfaction.

We are not left in life to grope our way in search of momentary thrills and pleasures. The message we must teach children in the 1990's and beyond is that they will be bombarded with moral relativism each year in schools and in the dimension of their "real life", both at home and with families.

Ultimately, God will require each of us to know the right answer. We will all face our own judgment day. The tide to relativism has invaded the classroom from the university to the elementary school. We can stop it at the front door of our house and the church!

In this book, there are many things that I cannot tell you beyond a shadow of a doubt. One thing I can tell you is that our highest calling is to acquaint our young people with these precious Truths!

Security wire around a marijuana patch, Cassville.

Springfield Police Officers practice CAT (Crisis Action Team) training. Left to right: Don Fuhr, Ron Hartman, Sgt. Steve Ijames, Mike Owen and Brian Atkins.

Springfield Police Officer participates in training exercise with an automatic rifle.

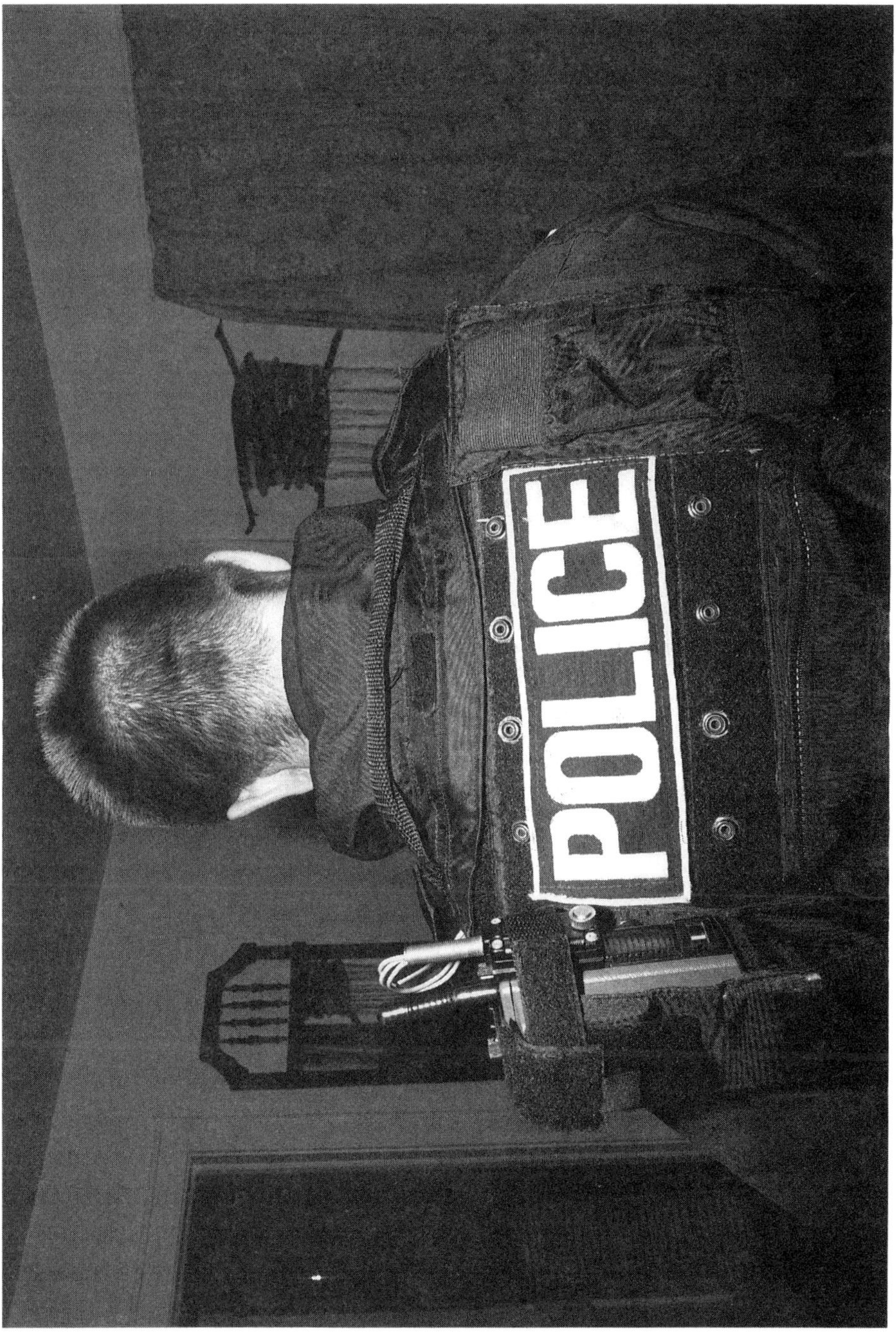
POLICE

Understanding the Lingo

GLOSSARY OF TERMS

A.A.	Alcoholics Anonymous organization
AC-DC	A bi-sexual
A.T.F.	A Bureau of the U.S. Treasury Department Alcohol, Tobacco, and Firearms charged with the collection of taxes on alcohol and tobacco and enforcement of firearms laws.
accessory	Encouraging or inciting another to commit a felony, concealing the fact of a crime or aiding the escape of its perpetrator.
acid	1-acetyl-d-lysergic acid diethylamide (LSD-25).
Alford Plea	You plead "guilty" not because you're guilty, but based on your belief a jury would convict you on the Prosecutor's facts, and the sentence you would receive might be greater than what you would receive from the Judge.
Algoa	Maximum security of the Missouri Intermedial Reformatory for males 17 to 25 years of age. (600 inmates)

alien	Any person not a citizen or national of the United States.
alibi	Legal defense alleging accused could not have committed the crime in question because he was somewhere other than at the scene of the crime.
amphetamine	Bennies, Black Beauties, Crystal, Meth, Roses, Uppers, Whites.
angel dust	The animal tranquilizer phencyclidine, (PCP), originally used by pushers as a substitute for tetrahydrocannabinol (THC), the active ingredient in marijuana. PCP can cause amnesia, coma and death.
Antabuse	Trade name for tetraethylthiuram disulfide, used in treating alcoholism. Another drug, Temposil (citrated calcium carbamide) safer but weaker. It makes you deathly sick if you consume alcohol.
appeal	A request that a case be removed to a higher court so the trial can be reviewed by the higher court.
appearance	Initial act of appearance in court and submitting to its authority.
arraignment	The defendant is read the charges, informed of his rights and required to enter a plea.
arrest warrant	Document issued by a Judge and clerk directing police to arrest an accused of an offense.
asylum	An alien present in the United States may request asylum.
B.A.C.	Reduced charge from D.W.I. Carries 6 points and often a smaller fine. Will not result in revocation of license. (Blood alcohol content in excess of .10).
backlog	Pending cases which exceed the capacity of a court and which may not be acted upon until the court has acted upon older cases.
back time	You're given credit for time served in county jail waiting trial or transfer. Mandatory that it is awarded you.

bad rap	Long prison sentence.
bag and tag	To seize evidence and place in an evidence envelope.
bag lady	Homeless person living on the streets.
bagman	(1) Racketeer designated to collect bets, bribes, or so-called loans or to pay off other racketeers or venal politicians; (2) Anyone holding or receiving money during the course of an illegal transaction; (3) Peddler of dangerous drugs.
bait and switch	Technique of advertising a big bargain and, when a customer tries to buy it, offering him a similar product that is supposed to be better and more expensive than what he came for, which, the seller will claim has been sold out.
barbiturates	Central nervous system depressants such as amobarbital (Amytal), Luminal (phenobarbital), Nembutal (pentrobarbital), Seconal (secobarbital), Tuinal (amobarbital and secobarbital). Protracted use affects blood pressure and pulse and may eventually bring on convulsion. Barbs, Christmas Trees, Downers, Mexican Reds, Pink Ladies, Red Devils, Reds, Yellow Jackets.
bench warrant	(1) Document issued by a Judge directing a person who has failed to obey a notice to appear to be brought before the court; (2) Court order to capture a criminal who has escaped detention, jumped bail, or violated parole or probation.
black box	(1) Device for bypassing the telephone company's switching system so that calls can be made to anywhere else in the U.S. without charge by, or knowledge of, the telephone company; (2) Technical device used in gathering intelligence which may range from a telephone wiretapping apparatus to an aerial satellite.
bong	Marijuana smoking device.

booking	Being asked routine questions, formally logged by the jail, fingerprinted, and photographed.
booster boxes	Boxes which appear to be carefully wrapped packages but actually have a hinged fast access side used to conceal shoplifted merchandise.
Border Patrol	INS enforcement officers checking crossings and borders and specified points of entry to stop people from illegally entering into the U.S.
bounty hunter	A person specializing in tracking down bail jumpers rewarded by bail bondsmen and law enforcement agencies.
bread	Cash
brick	Compressed brick-shaped block of hashish, marijuana, morphine or opium; bricks usually weigh either one pound or one kilogram.
bug	(1) Auditory surveillance maintained by some electronic listening device; (2) Burglar alarm protection.
bum rap	A charge filed by the Prosecutor who knows he does not have enough evidence to win at trial.
busted	To be arrested for criminal offenses, usually narcotics related.
C	(1) Abbreviation for cocaine; (2) One hundred dollar bill.
C.C.W.	Carrying a concealed weapon on or about your person, a Class C felony.
C & I	Careless and imprudent driving.
call-back	Although given a prison sentence, sentencing Judge has power to give you parole up to 120 days in prison, *but not* thereafter.
candy	Barbiturates.
candyman	Drug dealer.
case officer	Law enforcement officer supervising agents involved in a specific case.
Chillicothe	Cillicothe Correctional Center (100 inmates).

clean	(1) Not addicted; (2) Not carrying or hiding narcotics or stolen property; (3) Not in possession of firearms; (4) Not involved in illegal enterprises; (5) Not wanted by police.
closing	Closing argument in criminal trial when lawyers *argue* their case.
cocaine	Powerful stimulant drug. Blow, C. Nose Candy, Rock, Snow White.
coke	cocaine.
collar	To make an arrest.
come clean	Confess and incriminate yourself and others.
conjugal visit	Arrangement allowing a prisoner to enjoy a sexual relationship with a spouse.
conspiracy	Agreement between two or more persons to commit any crime. It is the agreement that is the crime. No need to prove the crime was committed.
cop a plea or cop out	To plead guilty to a lesser offense than that with which one is charged, and receive a lighter sentence.
court file	Your criminal file maintained by the Circuit or District clerk which is a matter of public record.
crank	Methamphetamine, a mind altering drug.
cross	To cross-examine a witness.
cut	(1) Share of the profits, hence to take a cut means to take a share of the profits; (2) To dilute drinks or drugs.
D.A.	District Attorney.
D.D.W.	Displaying a deadly and dangerous weapon in a rude, threatening, or angry manner.
D.E.A.	Drug Enforcement Administration.
D.O.C.	Missouri Department of Corrections (prison).
D.O.R.	Missouri Department of Revenue
D.F.S.	Division of Family Services (Welfare).
D.N.A.	Complicated chemical analysis.

D.T.'s	The shakes from alcohol or drug addiction withdrawal.
D.W.I.	Driving (or operating) a vehicle while intoxicated.
D.W.L.R.	Driving while your operating privileges (license) is revoked.
deportation	The formal removal of an alien from the United States when the presence of the alien is deemed inconsistent with the public welfare.
detox	Medical method of treating alcoholic and narcotic addicts (detoxification).
discovery	Once a Circuit Court felony information is filed, your attorney can look at the police reports.
docket call	Test of active pending cases called by the Judge.
docket sheet	A handwritten record of all court proceedings, written by the Judge, kept in the court file.
domestic	American grown marijuana.
doper	Habitual user of drugs.
drive-by	A shooting by car occupants and quick escape.
drop	(1) To swallow a drug; (2) Clandestine hiding place for drugs, mail or ransom money; (3) Drug administered by mouth.
dropsy	A fleeing suspect who throws away or abandons drugs while being pursued.
drunk tank	Jail cell reserved for those arrested while under influence of alcohol or other drugs.
dust	(1) Angel dust; (2) Heroin; (3) Money; (4) To mix marijuana and heroin for use in cigarettes.
E squad	Emergency squad. A select group of prison employees trained in methods of confrontation and negotiation for management of special problem inmates and interpersonal relationships to restore order when insurrections occur, which are utilized as a first line defense in the control and security of the institution.

entrapment	Device used by some officers which involves encouraging suspects to commit crimes so the officers can arrest them. Entrapment is illegal.
expungement	Legal erasing of a criminal's record to assist in his social rehabilitation and remove prejudice from the mind of potential employers. Rarely done.
extradition	Removal of fugitives from justice from the state where they are apprehended to the state where they may be tried for the commission of a crime. Many countries have specific treaties with others guaranteeing the extradition and wanted criminals.
fed	An investigative agent from the U.S. Government
felony	Crime punishable by imprisonment for more than a year (in prison).
flash	Narc showing money before a drug purchase.
Fordland	The Ozark Correctional Center (200 inmates in a minimum security setting).
Forensics	A chemist who often testifies in court.
freak out	(1) Drug induced hallucinations; (2) Violence or withdrawal.
frisk	Search a body for concealed weapons, contraband, or drugs.
front money	Advance payment for drugs.
funny farm	Insane asylum; psychiatric ward.
fuzz buster	Radar device used by motorists to give warning of speed traps.
gang	A somewhat organized group of some duration by turf concurs, symbols, special dress and colors promoting violence for status providing purposes.
gang crime incident	A crime in which there was a gang motivation as opposed to mere participation by a gang member.
glue sniffing	Sniffing volatile airplane glue, often affects the central nervous system and shows itself in the

	eyes as well as the muscular action. May result in death through suffocation.
gold dust	Cocaine.
good time	Getting a prison sentence reduced for being a good prisoner.
grand jury	Body of citizens selected and sworn to investigate criminal activity and conduct of public officials. To hear evidence against accused persons to determine if there is sufficient evidence to bring charges. Does not determine guilt, only that charges should be filed. Normally controlled by the Prosecutor.
grass	Marijuana.
Green Card	Temporary work permits given aliens.
grower	Person who grows marijuana.
habeas corpus	(Latin for "may you have the body"). Prisoner's right to be brought before a court so Judge may decide legality of detention.
habitual offender	The filing of criminal charges alleging the defendant has been previously convicted of felonies. Has the effect of removing sentencing from the jury and transferring it to the Judge with the additional effect of increasing the punishment.
half-way house	(1) Non-confining residential facility for adjudicated adults or juveniles; (2) Facility providing an alternative to confinement for persons not suitable for probation or needing a period of readjustment to the community after confinement; (3) A number of privately owned houses for housing inmates, minimum security, who are near the end of their sentence, preparing them for return to society.
hard drugs	Physically addictive drugs such as heroin, morphine, opium, cocaine, methamphetamine.
hash	Hashish (compressed marijuana).
hashish	Hash.
head shop	Store where paraphernalia of drug users such as cigarette paper, incense, opium pipes,

psychedelic posters, roach clips, and water pipes are sold.

heat — Attention directed against criminals by police.

hemp — Common name for the cannabis plant used to make hashish and marijuana.

heroin — Big H, Brown Sugar, Horse, Mexican Mud.

hibitch — Being tried as a habitual criminal with prior felony record.

Hoover sheet — F.B.I. rap sheet showing aliases, arrests, and convictions over a person's life.

hush money — Bribe given to induce someone not to give evidence or to testify.

hustler — Person obtaining alcohol, drugs, or money by stealing or whoring.

hypo — Hypodermic injection or hypodermic needle.

illegal alien — A foreign national who's entered the United States without inspection of a foreign national who after entering legally violates his status and remains in the United States without authority.

immigrant — An alien admitted as a lawful, permanent resident given the privilege of living permanently in the U.S.

immigrant visa — A document issued by the U.S. Counsel authorizing an alien to apply for admission as an immigrant to the U.S.

incognito — Living under an assumed name or disguised.

insanity — Lunacy, mental deficiency, disease, or incompetence, excluding responsibility, which will result in an acquittal, but require the defendant to be confined in a mental institution.

J.T. — Requesting a jury trial.

jailhouse lawyer — Legally well-informed prisoner.

jailhouse punk — Anyone who becomes a homosexual while in jail.

joy pop — Injection into an arm or leg muscle instead of a vein.

jump bail	Forfeit bail by not appearing in court at the time directed or by failing to comply with some other condition set before bail was granted. It is a new separate criminal offense.
K	Kilo (of marijuana).
kick the habit	Overcome a habit such as drinking, smoking, or using drugs.
kite	Obtain float credit by rapidly transferring funds from one bank to another so as to produce the illusion that ample funds are in several banks at the same time.
LSD	Acid, Blotter Acid, California Sunshine. Mind altering drug.
lab	An illicit laboratory manufacturing methamphetamine.
laundered money	Illegally obtained funds transferred by banking and other third party transactions until the original source of the money is no longer evident.
law day	Docket call where cases are reviewed once every 3-4 months.
libel	Written defamation.
lineup	Police conduct parade of prisoners, arranged to facilitate identification by victims of crime or eyewitnesses.
MSP	The Missouri State Penitentiary, largest institution in the Missouri Division of Corrections, (some buildings completed in 1836 being still in use) sitting on multi-level 47 acre site overlooking the Missouri River at Jefferson City, designed to house 2000 inmates and 550 employees.
madam	Brothel keeper; whoremistress.
mainline	Inject a drug into a vein.
make a run	Take an automobile; motorcycle, plane, or ship to another country or state with the object of returning with drugs and eluding suspicion.

Mann Act	The White Slave Traffic Act (1910) prohibiting transferring women across state lines for prostitution.
marijuana	Acapulco Gold, Cannabis, Columbian, Grass, Hemp, Mary Jane, Panama Red, Pot, Reefer, Smoke, Tea, Weed.
methaqualone	Qualude, Quads, Quas, Soapers, Sopes, Sopor
misdemeanor	Any crime not punishable by more than a year imprisonment in county jail.
misprision	(1) Concealment of a felony or of treason by anyone who is aware of either, although not a participant; (2) Seditous conduct; (3) Cover up; (4) Wrong performance of official duty.
Moberly	The Missouri Training Center for Men, a medium security facility near Moberly (900 male population).
morphine	Cube, First Line, Morf.
mouthpiece	Lawyer who represents organized crime figures.
mug shot	(1) Facial portrait; (2) Police file photograph of a criminal's face, full view and side view.
mule	Transportation of drugs.
MULES	A state computer with crime information Missouri Uniform Law Enforcement System.
municipal charge	A city charge, not a misdemeanor or felony, and not admissible against you for impeachment purposes.
murder one	Murder in the first degree—carries life or death. Requires premeditation.
murder two	Murder in the second degree—caries 10 to life.
N.A.	Narcotics Anonymous organization.
N.A.D.D.I.S.	Narcotics and Dangerous Drugs Information System (computerized criminal file).
N.C.I.C	National Crime Information Center computer which lists fugitives and stolen property. If property is shown to be stolen, it is know as a "hit".

narc	A narcotics agent or any law enforcement officer.
narc-out	To become a police informant.
naturalization	The granting of citizenship to a non-citizen.
Nolo contendra	A plea in federal court meaning that you throw yourself on the mercy of the court.
non-immigrant	An alien who seeks temporary entry to the United States for a specific purpose.
nose powder	Any drug powdered so it may be sniffed or snorted. Cocaine and hallucinogens such as MDA and heroin are often snorted.
O.D.	To consume too much of a drug, often resulting in death.
off shore islands	Certain Caribbean Islands where names and identities of bank deposits are secret and IRS cannot discover the information.
omnibus hearing	A short scheduling hearing in U.S. Magistrate Court occurring near the time of arraignment, where little is learned but lawyers are given deadlines to file pre-trial motions.
on ice	Imprisoned.
on the lam	Escaping or hiding from the police.
P&P	Office of Probation and Parole.
P.C.	To be arrested without a warrant only on a police officer's probable cause. Can be held for up to 20 hours.
P.G.	To enter a plea of guilty in court.
Pacific	The newest facility in the Missouri Division of Corrections, located on I-44 east of Pacific, Missouri, in St. Louis County to house approximately 510 medium security prisoners.
packing heat	Carrying a gun.
parole violations	A parolee's failure to conform to the conditions of his people. A violation usually results in a return to prison and loss of parole.
peyote	Buttons, Cactus, Mesc, Mescal, Mescal Buttons
phencyclidine	Angle Dust, Crystal, PCP, Rocket Fuel, Supergrass, TIC TAC

photo	Surveillance of the movements of surveillance suspects provided by photographic devices such as camera, which provides pictures useful in apprehending offenders.
piece	A pistol
plea bargaining	Exchange of judicial or prosecutorial concessions, such as a lesser charge, dismissal of other pending charges, a prosecutor's recommendation of a reduced sentence in return for a plea of guilty.
plead the Fifth	Refuse to answer questions on the grounds that answers might be self-incriminating.
pot	Marijuana
Potosi	Death row and lifers confined at Potosi.
prelim	A preliminary hearing.
Priors	Prior criminal convictions.
protective custody	Detention of persons to protect them from reprisal by criminal elements.
quick entry	No knock entry made by law enforcement officers in serving search warrants.
R.O.R.	Own recognizance release. Legal freeing of defendant from going to jail until case comes to court for hearing.
rap sheet	Arrest and criminal history.
rebuttal	Lawyer presents evidence opposing a witness.
receiving	Knowingly receiving stolen property.
red handed	Caught in the act of doing something illegal.
red herring	False issue raised to confuse the real issue.
refugee	A person outside of his country who is unable or unwilling to return to the country because of persecution or a well-founded fear of persecution because of his religion, nationality, membership in a particular social group or political opinion.
rehab	An outpatient or inpatient drug rehabilitation program.

remand	To send, or the act of sending a prisoner back to court for further hearing.
Renz	Renz Correctional Center in Jefferson City (270 inmates).
resin	Hashish or marijuana resin, containing the drug tetrahydrocannabinol.
restitution	Restoring money or property to its rightful owner or reimbursing for losses normally by court order.
reverse sting	Police sell stolen property or drugs under disguise for an extended period of time with video or audio recordings.
revolving door	Quickly returning sentenced defendants to society after early paroles, serving only a small fraction by the original sentence.
rigor mortis	(Latin for stiffening of death.) First appears in the face and jaws before proceeding downward. Rigor mortis of the entire body occurs within 8-12 hours after death, but 18 or more hours may pass before the body is completely enveloped. In 3-4 more hours rigor mortis in the upper half of the body disappears. It is with these figures estimates are made concerning the time of death of a homicide victim.
roach	Butt of a marijuana cigarette (resembles a wet cockroach once passed about and smoked.
roach clip	Device for holding a hashish or marijuana cigarette so it may be smoked to the end.
roll over	To turn *state's evidence*, become an informant and testify against another.
rolled	Drugs are seized and the arrested person agrees to make a controlled delivery to the intended destination.
runaway	Juvenile leaving the custody of his parents or without permission.
S.I.S.	Suspended Imposition of Sentence. Even though you plead guilty and are placed on probation you are not technically convicted

	and the charged are later dismissed and file closed.
sandbagging	When Prosecutor brings up a new argument in the final part of his closing argument that defense counsel has no chance to answer.
sanitize	(1) Make acceptable by removing objectional features, ideas, or words: (2) Protect participants by removal of all clues: (3) Protect the work of undercover agents.
Saturday Night Special	Cheap .38 caliber handgun
secure telephone	Telephone whose location cannot be detected even by checking with the telephone company. Conversations on such telephones cannot be intercepted.
sell a bill of goods	Defraud by selling something difficult to use or resell.
setup	A police trap.
shank	(1) Handmade knife or other pointed weapon; (2) Double edged dagger (often made by prisoners from eating utensils or bits of scrap metal); (3) Knife inflicted wound.
shave and a haircut	Obtaining quick probation from a Judge.
shock time	Judge grants probation but requires you to serve a short jail sentence.
shoot up	Inject drugs.
shrink	A psychiatrist.
slander	Spoken (oral) defamation.
smart money	Funds invested or money wagered by those in the know.
snitch	To become an informer.
spaced out	Mentally disorganized, especially by drugs.
speedball	Cocaine and heroin injection.
stake out	Disguised observation of illegal activity to arrest criminals in the act.
state's evidence	Testimony given by an informant against accomplices.

statch (rape)	Sexual intercourse with a female who has consented but is deemed to be legally incapable of consent because she is underage.
step on	To dilute a drug using Vitamin B-12, powdered sugar, baby powder, or other substance. Commonly done to increase the quantity and earn a larger profit.
sting	Police buy stolen property under the disguise for an extended period of time with video or audio recording.
Super-Max	High security prison unit at the Missouri State Pen, Jefferson City, for inmates seriously aggressive. Designed to minimize serious incidents.
surreptitious entry	Breaking and entering with a court order to aid in the collection of evidence.
suspended sentence	Court decision not to impose prison sentence but to grant probation.
SWAT Team	Specially trained police to react to dangerous emergency hostage situations.
tag	Motor vehicle license plate.
tag and bag	Collect and preserve evidence at crime scene by police.
temporary worker	Aliens admitted to the U.S. to perform specific work such as temporary labor where U.S. workers cannot be found.
time off	Time off for good behavior (while imprisoned), reduced from overall sentence.
Tipton	The State Correctional Center, Tipton, originally for confinement of female adult felons, now housing male inmates.
toke	To puff a hashish or marijuana cigarette.
two time loser	Going to prison for a second time.
under advisement	Judge has heard evidence and is considering his decision awaiting filing of legal briefs.
under the gun	Under observation or surveillance by the police.
under the table	Done illegally and secretly.

unethical	Contrary to the rules for correct conduct and legitimate practice.
upper	Stimulant drug
user	One who used dangerous drugs.
vag	Vagabond or vagrant—a person wandering from place to place without lawful or visible means of support. No longer illegal.
venue	Jurisdiction where a trial is held. Defendants ask for a change of venue because they believe the community will be hostile and unfair.
wad cutter	Bullet capable of cutting a clean hole in its target.
weight	Bulk quantity of hashish, heroin, LSD, marijuana, or any other drug.
welfare queen	Female criminal adept at using aliases to steal money from welfare programs.
white collar crime	Violations of criminal law by upper class. Expensive account padding, price fixing, product alterations, misrepresentations, and stealing office supplies and equipment are a few examples.
wire	Undercover narc or informant wearing a mike that transmits the sounds to a recorder.
wiretap	Use an electronic or eavesdropping device with or without a court order.
yellow jacket	(1) Barbiturates; (2) Nembutal capsules.
youth gang	A delinquent group of juveniles engaged in criminal income producing activity, usually drug trafficking.
zero tolerance	The forfeiture of a car, plane or boat upon finding only a tiny amount of drugs.

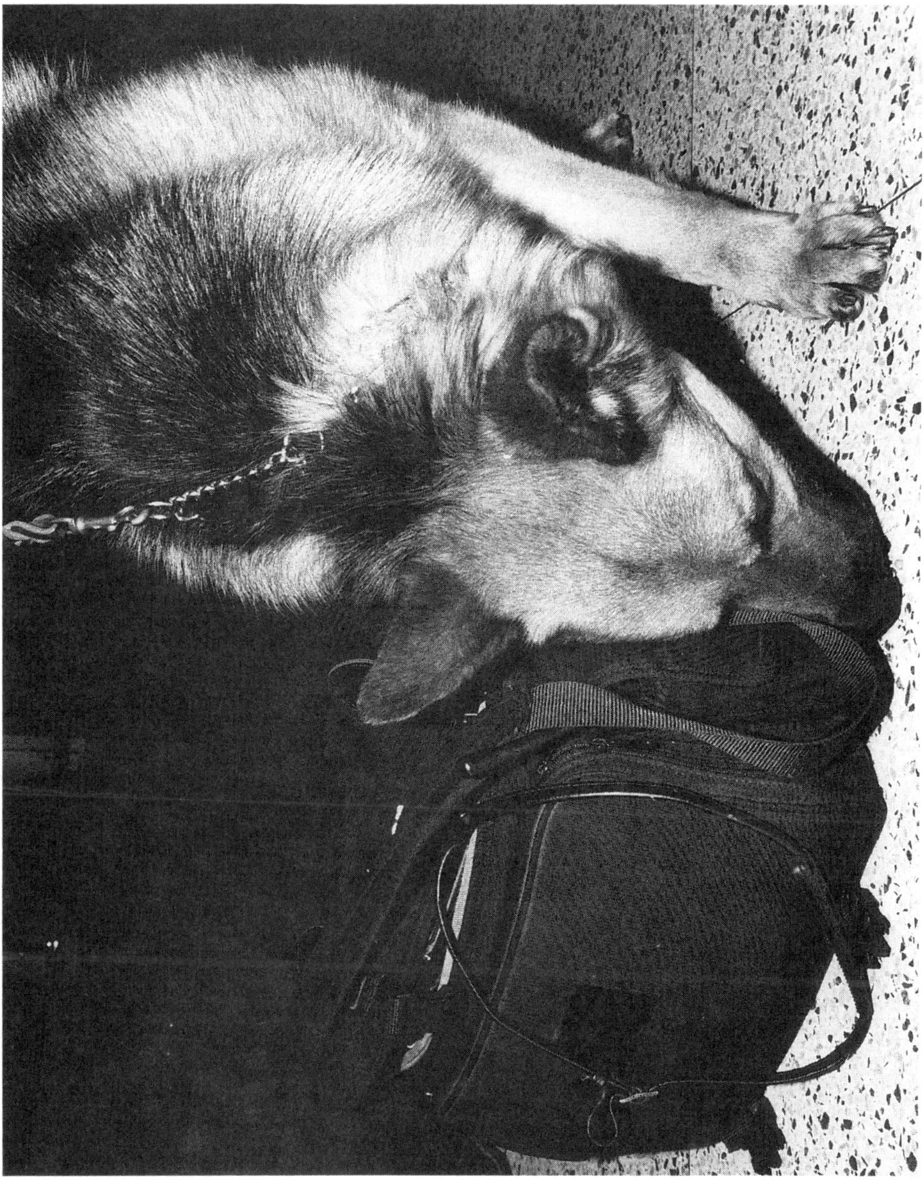

Narcotic search warrants also allow for emergency searches of adjoining rooms due to easy destructability of contraband (Cape Giradeau Police Department).

Two aerosol can, paint-sniffing suspects feel no pain, until they wake up in jail.

On the reverse side of a kidnap ransom envelope forensic specialists used infra-red lighting and the previous obliterated letters suddenly became clear.

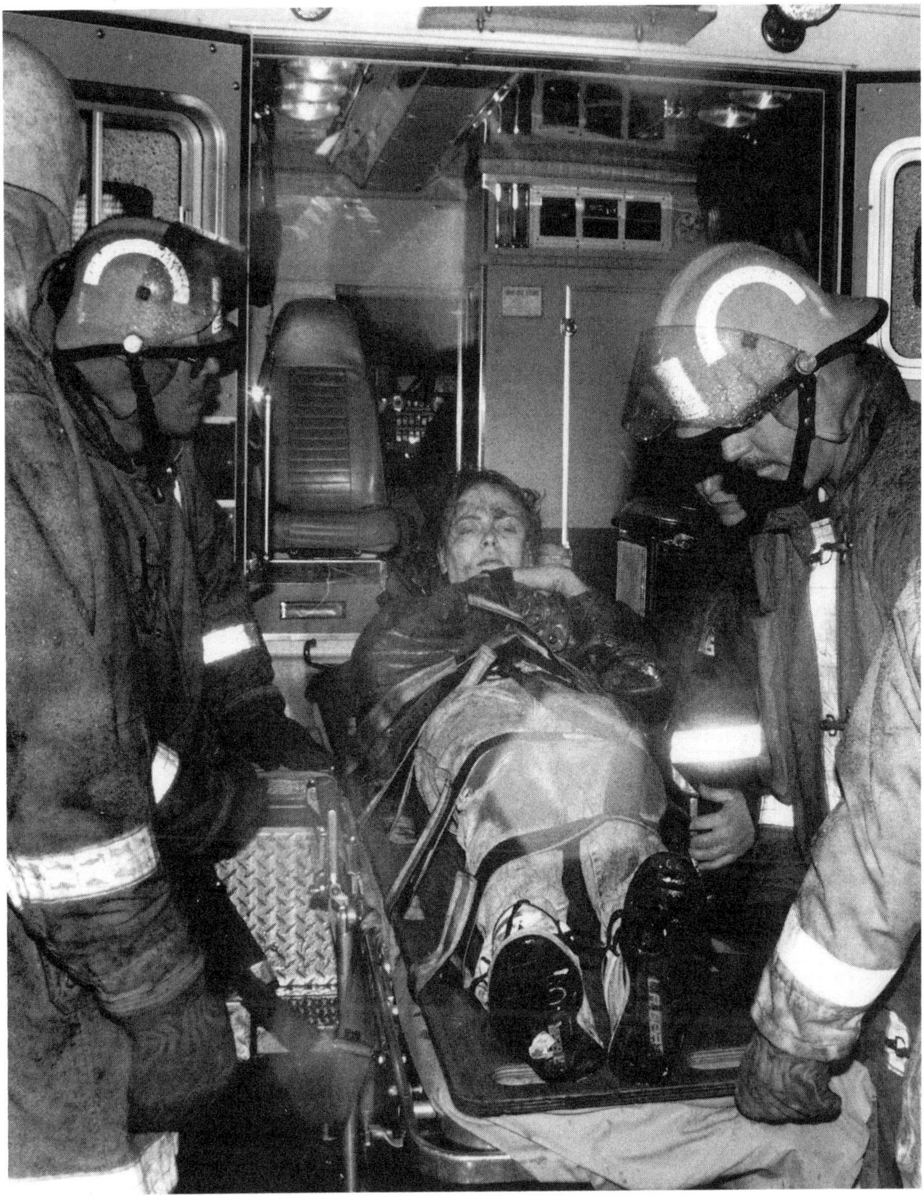